M000105190

Practical Mobile Forensics
Third Edition

A hands-on guide to mastering mobile forensics for the iOS, Android, and the Windows Phone platforms

Rohit Tamma
Oleg Skulkin
Heather Mahalik
Satish Bommisetty

BIRMINGHAM - MUMBAI

Practical Mobile Forensics
Third Edition

Copyright © 2018 Packt Publishing

All rights reserved. No part of this book may be reproduced, stored in a retrieval system, or transmitted in any form or by any means, without the prior written permission of the publisher, except in the case of brief quotations embedded in critical articles or reviews.

Every effort has been made in the preparation of this book to ensure the accuracy of the information presented. However, the information contained in this book is sold without warranty, either express or implied. Neither the authors, nor Packt Publishing or its dealers and distributors, will be held liable for any damages caused or alleged to have been caused directly or indirectly by this book.

Packt Publishing has endeavored to provide trademark information about all of the companies and products mentioned in this book by the appropriate use of capitals. However, Packt Publishing cannot guarantee the accuracy of this information.

Commissioning Editor: Vijin Boricha
Acquisition Editor: Rohit Rajkumar
Content Development Editor: Devika Battike
Technical Editor: Aditya Khadye
Copy Editor: Safis Editing
Project Coordinator: Judie Jose
Proofreader: Safis Editing
Indexer: Rekha Nair
Graphics: Tania Dutta
Production Coordinator: Arvindkumar Gupta

First published: July 2014
Second edition: May 2016
Third edition: January 2018

Production reference: 1220118

Published by Packt Publishing Ltd.
Livery Place
35 Livery Street
Birmingham
B3 2PB, UK.

ISBN 978-1-78883-919-8

www.packtpub.com

`mapt.io`

Mapt is an online digital library that gives you full access to over 5,000 books and videos, as well as industry leading tools to help you plan your personal development and advance your career. For more information, please visit our website.

Why subscribe?

- Spend less time learning and more time coding with practical eBooks and Videos from over 4,000 industry professionals

- Improve your learning with Skill Plans built especially for you

- Get a free eBook or video every month

- Mapt is fully searchable

- Copy and paste, print, and bookmark content

PacktPub.com

Did you know that Packt offers eBook versions of every book published, with PDF and ePub files available? You can upgrade to the eBook version at `www.PacktPub.com` and as a print book customer, you are entitled to a discount on the eBook copy. Get in touch with us at `service@packtpub.com` for more details.

At `www.PacktPub.com`, you can also read a collection of free technical articles, sign up for a range of free newsletters, and receive exclusive discounts and offers on Packt books and eBooks.

Contributors

About the authors

Rohit Tamma is a security program manager currently working with Microsoft. With over 8 years of experience in the field of security, his background spans management and technical consulting roles in the areas of application and cloud security, mobile security, penetration testing, and security training. Rohit has also coauthored couple of books, such as *Practical Mobile Forensics* and *Learning Android Forensics,* which explain various ways to perform forensics on the mobile platforms. You can contact him on Twitter at `@RohitTamma`.

Writing this book has been a great experience because it has taught me several things, which could not have been otherwise possible. I would like to dedicate this book to my parents for helping me in every possible way throughout my life.

Oleg Skulkin is a digital forensics "enthusional" (enthusiast and professional) from Russia with more than 6 years of experience, and is currently employed by Group-IB, one of the global leaders in preventing and investigating high-tech crimes and online fraud. He holds a number of certifications, including GCFA, MCFE, and ACE. Oleg is a coauthor of *Windows Forensics Cookbook,* and you can find his articles about different aspects of digital forensics both in Russian and foreign magazines. Finally, he is a very active blogger, and he updates the *Cyber Forensicator* blog daily.

I would like to thank my mom and wife for their support and understanding, my friend, Igor Mikhaylov, and my teammates from Group-IB Digital Forensics Lab: Valeriy Baulin, Sergey Nikitin, Vitaliy Trifonov, Roman Rezvuhin, Artem Artemov, Alexander Ivanov, Alexander Simonyan, Alexey Kashtanov, Pavel Zevahin, Vladimir Martyshin, Nikita Panov, Anastasiya Barinova, and Vesta Matveeva.

Heather Mahalik is the director of forensic engineering with ManTech CARD, where she leads the forensic effort focusing on mobile and digital exploitation. She is a senior instructor and author for the SANS Institute, and she is also the course leader for the FOR585 Advanced Smartphone Forensics course. With over 15 years of experience in digital forensics, she continues to thrive on smartphone investigations, digital forensics, forensic course development and instruction, and research on application analysis and smartphone forensics.

Satish Bommisetty is a security analyst working for a Fortune 500 company. His primary areas of interest include iOS forensics, iOS application security, and web application security. He has presented at international conferences, such as ClubHACK and C0C0n. He is also one of the core members of the Hyderabad OWASP chapter. He has identified and disclosed vulnerabilities within the websites of Google, Facebook, Yandex, PayPal, Yahoo!, AT&T, and more, and they are listed in their hall of fame.

About the reviewer

Igor Mikhaylov has been working as a forensics expert for 21 years. During this time, he has attended a lot of seminars and training classes in top forensic companies and forensic departments of government organizations. He has experience and skills in cellphones forensics, chip-off forensics, malware forensics, and other fields. He has worked on several thousand forensic cases.

He is the reviewer of *Windows Forensics Cookbook* by Oleg Skulkin and Scar de Courcier, Packt Publishing, 2017.

He is the author of *Mobile Forensics Cookbook*, Packt Publishing, 2017.

Packt is searching for authors like you

If you're interested in becoming an author for Packt, please visit `authors.packtpub.com` and apply today. We have worked with thousands of developers and tech professionals, just like you, to help them share their insight with the global tech community. You can make a general application, apply for a specific hot topic that we are recruiting an author for, or submit your own idea.

Table of Contents

Preface

The exponential growth in smartphones has revolutionized several aspects of our lives. Smartphones are one of the most quickly adopted consumer technologies in recent history. Despite their small size, smartphones are capable of performing many tasks, such as sending private messages and confidential emails, taking photos and videos, making online purchases, viewing sensitive information such as medical records and salary slips, completing banking transactions, accessing social networking sites, and managing business tasks. Hence, a mobile device is now a huge repository of sensitive data, which could provide a wealth of information about its owner. This has in turn led to the evolution of mobile device forensics, a branch of digital forensics, which deals with retrieving data from a mobile device. Today, there is a huge demand for specialized forensic experts, especially given the fact that the data retrieved from a mobile device is court-admissible.

Mobile forensics is all about using scientific methodologies to recover data stored within a mobile phone for legal purposes. Unlike traditional computer forensics, mobile forensics has limitations in obtaining evidence due to rapid changes in technology and the fast-paced evolution of mobile software. With different operating systems and a wide range of models being released onto the market, mobile forensics has expanded over the past few years. Specialized forensic techniques and skills are required in order to extract data under different conditions.

This book takes you through various techniques to help you learn how to forensically recover data from different mobile devices with the iOS, Android, and Windows Mobile operating systems. This book also covers behind the scenes details, such as how data is stored and what tools actually do in the background, giving you deeper knowledge on several topics. Step-by-step instructions enable you to try forensically recovering data yourself.

The book is organized in a manner that allows you to focus independently on chapters that are specific to your required platform.

Who this book is for

This book is intended for forensic examiners with little or basic experience in mobile forensics or open source solutions for mobile forensics. The book will also be useful to computer security professionals, researchers, and anyone seeking a deeper understanding of mobile internals. It will also come in handy for those who are trying to recover accidentally deleted data (photos, contacts, SMS messages, and more).

What this book covers

Chapter 1, *Introduction to Mobile Forensics*, introduces you to the concepts of mobile forensics, the core values, and the challenges involved. The chapter also provides an overview of practical approaches and best practices involved in performing mobile forensics.

Chapter 2, *Understanding the Internals of iOS Devices*, provides an overview of the popular Apple iOS devices, including an outline of different models and their hardware. The book explains iOS security features and device security and its impact on iOS forensics approaches, focusing on iOS 9-11. The chapter also gives an overview of the HFS+ and APFS filesystems and outlines the sensitive files that are useful for forensic examination.

Chapter 3, *Data Acquisition from iOS Devices*, covers various types of forensic acquisition methods that can be performed on iOS devices, including logical, filesystem, and physical, and guides you to prepare your desktop machine for forensic work. The chapter also discusses passcode bypass techniques.

Chapter 4, *Data Acquisition from iOS Backups*, provides detailed explanations of modern iOS backups and details what types of files are stored in a backup. The chapter also includes step-by-step guides on creating encrypted and unencrypted backups and introduces forensic tools capable of recovering data from backups.

Chapter 5, *iOS Data Analysis and Recovery*, discusses the types of data that is stored on iOS devices and its most common locations in the filesystem. Common file types used in iOS devices, such as plists and SQLite databases, are discussed in detail in order to provide an understanding of how data is stored on a device, which will help forensic examiners to efficiently recover data from those files.

Chapter 6, *iOS Forensic Tools*, introduces you to the most widely used commercial mobile forensic suites, Cellebrite UFED, Belkasoft Evidence Center, Magnet AXIOM, and Oxygen Forensic Detective, and contains step-by-step guides on how to use them in mobile forensic examinations.

Chapter 7, *Understanding Android*, introduces you to the Android model, filesystem, and its security features. This chapter provides an explanation of how data is stored on any android device, which will be useful when carrying out forensic investigations.

Chapter 8, *Android Forensic Setup and Pre-Data Extraction Techniques*, guides you through Android forensic setup and other techniques to use before extracting any information. Screen lock bypass techniques and gaining root access are also discussed in this chapter.

Chapter 9, *Android Data Extraction Techniques*, provides an explanation of physical, filesystem, and logical acquisition techniques to extract relevant information from an Android device. This chapter covers imaging the device and other advanced techniques, such as JTAG and Chip-Off.

Chapter 10, *Android Data Analysis and Recovery*, explains how to extract and analyze data from Android image files. The chapter also covers the possibilities and limitations of recovering deleted data from Android devices.

Chapter 11, *Android App Analysis, Malware, and Reverse Engineering*, includes an analysis of some of the most widely used Android apps to retrieve valuable data. The chapter also covers Android malware and techniques to reverse engineer an Android app to view its data.

Chapter 12, *Windows Phone Forensics*, provides a basic overview of forensic approaches when dealing with Windows Phones.

Chapter 13, *Parsing Third-Party Application Files*, guides you through how applications are stored on Android, iOS, and Windows devices and how commercial and open source tools parse through appiication data.

To get the most out of this book

The book details practical forensic approaches and explains techniques in a simple manner. The content is organized in a way that allows even a user with basic computer skills to examine a device and extract the required data. A Mac, Windows, or Linux computer would be helpful to successfully repeat the methods defined in this book. Where possible, methods for all computer platforms are provided.

Download the color images

We also provide a PDF file that has color images of the screenshots/diagrams used in this book. You can download it here: `https://www.packtpub.com/sites/default/files/downloads/PracticalMobileForensicsThirdEdition_ColorImages.pdf`.

Conventions used

There are a number of text conventions used throughout this book.

`CodeInText`: Indicates code words in text, database table names, folder names, filenames, file extensions, pathnames, dummy URLs, user input, and Twitter handles. Here is an example: "Alternatively, the `ideviceinfo` command-line tool available in the `libimobiledevice` software library (`http://www.libimobiledevice.org/`) can be used to identify the iPhone model and its iOS version."

Any command-line input or output is written as follows:

```
$ ruby -e "$(curl -fsSL
https://raw.githubusercontent.com/Homebrew/install/master/install)"
< /dev/null 2> /dev/null
```

Bold: Indicates a new term, an important word, or words that you see onscreen. For example, words in menus or dialog boxes appear in the text like this. Here is an example: "Launch Belkasoft Acquisition Tool and choose the **Mobile device** option:"

 Warnings or important notes appear like this.

 Tips and tricks appear like this.

Get in touch

Feedback from our readers is always welcome.

General feedback: Email `feedback@packtpub.com` and mention the book title in the subject of your message. If you have questions about any aspect of this book, please email us at `questions@packtpub.com`.

Errata: Although we have taken every care to ensure the accuracy of our content, mistakes do happen. If you have found a mistake in this book, we would be grateful if you would report this to us. Please visit `www.packtpub.com/submit-errata`, selecting your book, clicking on the Errata Submission Form link, and entering the details.

Piracy: If you come across any illegal copies of our works in any form on the Internet, we would be grateful if you would provide us with the location address or website name. Please contact us at `copyright@packtpub.com` with a link to the material.

If you are interested in becoming an author: If there is a topic that you have expertise in and you are interested in either writing or contributing to a book, please visit `authors.packtpub.com`.

Reviews

Please leave a review. Once you have read and used this book, why not leave a review on the site that you purchased it from? Potential readers can then see and use your unbiased opinion to make purchase decisions, we at Packt can understand what you think about our products, and our authors can see your feedback on their book. Thank you!

For more information about Packt, please visit `packtpub.com`.

1
Introduction to Mobile Forensics

There is no doubt that mobile devices have become part of our lives and revolutionized the way we do most of our activities. As a result, a mobile device is now a huge repository that holds sensitive and personal information about its owner. This has, in turn, led to the rise of mobile device forensics, a branch of digital forensics that deals with retrieving data from a mobile device. This book will help you understand forensic techniques on three main platforms—Android, iOS, and Windows. We will go through various methods that can be followed to collect evidence from different mobile devices.

In this chapter, we will cover the following topics:

- Introduction to mobile forensics
- Challenges in mobile forensics
- Mobile phone evidence extraction process
- Mobile forensic approaches
- Good forensic practices

Why do we need mobile forensics?

According to Statista reports, the number of mobile phone users in the world is expected to pass 5 billion by 2019. The world is witnessing technology and user migration from desktops to mobile phones. Most of the growth in the mobile market can be attributed to the continued demand for smartphones. The following graph, sourced from `https://www.statista.com/`, shows the actual and estimated growth of smartphones from the year 2009 to the year 2019:

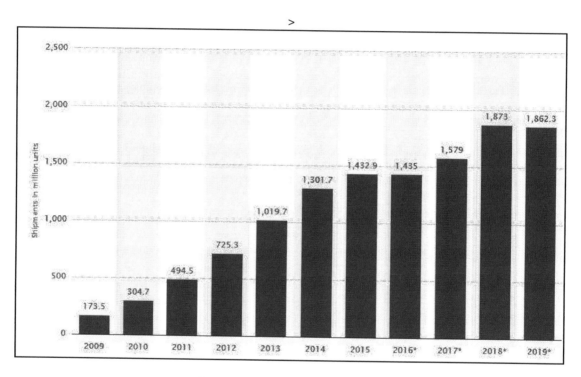

Growth of smartphones from 2009 to 2019 in million units

According to an Ericsson report, global mobile data traffic will reach 71 exabytes per month by 2022, from 8.8 exabytes in 2017, a compound annual growth rate of 42 percent. Smartphones of today, such as the Apple iPhone and the Samsung Galaxy series, are compact forms of computers with high performance, huge storage, and enhanced functionality. Mobile phones are the most personal electronic device that a user accesses. They are used to perform simple communication tasks, such as calling and texting, while still providing support for internet browsing, email, taking photos and videos, creating and storing documents, identifying locations with GPS services, and managing business tasks. As new features and applications are incorporated into mobile phones, the amount of information stored on the devices is continuously growing. Mobile phones become portable data carriers, and they keep track of all your movements. With the increasing prevalence of mobile phones in people's daily lives and in crime, data acquired from phones becomes an invaluable source of evidence for investigations relating to criminal, civil, and even high-profile cases. It is rare to conduct a digital forensic investigation that does not include a phone. Mobile device call logs and GPS data were used to help solve the attempted bombing in Times Square, New York, in 2010. The details of the case can be found at: `https://www.forensicon.com/forensics-blotter/cell-phone-email-forensics-investigation-cracks-nyc-times-square-car-bombing-case/`.

The science behind recovering digital evidence from mobile phones is called **mobile forensics**. Digital evidence is defined as information and data that is stored on, received, or transmitted by an electronic device that is used for investigations. Digital evidence encompasses any and all digital data that can be used as evidence in a case.

Mobile forensics

Digital forensics is a branch of forensic science focusing on the recovery and investigation of raw data residing in electronic or digital devices. The goal of the process is to extract and recover any information from a digital device without altering the data present on the device. Over the years, digital forensics has grown, along with the rapid growth of computers and various other digital devices. There are various branches of digital forensics based on the type of digital device involved, such as computer forensics, network forensics, mobile forensics, and so on.

Mobile forensics is a branch of digital forensics related to the recovery of digital evidence from mobile devices. **Forensically sound** is a term used extensively in the digital forensics community to qualify and justify the use of a particular forensic technology or methodology. The main principle for a sound forensic examination of digital evidence is that the original evidence must not be modified. This is extremely difficult with mobile devices. Some forensic tools require a communication vector with the mobile device, and thus a standard write protection will not work during forensic acquisition. Other forensic acquisition methods may involve removing a chip or installing a bootloader on the mobile device prior to extracting data for forensic examinations. In cases where the examination or data acquisition is not possible without changing the configuration of the device, the procedure and the changes must be tested, validated, and documented. Following proper methodology and guidelines is crucial in examining mobile devices as it yields the most valuable data. As with any evidence gathering, not following the proper procedure during the examination can result in loss or damage of evidence or render it inadmissible in court.

The mobile forensics process is broken down into three main categories—**seizure**, **acquisition**, and **examination/analysis**. Forensic examiners face some challenges while seizing the mobile device as a source of evidence. At the crime scene, if the mobile device is found switched off, the examiner should place the device in a **Faraday bag** to prevent changes should the device automatically power on. Faraday bags are specifically designed to isolate the phone from the network. A Faraday bag can be found at: `http://www.amazon.com/Black-Hole-Faraday-Bag-Isolation/dp/B0091WILY0`.

If the phone is found switched on, switching it off has a lot of concerns attached to it. If the phone is locked by a PIN or password, or encrypted, the examiner will be required to bypass the lock or determine the PIN to access the device. Mobile phones are networked devices and can send and receive data through different sources, such as telecommunication systems, Wi-Fi access points, and Bluetooth. So, if the phone is in a running state, a criminal can securely erase the data stored on the phone by executing a remote wipe command. When a phone is switched on, it should be placed in a Faraday bag. If possible, prior to placing the mobile device in the Faraday bag, disconnect it from the network to protect the evidence by enabling the flight mode and disabling all network connections (Wi-Fi, GPS, hotspots, and so on). This will also preserve the battery, which will drain while in a Faraday bag, and protect against leaks in the Faraday bag. Once the mobile device is seized properly, the examiner may need several forensic tools to acquire and analyze the data stored on the phone.

Mobile device forensic acquisition can be performed using multiple methods, which are defined later. Each of these methods affects the amount of analysis required, which will be discussed in greater detail in the upcoming chapters. Should one method fail, another must be attempted. Multiple attempts and tools may be necessary in order to acquire the maximum data from the mobile device.

Mobile phones are dynamic systems that present a lot of challenges to the examiner in extracting and analyzing digital evidence. The rapid increase in the number of different kinds of mobile phones from different manufacturers makes it difficult to develop a single process or tool to examine all types of devices. Mobile phones are continuously evolving as existing technologies progress and new technologies are introduced. Furthermore, each mobile is designed with a variety of embedded operating systems. Hence, special knowledge and skills are required from forensic experts to acquire and analyze the devices.

Challenges in mobile forensics

One of the biggest forensic challenges when it comes to the mobile platform is the fact that data can be accessed, stored, and synchronized across multiple devices. As the data is volatile and can be quickly transformed or deleted remotely, more effort is required for the preservation of this data. Mobile forensics is different from computer forensics and presents unique challenges to forensic examiners.

Law enforcement and forensic examiners often struggle to obtain digital evidence from mobile devices. The following are some of the reasons:

- **Hardware differences**: The market is flooded with different models of mobile phones from different manufacturers. Forensic examiners may come across different types of mobile models, which differ in size, hardware, features, and operating system. Also, with a short product development cycle, new models emerge very frequently. As the mobile landscape is changing each passing day, it is critical for the examiner to adapt to all the challenges and remain updated on mobile device forensic techniques across various devices.

- **Mobile operating systems**: Unlike personal computers, where Windows has dominated the market for years, mobile devices widely use more operating systems, including Apple's iOS, Google's Android, RIM's BlackBerry OS, Microsoft's Windows Phone OS, HP's webOS, and many others. Even within these operating systems, there are several versions, which makes the task of the forensic investigator even more difficult.

- **Mobile platform security features**: Modern mobile platforms contain built-in security features to protect user data and privacy. These features act as a hurdle during forensic acquisition and examination. For example, modern mobile devices come with default encryption mechanisms from the hardware layer to the software layer. The examiner might need to break through these encryption mechanisms to extract data from the devices. The FBI versus Apple encryption dispute was a watershed moment in this regard, where the security implementation of Apple prevented the FBI from breaking into the iPhone seized from an attacker in the San Bernardino case.

- **Preventing data modification**: One of the fundamental rules in forensics is to make sure that data on the device is not modified. In other words, any attempt to extract data from the device should not alter the data present on that device. But this is not practically possible with mobiles because just switching on a device can change the data on that device. Even if a device appears to be in an off state, background processes may still run. For example, in most mobiles, the alarm clock still works even when the phone is switched off. A sudden transition from one state to another may result in the loss or modification of data.

- **Anti-forensic techniques**: Anti-forensic techniques, such as data hiding, data obfuscation, data forgery, and secure wiping, make investigations on digital media more difficult.

- **Passcode recovery**: If the device is protected with a passcode, the forensic examiner needs to gain access to the device without damaging the data on the device. While there are techniques to bypass the screen lock, they may not always work on all the versions.

- **Lack of resources**: As mentioned earlier, with the growing number of mobile phones, the tools required by a forensic examiner would also increase. Forensic acquisition accessories, such as USB cables, batteries, and chargers for different mobile phones, have to be maintained in order to acquire those devices.

- **Dynamic nature of evidence**: Digital evidence may be easily altered either intentionally or unintentionally. For example, browsing an application on the phone might alter the data stored by that application on the device.

- **Accidental reset**: Mobile phones provide features to reset everything. Resetting the device accidentally while examining it may result in the loss of data.

- **Device alteration**: The possible ways to alter devices may range from moving application data or renaming files, to modifying the manufacturer's operating system. In this case, the expertise of the suspect should be taken into account.

- **Communication shielding**: Mobile devices communicate over cellular networks, Wi-Fi networks, Bluetooth, and infrared. As device communication might alter the device data, the possibility of further communication should be eliminated after seizing the device.
- **Lack of availability of tools**: There is a wide range of mobile devices. A single tool may not support all the devices or perform all the necessary functions, so a combination of tools needs to be used. Choosing the right tool for a particular phone might be difficult.
- **Malicious programs**: The device might contain malicious software or malware, such as a virus or a Trojan. Such malicious programs may attempt to spread over other devices over either a wired interface or a wireless one.
- **Legal issues**: Mobile devices might be involved in crimes, which can cross geographical boundaries. In order to tackle these multijurisdictional issues, the forensic examiner should be aware of the nature of the crime and the regional laws.

The mobile phone evidence extraction process

Evidence extraction and forensic examination of each mobile device may differ. However, following a consistent examination process will assist the forensic examiner to ensure that the evidence extracted from each phone is well-documented and that the results are repeatable and defendable. There is no well-established standard process for mobile forensics.

However, the following figure provides an overview of process considerations for the extraction of evidence from mobile devices. All methods used when extracting data from mobile devices should be tested, validated, and well-documented:

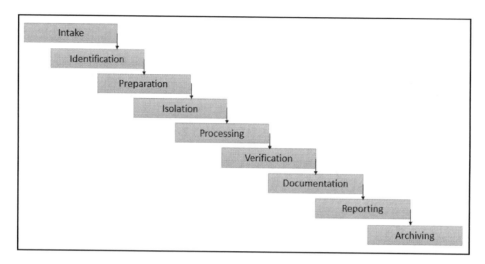

Mobile phone evidence extraction process

 A great resource for handling and processing mobile devices can be found at: http://digital-forensics.sans.org/media/mobile-device-forensic-process-v3.pdf.

As shown in the preceding figure, forensics on a mobile device includes several phases, from the evidence intake phase to the archiving phase. The following sections provide an overview of various considerations across all the phases.

The evidence intake phase

The evidence intake phase is the starting phase and entails request forms and paperwork to document ownership information and the type of incident the mobile device was involved in, and it outlines the type of data or information the requester is seeking. Developing specific objectives for each examination is the critical part of this phase. It serves to clarify the examiner's goals. Also, while seizing the device, care should be taken not to modify any data present on the device. At the same time, any opportunity that might help the investigation should not be missed. For example, at the time of seizing the device, if the device is unlocked, then try to disable the passcode.

The identification phase

The forensic examiner should identify the following details for every examination of a mobile device:

- The legal authority
- The goals of the examination
- The make, model, and identifying information for the device
- Removable and external data storage
- Other sources of potential evidence

We will discuss each of them in the following sections.

The legal authority

It is important for the forensic examiner to determine and document what legal authority exists for the acquisition and examination of the device, as well as any limitations placed on the media prior to the examination of the device. For example, if the mobile device is being searched pursuant to a warrant, the examiner should be mindful of confining the search to the limitations of the warrant.

The goals of the examination

The examiner will identify how in-depth the examination needs to be based upon the data requested. The goal of the examination makes a significant difference in selecting the tools and techniques to examine the phone and increases the efficiency of the examination process.

The make, model, and identifying information for the device

As part of the examination, identifying the make and model of the phone assists in determining what tools would work with the phone. For all phones, the manufacturer, model number, carrier, and the current phone number associated with the cellular phone should be identified and documented.

Removable and external data storage

Many mobile phones provide an option to extend the memory with removable storage devices, such as the Trans Flash Micro SD memory expansion card. In cases when such a card is found in a mobile phone that is submitted for examination, the card should be removed and processed using traditional digital forensic techniques. It is wise to also acquire the card while in the mobile device to ensure that data stored on both the handset memory and card are linked for easier analysis. This will be discussed in detail in upcoming chapters.

Other sources of potential evidence

Mobile phones act as good sources of fingerprint and other biological evidence. Such evidence should be collected prior to the examination of the mobile phone to avoid contamination issues, unless the collection method will damage the device. Examiners should wear gloves when handling the evidence.

The preparation phase

Once the mobile phone model is identified, the preparation phase involves research regarding the particular mobile phone to be examined and the appropriate methods and tools to be used for acquisition and examination. This is generally done based on the device model, underlying operating system, its version, and so on. Also, choosing tools for examination of a mobile device will be determined by factors such as the goal of the examination, resources available, the type of cellular phone to be examined, and the presence of any external storage capabilities.

The isolation phase

Mobile phones are, by design, intended to communicate via cellular phone networks, Bluetooth, infrared, and wireless (Wi-Fi) network capabilities. When the phone is connected to a network, new data is added to the phone through incoming calls, messages, and application data, which modifies the evidence on the phone. Complete destruction of data is also possible through remote access or remote wiping commands. For this reason, isolation of the device from communication sources is important prior to the acquisition and examination of the device. Network isolation can be done by placing the phone in radio frequency shielding cloth and then putting the phone in airplane or flight mode. The airplane mode disables a device's communication channels, such as cellular radio, Wi-Fi, and Bluetooth. However, if the device is screen-locked, then this is not possible. Also, since Wi-Fi is now available in airplanes, some devices now have Wi-Fi access enabled in airplane mode. An alternate solution is isolation of the phone through the use of Faraday bags, which block radio signals to or from the phone. Faraday bags contain materials that block external static electrical fields (including radio waves). Thus, Faraday bags shield seized mobile devices from external interference to prevent wiping and tracking. To work more conveniently with the seized devices, Faraday tents and rooms also exist.

The processing phase

Once the phone has been isolated from communication networks, the actual processing of the mobile phone begins. The phone should be acquired using a tested method that is repeatable and is as forensically sound as possible. Physical acquisition is the preferred method as it extracts the raw memory data and the device is commonly powered off during the acquisition process. On most devices, the smallest number of changes occur to the device during physical acquisition. If physical acquisition is not possible or fails, an attempt should be made to acquire the filesystem of the mobile device. A logical acquisition should always be obtained as it may contain only the parsed data and provide pointers to examine the raw memory image. These acquisition methods are discussed in detail in later chapters.

The verification phase

After processing the phone, the examiner needs to verify the accuracy of the data extracted from the phone to ensure that data has not been modified. The verification of the extracted data can be accomplished in several ways.

Comparing extracted data to the handset data

Check whether the data extracted from the device matches the data displayed by the device. The data extracted can be compared to the device itself or a logical report, whichever is preferred. Remember, handling the original device may make changes to the only evidence—the device itself.

Using multiple tools and comparing the results

To ensure accuracy, use multiple tools to extract the data and compare results.

Using hash values

All image files should be hashed after acquisition to ensure that data remains unchanged. If filesystem extraction is supported, the examiner extracts the filesystem and then computes hashes for the extracted files. Later, any individually extracted file hash is calculated and checked against the original value to verify the integrity of it. Any discrepancy in a hash value must be explainable (for example, the device was powered on and then acquired again, thus the hash values are different).

The documenting and reporting phase

The forensic examiner is required to document throughout the examination process in the form of contemporaneous notes relating to what was done during the acquisition and examination. Once the examiner completes the investigation, the results must go through some form of peer review to ensure that the data is checked and the investigation is complete. The examiner's notes and documentation may include information such as the following:

- The examination start date and time
- The physical condition of the phone
- Photos of the phone and individual components
- Phone status when received—turned on or off
- Phone make and model
- Tools used for the acquisition
- Tools used for the examination
- Data found during the examination
- Notes from peer review

The presentation phase

Throughout the investigation, it is important to make sure that the information extracted and documented from a mobile device can be clearly presented to any other examiner or to a court. Creating a forensic report of data extracted from the mobile device during acquisition and analysis is important. This may include data in both paper and electronic formats. Your findings must be documented and presented in a manner that the evidence speaks for itself when in court. The findings should be clear, concise, and repeatable. Timeline and link analysis, features offered by many commercial mobile forensic tools, will aid in reporting and explaining findings across multiple mobile devices. These tools allow the examiner to tie together the methods behind the communication of multiple devices.

The archiving phase

Preserving the data extracted from the mobile phone is an important part of the overall process. It is also important that the data is retained in a usable format for the ongoing court process, for future reference, should the current evidence file become corrupt, and for record-keeping requirements. Court cases may continue for many years before the final judgment is arrived at, and most jurisdictions require that data be retained for long periods of time for the purposes of appeals. As the field and methods advance, new methods for pulling data out of a raw, physical image may surface, and then the examiner can revisit the data by pulling a copy from the archives.

Practical mobile forensic approaches

Similar to any forensic investigation, there are several approaches that can be used for the acquisition and examination/analysis of data from mobile phones. The type of mobile device, the operating system, and the security setting generally dictate the procedure to be followed in a forensic process. Every investigation is distinct with its own circumstances, so it is not possible to design a single definitive procedural approach for all cases. The following details outline the general approaches followed in extracting data from mobile devices.

Overview of mobile operating systems

One of the major factors in the data acquisition and examination/analysis of a mobile phone is the operating system. From low-end mobile phones to smartphones, mobile operating systems have come a long way with a lot of features. Mobile operating systems directly affect how the examiner can access the mobile device. For example, Android OS gives terminal-level access whereas iOS does not give such an option. A comprehensive understanding of the mobile platform helps the forensic examiner make sound forensic decisions and conduct a conclusive investigation. While there is a large range of smart mobile devices, with the demise of Blackberry, currently two main operating systems dominate the market, namely Google Android and Apple iOS (followed by Windows Phone at a distant third). More information can be found at: `https://www.idc.com/promo/smartphone-market-share/os`. This book covers forensic analysis of these three mobile platforms. We will provide a brief overview of the leading mobile operating systems.

Android

Android is a Linux-based operating system, and it's a Google open source platform for mobile phones. Android is the world's most widely used smartphone operating system. Sources show that Apple's iOS stands second (`https://www.idc.com/promo/smartphone-market-share/os`). Android has been developed by Google as an open and free option for hardware manufacturers and phone carriers. This makes Android the software of choice for companies who require a low-cost, customizable, lightweight operating system for their smart devices without developing a new OS from scratch. Android's open nature has further encouraged developers to build a large number of applications and upload them onto Google Play. Later, end users can download the application from Android Market, which makes Android a powerful operating system. It is estimated that Google Play Store has 3.3 million apps at the time of writing this book. More details on Android are covered in `Chapter 7`, *Understanding Android*.

iOS

iOS, formerly known as the iPhone operating system, is a mobile operating system developed and distributed solely by Apple Inc. iOS is evolving into a universal operating system for all Apple mobile devices, such as iPad, iPod touch, and iPhone. iOS is derived from OS X, with which it shares the Darwin foundation, and is therefore a Unix-like operating system. iOS manages the device hardware and provides the technologies required to implement native applications. iOS also ships with various system applications, such as Mail and Safari, which provide standard system services to the user. iOS native applications are distributed through AppStore, which is closely monitored by Apple. More details about iOS are covered in Chapter 2, *Understanding the Internals of iOS Devices*.

Windows Phone

Windows Phone is a proprietary mobile operating system developed by Microsoft for smartphones and pocket PCs. It is the successor to Windows Mobile and primarily aimed at the consumer market rather than the enterprise market. The Windows Phone OS is similar to the Windows desktop OS, but it is optimized for devices with a small amount of storage. Windows Phone basics and forensic techniques are discussed in Chapter 12, *Windows Phone Forensics*.

Mobile forensic tool leveling system

Mobile phone forensic acquisition and analysis involves manual effort and the use of automated tools. There are a variety of tools that are available for performing mobile forensics. All the tools have their pros and cons, and it is fundamental that you understand that no single tool is sufficient for all purposes. So, understanding various types of mobile forensic tools is important for forensic examiners.

When identifying the appropriate tools for the forensic acquisition and analysis of mobile phones, a mobile device forensic tool classification system developed by Sam Brothers (shown in the following figure) comes in handy for examiners:

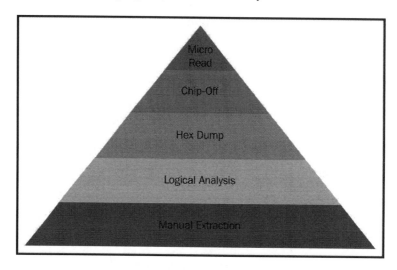

Cellular phone tool leveling pyramid (Sam Brothers, 2009)

The objective of the mobile device forensic tool classification system is to enable an examiner to categorize forensic tools based on the examination methodology of the tool. Starting at the bottom of the classification and working upward, the methods and the tools generally become more technical, complex, and forensically sound, and require longer analysis times. There are pros and cons of performing an analysis at each layer. The forensic examiner should be aware of these issues and should only proceed with the level of extraction that is required. Evidence can be destroyed completely if the given method or tool is not properly utilized. This risk increases as you move up in the pyramid. Thus, proper training is required to obtain the highest success rate in data extraction from mobile devices.

Each existing mobile forensic tool can be classified under one or more of the five levels. The following sections contain a detailed description of each level.

Manual extraction

The manual extraction method involves simply scrolling through the data on the device and viewing the data on the phone directly through the use of the device's keypad or touchscreen. The information discovered is then photographically documented. The extraction process is fast and easy to use, and it will work on almost every phone. This method is prone to human error, such as missing certain data due to unfamiliarity with the interface. At this level, it is not possible to recover deleted information and grab all the data. There are some tools, such as Project-A-Phone, that have been developed to aid an examiner to easily document a manual extraction. However, this might also result in the modification of data. For example, viewing an unread SMS can mark it as read.

Logical extraction

Logical extraction involves connecting the mobile device to forensic hardware or to a forensic workstation via a USB cable, a RJ-45 cable, infrared, or Bluetooth. Once connected, the computer initiates a command and sends it to the device, which is then interpreted by the device processor. Next, the requested data is received from the device's memory and sent back to the forensic workstation. Later, the examiner can review the data. Most of the forensic tools currently available work at this level of the classification system. The extraction process is fast, easy to use, and requires little training for the examiners. On the flip side, the process may write data to the mobile and might change the integrity of the evidence. In addition, deleted data is not generally accessible with this procedure.

Hex dump

A hex dump, also referred to as a physical extraction, is achieved by connecting the device to the forensic workstation and pushing unsigned code or a bootloader into the phone and instructing the phone to dump memory from the phone to the computer. Since the resulting raw image is in binary format, technical expertise is required to analyze it. The process is inexpensive, provides more data to the examiner, and allows the recovery of deleted files from the device-unallocated space on most devices.

Chip-off

Chip-off refers to the acquisition of data directly from the device's memory chip. At this level, the chip is physically removed from the device and a chip reader or a second phone is used to extract data stored on it. This method is more technically challenging, as a wide variety of chip types are used in mobiles. The process is expensive and requires hardware-level knowledge as it involves the desoldering and heating of the memory chip. Training is required to successfully perform a chip-off extraction. Improper procedures may damage the memory chip and render all data unsalvageable. When possible, it is recommended that the other levels of extraction are attempted prior to chip-off, since this method is destructive in nature. Also, the information that comes out of memory is in a raw format and has to be parsed, decoded, and interpreted. The chip-off method is preferred in situations where it is important to preserve the state of memory exactly as it exists on the device. It is also the only option when a device is damaged but the memory chip is intact.

The chips on the device are often read using the **Joint Test Action Group (JTAG)** method. The JTAG method involves connecting to **Test Access Ports (TAPs)** on a device and instructing the processor to transfer the raw data stored on memory chips. The JTAG method is generally used with devices that are operational but inaccessible using standard tools. Both of these techniques also work even when the device is screen-locked.

Micro read

The micro read process involves manually viewing and interpreting data seen on the memory chip. The examiner uses an electron microscope and analyzes the physical gates on the chip and then translates the gate status to 0s and 1s to determine the resulting ASCII characters. The whole process is time-consuming and costly, and it requires extensive knowledge and training on memory and the filesystem. Due to the extreme technicalities involved in micro read, it would be only attempted for high-profile cases equivalent to a national security crisis after all other level extraction techniques have been exhausted. The process is rarely performed and is not well-documented at this time. Also, there are currently no commercial tools available to perform a micro read.

Data acquisition methods

Data acquisition is the process of imaging or otherwise extracting information from a digital device and its peripheral equipment and media. Acquiring data from a mobile phone is not as simple as a standard hard drive forensic acquisition. The following points break down the three types of forensic acquisition methods for mobile phones—**physical**, **logical**, and **manual**. These methods may have some overlap with a couple of levels discussed in the mobile forensics tool leveling system. The amount and type of data that can be collected will vary depending on the type of acquisition method being used. While we cover these methods in detail in the upcoming chapters, the following is a brief description of them.

Physical acquisition

Physical acquisition of a mobile device is nothing but a bit-by-bit copy of the physical storage. Physical extraction acquires information from the device by direct access to the flash memory. Flash memory is a non-volatile memory and is primarily used in memory cards and USB flash drives as solid-state storage. The process creates a bit-for-bit copy of an entire filesystem, similar to the approach taken in computer forensic investigations. A physical acquisition is able to acquire all of the data present on a device, including the deleted data and access to unallocated space on most devices.

Logical acquisition

Logical acquisition is about extracting the logical storage objects, such as files and directories, that reside on the filesystem. Logical acquisition of mobile phones is performed using the device manufacturer application programming interface to synchronize the phone's contents with a computer. Many of the forensic tools perform a logical acquisition. It is much easier for a forensic tool to organize and present the data extracted through logical acquisition. However, the forensic analyst must understand how the acquisition occurs and whether the mobile is modified in any way during the process. Depending on the phone and forensic tools used, all or some of the data is acquired. A logical acquisition is easy to perform and only recovers the files on a mobile phone and does not recover data contained in unallocated space.

Manual acquisition

With mobile phones, physical acquisition is usually the best option, and logical acquisition is the second-best option. Manual extraction should be the last option when performing the forensic acquisition of a mobile phone. Both logical and manual acquisition can be used to validate findings in the physical data. During manual acquisition, the examiner utilizes the user interface to investigate the contents of the phone's memory. The device is used normally through keypad or touchscreen and menu navigation, and the examiner takes pictures of each screen's contents. Manual extraction introduces a greater degree of risk in the form of human error, and there is a chance of deleting the evidence. Manual acquisition is easy to perform and only acquires the data that appears on a mobile phone.

Potential evidence stored on mobile phones

The range of information that can be obtained from mobile phones is detailed in this section. Data on a mobile phone can be found in a number of locations--SIM card, external storage card, and phone memory. In addition, the service provider also stores communication-related information. The book primarily focuses on data acquired from the phone memory. Mobile device data extraction tools recover data from the phone's memory. Even though data recovered during a forensic acquisition depends on the mobile model, in general, the following data is common across all models and useful as evidence. Note that most of the following artifacts contain date- and timestamps:

- **Address book**: This contains contact names, phone numbers, email addresses, and so on
- **Call history**: This contains dialed, received, missed calls, and call duration
- **SMS**: This contains sent and received text messages
- **MMS**: This contains media files such as sent and received photos and videos
- **E-mail**: This contains sent, drafted, and received email messages
- **Web browser history**: This contains the history of websites that were visited
- **Photos**: This contains pictures that were captured using the mobile phone camera, those downloaded from the internet, and the ones transferred from other devices

- **Videos**: This contains videos that are captured using the mobile camera, those downloaded from the internet, and the ones transferred from other devices
- **Music**: This contains music files downloaded from the internet and those transferred from other devices
- **Documents**: This contains documents created using the device's applications, those downloaded from the internet, and the ones transferred from other devices
- **Calendar**: This contains calendar entries and appointments
- **Network communication**: This contains GPS locations
- **Maps**: This contains places the user visited, looked-up directions, and searched and downloaded maps
- **Social networking data**: This contains data stored by applications, such as Facebook, Twitter, LinkedIn, Google+, and WhatsApp
- **Deleted data**: This contains information deleted from the phone

Examination and analysis

This is the ultimate step in the investigation, which aims to uncover data that is present on the device. Examination is done by applying well-tested and scientific methods to conclusively establish the results. The analysis phase is focused on separating relevant data from the rest and to probe data which is of value to the underlying case. The examination process starts with a copy of the evidence acquired using some of the techniques described above, which will be covered in detail in the next chapters. Examination and analysis using third-party tools is generally performed by importing the device's memory dump into a mobile forensics tool which will automatically retrieve the results. Understanding the case is also crucial to perform a targeted analysis of the data. For example, a case about child pornography may require focusing on all of the images present on the device rather than looking at other artifacts.

It is important that the examiner has fair knowledge of how the forensic tools which are used for examination work. Proficient use of the features and options available in the tool will drastically speed up the examination process. Sometimes, due to programming flaws in the software, the tool may not be able to recognize or convert bits into a format comprehensible by the examiner. Hence, it is crucial that the examiner has the necessary skills to identify such situations and use alternate tools or software to construct the results. In some cases, the individual may purposefully tamper with the device information or may delete/hide some of the crucial data. Forensic analysts should understand the limitations of the tool and sometimes compensate for them to achieve the best possible results. To analyze the extracted data, the US Department of Justice has published the following suggestions (referenced directly from: `https://www.ncjrs.gov/pdffiles1/nij/199408.pdf`) in the publication *Forensic Examination of Digital Evidence - A Guide for Law Enforcement*:

- **Ownership and possession**: Identify the individuals who created, modified, or accessed a file, and the ownership and possession of questioned data by placing the subject with the device at a particular time and date, locating files of interest in non-default locations, recovering passwords that indicate possession, and identifying contents of files that are specific to a user.

- **Application and file analysis**: Identify information relevant to the investigation by examining file content, correlating files to installed applications, identifying relationships between files (for example, email files to email attachments), determining the significance of unknown file types, examining system configuration settings, and examining file metadata (for example, documents containing authorship identification).

- **Timeframe analysis**: Determine when events occurred on the system to associate usage with an individual by reviewing any logs present and the date-/timestamps in the filesystem, such as the last modified time. Besides call logs, the date/time and content of messages and email can prove useful. Such data can also be corroborated with billing and subscriber records kept by the service provider.

- **Data hiding analysis**: Detect and recover hidden data that may indicate knowledge, ownership, or intent by correlating file headers to file extensions to show intentional obfuscation; gaining access to password-protected, encrypted, and compressed files; and gaining access to steganographic information detected in images.

Rules of evidence

Courtrooms rely more and more on the information inside a mobile phone as vital evidence. Prevailing evidence in court requires a good understanding of the rules of evidence. Mobile forensics is a relatively new discipline and laws dictating the validity of evidence are not widely known and they also differ from country to country. However, there are five general rules of evidence that apply to digital forensics and need to be followed in order for evidence to be useful. Ignoring these rules makes evidence inadmissible, and your case could be thrown out. These five rules are: admissible, authentic, complete, reliable, and believable:

- **Admissible**: This is the most basic rule and a measure of evidence validity and importance. The evidence must be preserved and gathered in such a way that it can be used in court or elsewhere. Many errors can be made that could cause a judge to rule a piece of evidence as inadmissible. For example, evidence that is gathered using illegal methods is commonly ruled inadmissible.
- **Authentic**: The evidence must be tied to the incident in a relevant way to prove something. The forensic examiner must be accountable for the origin of the evidence.
- **Complete**: When evidence is presented, it must be clear and complete, and should reflect the whole story. It is not enough to collect evidence that just shows one perspective of the incident. Presenting incomplete evidence is more dangerous than not providing any evidence at all, as it could lead to a different judgment.
- **Reliable**: Evidence collected from the device must be reliable. This depends on the tools and methodology used. The techniques used and evidence collected must not cast doubt on the authenticity of the evidence. If the examiner used some techniques that cannot be reproduced, the evidence is not considered unless they were directed to do so. This would include possible destructive methods such as chip-off extraction.
- **Believable**: A forensic examiner must be able to explain, with clarity and conciseness, what processes they used and the way the integrity of the evidence was preserved. The evidence presented by the examiner must be clear, easy to understand, and believable by the jury.

Good forensic practices

Good forensic practices apply to the collection and preservation of evidence. Following good forensic practices ensures that evidence will be accepted in a court as being authentic and accurate. Modification of evidence, either intentionally or accidentally, can affect the case. So, understanding the best practices is critical for forensic examiners.

Securing the evidence

With advanced smartphone features such as **Find My iPhone** and remote wipes, securing a mobile phone in a way that it cannot be remotely wiped is of great importance. Also, when the phone is powered on and has service, it constantly receives new data. To secure the evidence, use the right equipment and techniques to isolate the phone from all networks. With isolation, the phone is prevented from receiving any new data that would cause active data to be deleted. Depending on the case, sometimes traditional forensic measures, such as fingerprints or DNA testing, may also need to be applied to establish a connection between a mobile device and its owner. If the device is not handled in a secure manner, physical evidence may be unintentionally tampered with and may be rendered useless. It is also important to collect any peripherals, associated media, cables, power adapters, and other accessories that are present at the scene. At the scene of investigation, if the device is found to be connected to a personal computer, pulling it directly would stop the data transfer. Instead, it is recommended to capture the memory of the personal computer before pulling the device, as this contains significant details in many cases.

Preserving the evidence

As evidence is collected, it must be preserved in a state that is acceptable in court. Working directly on the original copies of evidence might alter it. So, as soon as you recover a raw disk image or files, create a read-only master copy and duplicate it. In order for evidence to be admissible, there must be a method to verify that the evidence presented is exactly the same as the original collected. This can be accomplished by creating a forensic hash value of the image. A forensic hash is used to ensure the integrity of an acquisition by calculating a cryptographically strong and non-reversible value of the image/data. After duplicating the raw disk image or files, compute and verify the hash values for the original and the copy to ensure that the integrity of the evidence is maintained. Any changes in hash values should be documented and explainable. All further processing or examination should be performed on copies of the evidence. Any use of the device might alter the information stored on the handset. So, only perform the tasks that are absolutely necessary.

Documenting the evidence and changes

Whenever possible, a record of all visible data should be created. It is recommended to photograph the mobile device along with any of the other media found, such as cables, peripherals, and so on. This will be helpful in case questions arise later on about the environment. Do not touch or lay hands on the mobile device when photographing it. Ensure that you document all the methods and tools that are used to collect and extract the evidence. Detail your notes so that another examiner can reproduce them. Your work must be reproducible; if not, a judge may rule it inadmissible. It's important to document the entire recovery process, including all the changes made during the acquisition and examination. For example, if the forensic tool used for the data extraction sliced up the disk image to store it, this must be documented. All changes to the mobile device, including power cycling and syncing, should be documented in your case notes.

Reporting

Reporting is the process of preparing a detailed summary of all the steps taken and conclusions reached as part of the examination. Reporting should include details about all the important actions performed by the examiner, results of the acquisition, and any inferences drawn from the results. Most of the forensic tools come with built-in reporting features which will autogenerate the reports while providing scope for customization at the same time. In general, the report may contain the following details:

- Details of the reporting agency
- Case identifier
- Forensic investigator
- Identity of the submitter
- Date of evidence receipt
- Details of the device seized for examination including serial number, make, and model
- Details of the equipment and tools used in the examination
- Description of steps taken during examination
- Chain of custody documentation
- Details of findings or issues identified
- Evidence recovered during the examination, ranging from chat messages, browser history, and call logs to deleted messages, and so on

- Any images captured during the examination
- Examination and analysis information
- Report conclusion

Summary

Mobile devices store a wide range of information, such as SMS, call logs, browser history, chat messages, location details, and so on. Mobile device forensics includes many approaches and concepts that fall outside the boundaries of traditional digital forensics. Extreme care should be taken while handling the device, right from the evidence intake phase to the archiving phase. Examiners responsible for mobile devices must understand the different acquisition methods and the complexities of handling the data during analysis. Extracting data from a mobile device is half the battle. The operating system, security features, and type of smartphone will determine the amount of access you have to the data. It is important to follow sound forensic practices and make sure that the evidence is unaltered during the investigation.

The next chapter will provide an insight into iOS forensics. You will learn about the filesystem layout, security features, and the way files are stored on an iOS device.

2
Understanding the Internals of iOS Devices

In October 2017 alone, Apple sold more than 170,000 iPhones and more than 33,000 iPads according to released sales records. While iOS is the leading operating system for tablets worldwide, Android continues to be the leading operating system for smartphones worldwide. Regardless of the statistics, if you are a forensic examiner, the chances are that you will need to conduct an examination of an iOS device.

In order to perform a forensic examination of an iOS device, the examiner must understand the internal components and inner workings of that device. Developing an understanding of the underlying components of a mobile device will help the forensic examiner understand the criticalities involved in the forensic process, including what data can be acquired, where the data is stored, and what methods can be used to access the data from that device. So, before we delve into the examination of iOS devices, it is necessary to know the different models that exist and their internal components. Throughout this book, we will perform forensic acquisition and analysis on iOS devices, including the iPhone, iPad, and Apple Watch.

The goal of this chapter is to introduce you to the iOS device technology. We will cover details that may often get overlooked, but will help you during your forensic investigation. You must understand the different iOS devices and how data is stored on the devices before you can successfully extract it.

In this chapter, we will cover the following topics in detail:

- iPhone models and hardware
- iPad models and hardware
- Apple Watch models and hardware

- iOS overview
- HFS Plus overview
- APFS overview
- Jailbreaking

iPhone models

The iPhone is among the most popular smartphones on the market. Apple released the first-generation iPhone in June 2007. Ever since the first release, the iPhone has gained a lot of popularity due to its advanced functionality and usability. The introduction of the iPhone has redefined the entire world of mobile computing. Consumers started looking for faster and more efficient phones. Various iPhone models exist now, with different features and storage capabilities to serve consumer requirements.

The iPhones released since the second edition of *Practical Mobile Forensics*, the iPhone SE, 7, 7 Plus, 8, 8 Plus, and X, remain difficult when dealing with physical forensic acquisition methods. Just like the devices released since the iPhone 5, there is no method or tool available to physically recover data from these devices, unless they are jailbroken. However, the filesystem and a logical acquisition can be obtained if the iPhone is unlocked. Acquisition methods for data extraction are available and will be discussed in `Chapter 3`, *Data Acquisition from iOS Devices*, and `Chapter 4`, *Data Acquisition from iOS Backups*.

Identifying the correct hardware model

Before examining an iPhone, it is necessary to identify the correct hardware model and the firmware version installed on the device. Knowing the iPhone's details helps you to understand the criticalities and possibilities of obtaining evidence from the iPhone. For example, in many cases, the device passcode is required in order to obtain the filesystem or logical image. Even if the device is supported physically, the passcode is needed to decrypt artifacts such as emails and passwords. Depending on the iOS version, device model, and passcode complexity, it may be possible to obtain the device passcode using a brute-force attack.

There are various ways to identify the hardware of a device. The easiest way to identify the hardware of a device is by observing the model number displayed on the back of the device. Apple's knowledge base articles can be helpful for this purpose. Details on identifying iPhone models can be found at `https://support.apple.com/en-in/HT201296`.

The firmware version of an iPhone can be found by accessing the **Settings** option and then navigating to **General** | **About** | **Version**, as shown in the following screenshot. The purpose of the firmware is to enable certain features and assist with the general functioning of the device:

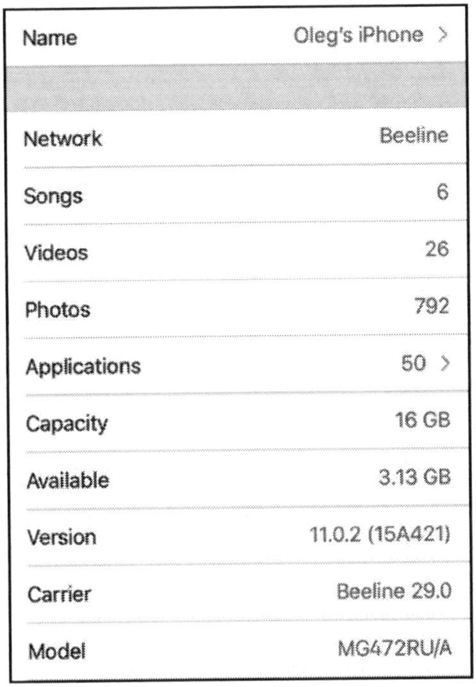

Name	Oleg's iPhone >
Network	Beeline
Songs	6
Videos	26
Photos	792
Applications	50 >
Capacity	16 GB
Available	3.13 GB
Version	11.0.2 (15A421)
Carrier	Beeline 29.0
Model	MG472RU/A

The iPhone About screen, displaying firmware version 11.0.2 (15A421)

Alternatively, the `ideviceinfo` command-line tool available in the `libimobiledevice` software library (`http://www.libimobiledevice.org/`) can be used to identify the iPhone model and its iOS version. The library allows you to communicate with an iPhone even if the device is locked by a passcode. The easiest way to get it is to use Homebrew, a free and open source software package management system for Apple's macOS operating system.

To obtain the iPhone model and its iOS version information on macOS 10.12.6, follow these steps:

1. Open the Terminal application.
2. From the command line, run the following command to download and install Homebrew:

```
$ ruby -e "$(curl -fsSL
https://raw.githubusercontent.com/Homebrew/install/master/install)"
< /dev/null 2> /dev/null
```

3. Once it's installed, you are ready to install the libimobiledevice library:

```
$ brew install libimobiledevice
```

4. Connect the iPhone to your Mac workstation using a USB cable and run the ideviceinfo command with the -s option:

```
$ ideviceinfo -s
```

The output of the ideviceinfo command displays the iPhone identifier, internal name, and the iOS version, as shown here:

```
Olegs-MacBook-Air:~ olegskulkin$ ideviceinfo -s
BasebandCertId: 3840149528
BasebandKeyHashInformation:
 AKeyStatus: 2
 SKeyHash: u+/tcCwvaQ+1Y9t40I4yegCEmB28mALlaROhaIVGBWo=
 SKeyStatus: 0
BasebandSerialNumber: COM6Tw==
BasebandVersion: 6.17.00
BoardId: 6
BuildVersion: 15A421
ChipID: 28672
DeviceClass: iPhone
DeviceColor: #3b3b3c
DeviceName: Oleg's iPhone
DieID: 62230050064422
HardwareModel: N61AP
HasSiDP: true
PartitionType: GUID_partition_scheme
ProductName: iPhone OS
ProductType: iPhone7,2
ProductVersion: 11.0.2
ProductionSOC: true
ProtocolVersion: 2
TelephonyCapability: true
UniqueChipID: 62230050064422
UniqueDeviceID: 4fecf6418e3fc6dc6fb787de53f51a557267b3af
WiFiAddress: 64:9a:be:81:73:54
Olegs-MacBook-Air:~ olegskulkin$
```

Output from libimobiledevice displaying firmware version 11.0.2 (15A421)

Free tools, such as **iExplorer** and others, will provide access to similar iOS device information on a Windows PC, as shown in the following screenshot. Both Mac and Windows methods for recovering iPhone device information will work on iPad devices as well. Here, iExplorer is being used to obtain device information from the iPhone:

iExplorer displaying iPhone identifiers

Every release of the iPhone comes with improved or newly-added features. As previously stated in this chapter, knowing the iPhone's details helps you understand the criticalities and possibilities of obtaining evidence from the iPhone. The examiner must know the model of the device to ensure that their tools and methodologies support that iPhone. They must determine the internal storage size of the iPhone to ensure that the evidence container is large enough for the entire forensic image. Most tools will not alert the examiner that there is not enough disk space on the evidence drive until space has run out. This will waste time and force the examiner to acquire the device a second time. Finally, the network capabilities of the device must be noted, so the examiner can properly isolate the device to prevent remote access or wiping during examination. This will be discussed further in Chapter 3, *Data Acquisition from iOS Devices*.

The following table shows the specifications and features of legacy iPhone models:

Specification	iPhone	iPhone 3G	iPhone 3GS
System on chip	Samsung Chip	Samsung Chip	Samsung Chip
Onboard RAM	128 MB	128 MB	256 MB
Connectivity	Wi-Fi, Bluetooth 2.0, GSM	Wi-Fi, Bluetooth 2.0, GSM/UMTS/HSDPA, GPS	Wi-Fi, Bluetooth 2.1, GSM, UMTS/HSDPA, GPS
Camera (megapixel)	2	2	3
Front camera	N/A	N/A	N/A
Storage (GB)	4, 8, 16	8, 16	8, 16, 32
Colors	Black	Black, white (white not in 8 GB)	Black, white (white not in 8 GB)
Connector	USB 2.0 dock connector	USB 2.0 dock connector	USB 2.0 dock connector
SIM card form-factor	Mini SIM	Mini SIM	Mini SIM
Siri support	No	No	No

Specifications of legacy iPhone models

The later iPhone releases and features are shown in the following table:

Specification	iPhone 4	iPhone 4S	iPhone 5	iPhone 5C	iPhone 5S
System on chip	Apple A4	Apple A5	Apple A6	Apple A6	Apple A7
Onboard RAM	512 MB	512 MB	1 GB	1 GB	1 GB
Connectivity	Wi-Fi, Bluetooth 2.1, GSM, UMTS/HSDPA/HSUPA, GPS	Wi-Fi, Bluetooth 4, GSM, UMTS/HSDPA/HSUPA, GPS	Wi-Fi, Bluetooth 4, UMTS/HSDPA+/DC-HSDPA, GSM, GPS	Wi-Fi, Bluetooth 4, UMTS/HSDPA+/DC-HSDPA/LTE, GSM, GPS	Wi-Fi, Bluetooth 4, UMTS/HSDPA+/DC-HSDPA/LTE/TD-LTE, GSM, GPS
Camera (megapixel)	5	8	8	8	8
Storage (GB)	8, 16, 32	8, 16, 32, 64	16, 32, 64	8, 16, 32, 64	8, 16, 32, 64
Colors	Black	Black, white	Black, white	White, pink, yellow, blue, or green	Silver, space gray, or gold
Connector	USB 2.0 dock connector	USB 2.0 dock connector	Lightning connector	Lightning connector	Lightning connector
SIM card form factor	Micro SIM	Micro SIM	Nano-SIM	Nano-SIM	Nano-SIM
Siri support	No	Yes	Yes	Yes	Yes

One of the major changes in the iPhone 5, iPhone 5C, and iPhone 5S is the Lightning connector, which is used to charge and synchronize the device with the computer. Devices prior to the iPhone 5 use a 30-pin USB dock connector, whereas the newer iPhones use an 8-pin Lightning connector.

The most recent iPhone releases and features are shown in the following tables:

Specification	iPhone 6	iPhone 6 Plus	iPhone 6S	iPhone 6S Plus
System on chip	Apple A8	Apple A8	Apple A9	Apple A9
CPU	1.4 GHz	1.4 GHz	1.8 GHz	1.8 GHz
Onboard RAM	1 GB	1 GB	2 GB	
Screen size (in inches)	4.7	5.5	4.7	5.5
Connectivity	Wi-Fi, Bluetooth 4.2, UMTS/HSDPA+/DC-HSDPA/LTE, CDMA, GSM, GPS	Wi-Fi, Bluetooth 4.2, UMTS/HSDPA+/DC-HSDPA/LTE, CDMA, GSM, GPS	Wi-Fi, Bluetooth 4.2, UMTS/HSDPA+/DC-HSDPA/LTE, CDMA, GSM, GPS	Wi-Fi, Bluetooth 4.2, UMTS/HSDPA+/DC-HSDPA/LTE, CDMA, GSM, GPS
Camera (megapixel)	8	8	12	12
Storage (GB)	16, 64, 128	16, 64, 128	16, 64, 128	16, 64, 128
Colors	Silver, Gold, Space Gray	Silver, Gold, Space Gray	Silver, Rose Gold, Gold, Space Gray	Silver, Rose Gold, Gold, Space Gray
Connector	Lightning connector	Lightning connector	Lightning connector	Lightning connector
SIM card form-factor	Nano-SIM	Nano-SIM	Nano-SIM	Nano-SIM
Siri support	Yes	Yes	Yes	Yes

The iPhone models released after the second edition of the book are shown in the following table:

Specification	iPhone SE	iPhone 7	iPhone 7 Plus	iPhone 8	iPhone 8 Plus	iPhone X
System on chip	Apple A9	Apple A10	Apple A10	Apple A11	Apple A11	Apple A11
CPU	1.85 GHz	2.33 GHz	2.33 GHz	2.39 GHz	2.39 GHz	2.39 GHz
Onboard RAM	2 GB	2 GB	3 GB	2 GB	3 GB	3 GB
Connectivity	Wi-Fi: 802.11a/b/g/n/ac	Wi-Fi: 802.11a/b/g/n/ac with MIMO	Wi-Fi: 802.11a/b/g/n/ac with MIMO	Wi-Fi: 802.11a/b/g/n/ac with MIMO	Wi-Fi: 802.11a/b/g/n/ac with MIMO	Wi-Fi: 802.11ac with MIMO
Camera (megapixel)	12	12	12	12	12	12
Storage (GB)	16, 32, 64 & 128	32, 128 & 256	32, 128 & 256	64 & 256	64 & 256	64 & 256
Colors	Silver, Space Gray, Gold, Rose Gold	Black, Silver, Gold, Rose Gold, Jet Black, Red	Black, Silver, Gold, Rose Gold, Jet Black, Red	Silver, Space Gray, Gold	Silver, Space Gray, Gold	Silver, Space Gray
Connector	Lightning connector	Lightning connector	Lightning connector	Lightning connector	Lightning connector	Lightning connector
SIM card form-factor	Nano-SIM	Nano-SIM	Nano-SIM	Nano-SIM	Nano-SIM	Nano-SIM
Siri support	Yes	Yes	Yes	Yes	Yes	Yes

Again, some familiarity with iPhone device hardware will aid the examiner in determining how to handle the device during a forensic investigation. Certain models enforce full disk encryption, while older models do not. Encrypted devices require additional steps during acquisition if access is even possible. The examiner must be prepared for all hurdles they may be required to clear during the acquisition and analytical stages of the investigation. In addition, knowing the capabilities that the iPhone has, and the initial and current OS version, makes a difference in the data you will be able to recover from the device. Apple is not consistent with data storage locations across iOS versions. Thus, the examiner must know the original version installed when the phone was first in use to ensure that the forensic tools do not overlook data that could aid in the investigation. Topics such as iOS upgrades will be discussed in Chapter 5, *iOS Data Analysis and Recovery*.

iPhone hardware

The iPhone is a collection of modules, chips, and electronic components from different manufacturers. Due to the complexities of the iPhone, the list of hardware components is extensive and each device should be researched for internal components.

The following images show the internals of the iPhone 8. The images were taken after dismantling the iPhone 8. Internal images for all iPhones can be found in the teardown section at https://www.ifixit.com/Device/iPhone.

This is the front of the dismantled iPhone 8:

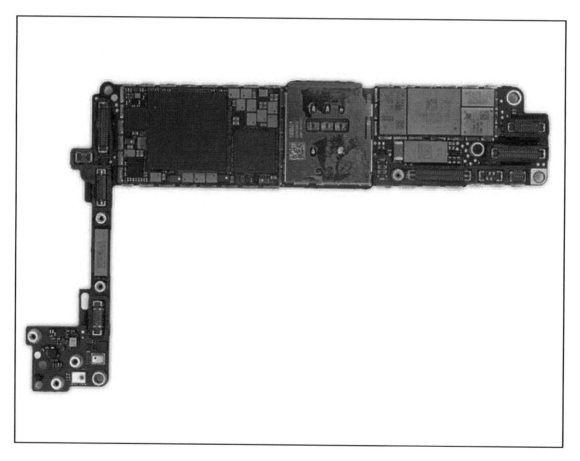

The iPhone 8 teardown image—front (https://www.ifixit.com/Teardown/iPhone+8+Teardown/97481)

This is the back of the dismantled iPhone 8:

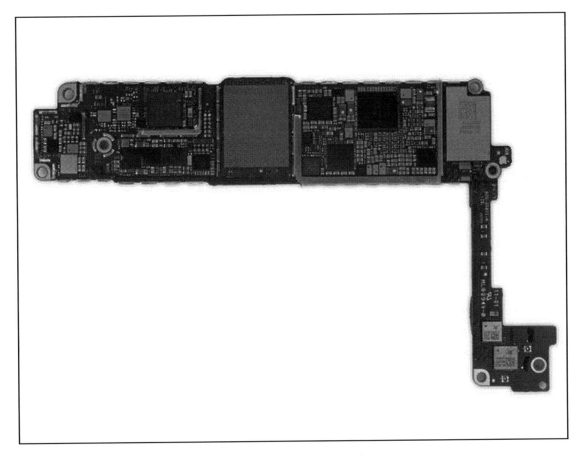

The iPhone 8 teardown image—back (https://www.ifixit.com/Teardown/iPhone+8+Teardown/97481)

iPad models

The Apple iPhone changed the way cell phones are produced and used. Similarly, the iPad, a version of the tablet computer introduced in January 2010, squashed the sales of notebooks. With the iPad, individuals can shoot videos, take photos, play music, read books, browse the internet, and do much more. Various iPad models exist now, with different features and storage capabilities. Details on identifying iPad models can be found at https://support.apple.com/en-in/HT201471.

The most recent iPad models are listed in the following table:

Device	Model	Initial OS	Identifier	Release date
iPad Pro 9.7-inch	A1673 A1674 A1675	9.3	iPad6,3 iPad6,4	March 31, 2016
iPad Pro 12.9-inch (2nd generation)	A1670 A1671	10.3.2	iPad7,1 iPad7,2	June 13, 2017
iPad Pro 10.5-inch	A1701 A1709	10.3.2	iPad7,3 iPad7,4	June 13, 2017

As with the iPhone, not all versions of the iPad are supported for physical acquisition. In addition, Apple has changed data storage locations in iOS versions, which affects the iPad devices as well. The examiner must be aware of the different models, the released and currently installed iOS version, storage capability, network access vectors, and more.

Every release of the iPad comes with improved or newly-added features. The following table shows the specifications and features of the most recent iPad models:

Specification	iPad Pro 9.7-inch	iPad Pro 12.9-inch (2nd generation)	iPhone 7 Plus
System on chip	Apple A9X	Apple A10X	Apple A10X
CPU	2.16 GHz	2.39 GHz	2.39 GHz
Onboard RAM	2 GB	4 GB	4 GB
Camera (megapixel)	12	12	12
Storage (GB)	32, 128 & 256	64, 256 & 512	64, 256 & 512
Colors	Silver, Space Gray, Gold, Rose Gold	Silver, Space Gray, Gold	Silver, Space Gray, Gold, Rose Gold
Connector	Lightning connector	Lightning connector	Lightning connector
Siri support	Yes	Yes	Yes

Understanding the iPad hardware

One of the key factors of the success of Apple iOS devices is the proper selection of its hardware components. Just like the iPhone, the iPad is also a collection of modules, chips, and electronic components from different manufacturers. Internal images for all iPads can be found in the teardown section of `https://www.ifixit.com/Device/iPad`.

The following images show the internals of the iPad Pro. The images were taken after dismantling the iPad Pro cellular model and were obtained from `https://www.ifixit.com/Teardown/iPad+Pro+10.5-Inch+Teardown/92534`:

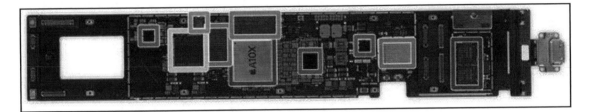

The iPad Pro teardown image (https://www.ifixit.com/Teardown/iPad+Pro+10.5-Inch+Teardown/92534)

The following image shows the other side of the iPad Pro:

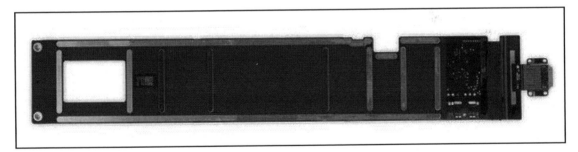

The iPad Pro teardown image (https://www.ifixit.com/Teardown/iPad+Pro+10.5-Inch+Teardown/92534)

Apple Watch models

The Apple Watch was released in spring 2015. This smartwatch enables users to sync iPhone data to the watch and leverage the watch as a way to interact with the iPhone and as a singular device. The Apple Watch enables users to answer calls, send and respond to SMS, iMessage and email, access third-party applications, use Apple maps, and more. The Apple Watch can only be paired with an iPhone capable of running iOS 8.2 or later, not an iPad. The first release of Watch OS required the watch to be within Bluetooth range of the iPhone for full functionality, but Watch OS 2.X allows the watch to function independently on Wi-Fi. The Apple Watch 3 was first introduced on September 12, 2017 and released on September 22 with iPhone 8. It requires iOS 11 or later running on an iPhone 5S or newer. The third series has built-in LTE cellular connectivity and allows both voice and data communication:

Device	Initial OS	Identifier	Release date
Apple Watch (1st generation)	watchOS 1.0	Watch1,1 Watch1,2	April 24, 2015
Apple Watch (Series 1)	watchOS 3.0	Watch2,6, Watch2,7	September 16, 2016
Apple Watch (Series 2)	watchOS 3.0	Watch2,3, Watch2,4	September 16, 2016
Apple Watch (Series 3)	watchOS 4.0	Watch3,1, Watch3,2, Watch3,3, Watch3,4	September 22, 2017 October 5, 2017 September 22, 2017

The features of the current Apple Watch are listed here:

Specification	Apple Watch (1st generation)	Apple Watch (Series 1)	Apple Watch (Series 2)	Apple Watch (Series 3)
System on chip	Apple S1	Apple S1P	Apple S2	Apple S3
Onboard RAM	512 MB	Unknown	Unknown	Unknown
Storage (GB)	8	8	Unknown	16

Understanding the Apple Watch hardware

While there are two sizes of the Apple Watch, the hardware is similar for each. Apple has not disclosed the complete Watch specifications, which forces us to rely on the little we currently know.

The following image shows the internals of the Apple Watch. The images were taken after dismantling the Apple Watch, and were obtained from `https://www.ifixit.com/`
`Teardown/Apple+Watch+Series+3+Teardown/97521`:

Apple Watch Series 3 (https://www.ifixit.com/Teardown/Apple+Watch+Series+3+Teardown/97521)

The following image shows the reverse side of the Apple Watch Series 3:

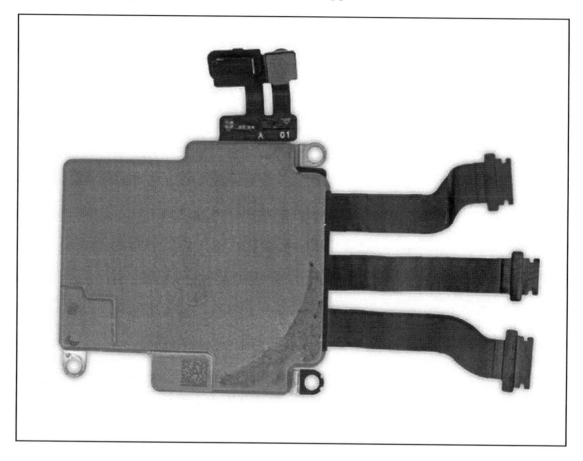

Apple Watch Series 3 (https://www.ifixit.com/Teardown/Apple+Watch+Series+3+Teardown/97521)

The filesystem

To better understand the forensic process of an iOS device, it is good to know about the filesystem that is used. The filesystem used in the iPhone and other Apple iOS devices is HFSX, a variation of HFS Plus with one major difference. HFSX is case-sensitive whereas HFS Plus is case-insensitive. Other differences will be discussed later in this chapter. OS X uses HFS Plus by default and iOS uses HFSX. **Apple File System (APFS)** was introduced in June 2016 as a replacement for HFS+, and released for iOS devices with the release of iOS 10.3, and for macOS devices with the release of macOS 10.13.

The HFS Plus filesystem

In 1996, Apple developed a new filesystem, **Hierarchical File System (HFS)**, to accommodate the storage of large datasets. In a HFS filesystem, the storage medium is represented as volumes. HFS volumes are divided into logical blocks of 512 bytes. The logical blocks are numbered from first to last on a given volume and will remain static with the same size as physical blocks, that is, 512 bytes. These logical blocks are grouped together into allocation blocks, which are used by the HFS filesystem to track data in a more efficient way. HFS uses a 16-bit value to address allocation blocks, which limits the number of allocation blocks to 65,535. To overcome the inefficient allocations of disk space and some of the limitations of HFS, Apple introduced the HFS Plus filesystem (`http://dubeiko.com/development/FileSystems/HFSPLUS/tn1150.html`).

The HFS Plus filesystem was designed to support larger file sizes. HFS volumes are divided into sectors that are usually 512 bytes in size. These sectors are grouped together into allocation blocks. The number of allocation blocks depends on the total size of the volume. HFS Plus uses block addresses of 32 bits to address allocation blocks. HFS Plus uses journaling by default. Journaling is the process of logging every transaction to the disk, which helps prevent filesystem corruption. The key characteristics of the HFS Plus filesystem are: efficient use of disk space, Unicode support for filenames, support for name forks, file compression, journaling, dynamic resizing, dynamic defragmentation, and an ability to boot on operating systems other than macOS.

The HFS Plus volume

The HFS Plus volume contains a number of internal structures to manage the organization of data. These structures include a header, an alternate header, and five special files: an allocation file, an extents overflow file, a catalog file, an attributes file, and a startup file. Among the five files, three files (the extents overflow file, the catalog file, and the attribute file) use a B-tree structure, a data structure that allows data to be efficiently searched, viewed, modified, or removed. The HFS Plus volume structure is shown in the following figure:

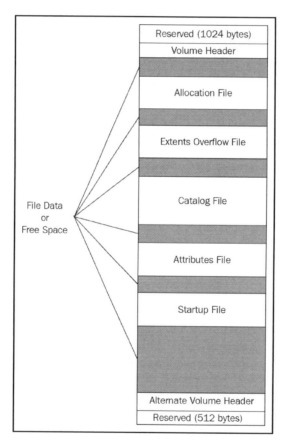

The HFS Plus volume structure

The volume structure is described as follows:

- **1024 bytes:** This is reserved for boot load information.
- **Volume header:** This stores volume information, such as the size of allocation blocks, a timestamp of when the volume was created, and metadata about each of the five special files.
- **Allocation file:** This file is used to track which allocation blocks are in use by the system. The file format consists of one bit for every allocation block. If the bit is set, the block is in use. If it is not set, the block is free.
- **Extents Overflow file:** This file records the allocation blocks that are allocated when the file size exceeds eight blocks, which helps in locating the actual data when referred. Bad blocks are also recorded in the file.
- **Catalog file:** This file contains information about the hierarchy of files and folders, which is used to locate any file and folder within the volume.
- **Attribute file:** This file contains inline data attribute records, fork data attribute records, and extension attribute records.
- **Startup file:** This file holds the information needed to assist in booting a system that does not have HFS Plus support.
- **Alternate Volume header:** This is a backup of the volume header, and it is primarily used for disk repair.
- **512 bytes:** This is reserved for use by Apple, and it is used during the manufacturing process.

The APFS filesystem

APFS is a new filesystem for iOS, macOS, tvOS, and watchOS. It is a 64-bit filesystem and supports over 9 quintillion files on a single volume. Here is the list of its main features:

- **Clones:** Instantaneous copies of files or directories. Modifications are written elsewhere and continue to share the unmodified blocks; changes are saved as deltas of the cloned file.
- **Snapshots:** Points-in-time, read-only instances of the filesystem.
- **Space sharing:** Allows multiple filesystems to share the same underlying free space on a physical volume.

- **Encryption:** There are three modes:
    - No encryption
    - Single-key encryption
    - Multi-key encryption with per-file keys for file data and a separate key for sensitive metadata

    Depending on the hardware, AES-XTS or AES-CBC encryption mode is used.

- **Crash protection:** A novel copy-on-write metadata scheme, it's used to ensure that filesystem updates are crash-protected.
- **Sparse files:** Allow the logical size of files to be greater than the physical space they occupy on disk.
- **Fast directory sizing:** Quickly computes the total space used by a directory hierarchy, allowing it to be updated as the hierarchy evolves.

The APFS structure

So, APFS is structured in a single container, which may contain one or more volumes. The APFS structure is presented in the following figure:

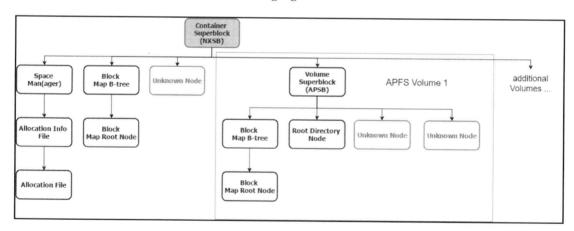

APFS structure overview (https://blog.cugu.eu/post/apfs/)

Each filesystem structure in APFS starts with a block header. The block header starts with a checksum (Fletcher's checksum algorithm is used) for the whole block, and also contains the copy-on-write version of the block, the block ID, and the block type.

The **container superblock** contains information on the block size, the number of blocks, and pointers to the space manager for this task, the block IDs of all volumes, and a pointer to a block map B-tree (contains entries for each volume with its ID and offset).

Nodes are used for storing different kinds of entries. They can be part of a B-tree or exist on their own, and can either contain flexible or fixed-sized entries.

The **space manager** manages allocated blocks in the APFS container, and stores the number of free blocks and a pointer to the allocation info file.

The **allocation info file** stores the allocation file's length, version and the offset.

B-trees manage multiple nodes, and contain the offset of the root node.

A **volume superblock** contains the name of the volume, an ID and a timestamp.

As for **allocation files**, they are simple bitmaps, and do not have a block header and type ID.

Disk layout

By default, the filesystem is configured as two logical disk partitions: system (root or firmware) partition and user data partition.

The system partition contains the OS and all of the preloaded applications used with the iPhone. The system partition is mounted as read-only unless an OS upgrade is in progress or the device is jailbroken. The partition is updated only when a firmware upgrade is performed on the device. During this process, the entire partition is formatted by iTunes without affecting any of the user data. The system partition takes only a small portion of storage space, normally between 0.9 GB and 2.7 GB, depending on the size of the NAND drive. As the system partition was designed to remain in factory state for the entire life of the iPhone, there is typically little useful evidentiary information that can be obtained from it. If the iOS device is jailbroken, files containing information regarding the jailbreak and user data may be resident on the system partition. Jailbreaking an iOS device allows the user root access to the device, but voids the manufacturer warranty. Jailbreaking will be discussed later in this chapter.

The user data partition contains all user-created data, ranging from music and contacts to third-party application data. The user data partition occupies most of the NAND memory and is mounted at /private/var on the device. Most of the evidentiary information can be found in this partition. During a physical acquisition, both the user data and system partitions should be captured and saved as a .dmg or .img file. Most Windows tools and acquisition methods will create an .img file, while macOS X tools and acquisition methods will create a .dmg file. Both of the output image files are supported by most commercial forensic analysis tools.

These raw image files can be mounted as read-only for forensic analysis, which is covered in detail in Chapter 3, *Data Acquisition from iOS Devices* and Chapter 5, *iOS Data Analysis and Recovery*.

iPhone operating system

iOS is Apple's most advanced and feature-rich proprietary mobile operating system. It was released with the first generation of the iPhone. When introduced, it was named iPhone OS, and it was later renamed iOS to reflect the unified nature of the operating system that powers all Apple iOS devices, such as the iPhone, iPod touch, iPad, and Apple TV. iOS is derived from core OS X technologies and streamlined to be compact and efficient for mobile devices.

It utilizes a multi-touch interface, where simple gestures are used to operate and control the device, such as swiping your finger across the screen to move to the successive page or pinching your fingers to zoom. In simple terms, iOS assists with the general functioning of the device. iOS is really macOS X with the following significant differences:

- The architecture for which the kernel and binaries are compiled is ARM-based rather than Intel x86_64
- The OS X kernel is open source, whereas the iOS kernel remains closed
- Memory management is much tighter
- The system is hardened and does not allow access to the underlying APIs

The iOS architecture

iOS acts as an intermediary between the underlying hardware components and the applications that appear on the screen. The applications do not talk to the underlying hardware directly. Instead, they communicate through a well-defined system interface that protects the applications from hardware changes. This abstraction makes it easy to build applications that work on devices with different hardware capabilities.

The iOS architecture consists of four layers—the Cocoa Touch layer, Media layer, Core Services layer, and Core OS layer—as shown in the following figure. Each layer consists of several frameworks that help to build an application:

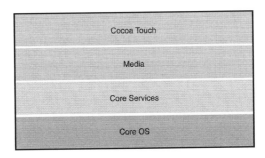

The iOS layers

- **The Cocoa Touch layer:** The Cocoa Touch layer contains the key frameworks required to develop the visual interface for iOS applications. Frameworks in this layer provide the basic application infrastructure and support key technologies, such as multitasking, touch-based input, and many high-level system services.
- **The Media layer:** The Media layer provides the graphics and audio and video frameworks to create the best multimedia experience available on a mobile device. The technologies in this layer help developers to build applications that look and sound great.
- **The Core Services layer:** The Core Services layer provides the fundamental system services that are required for the applications. Not all of these services are used by developers, though many parts of the system are built on top of them. This layer contains technologies to support features such as location, iCloud, and social media.
- **The Core OS layer:** The Core OS layer is the base layer and sits directly on top of the device hardware. This layer deals with low-level functionalities and provides services such as networking (BSD sockets), memory management, threading (POSIX threads), filesystem handling, external accessories access, and inter-process communication.

iOS security

Newer versions of iOS were designed with security at its core. At the highest level, the iOS security architecture appears as shown in the following figure:

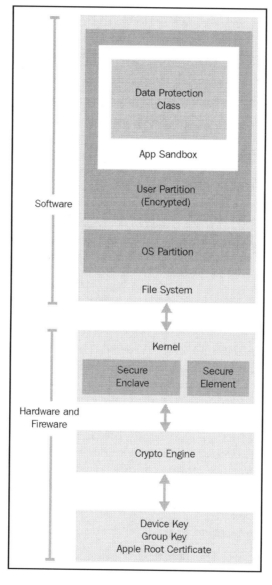

The iOS security architecture

Apple iOS devices such as iPhone, iPad, and iPod touch are designed with layers of security. Low-level hardware features safeguard from malware attacks, and the high-level OS features prevent unauthorized use. A brief overview of the iOS security features is provided in the following sections.

Passcodes, Touch ID, and Face ID

Passcodes restrict unauthorized access to the device. Once a passcode is set, each time you turn on or wake up the device, it will ask for the passcode to access the device. iOS devices support simple as well as complex passcodes. iOS 9 released the option to use a six-digit simple passcode instead of the legacy four-digit option. iPhone 5S and later also supports Touch ID fingerprints as a passcode, which are backed up with a simple or complex passcode. iPhone X will support a new biometric way of locking the device, Face ID, so users can use their faces as the passcodes. And it's even more secure, as the chance that a stranger will unlock your iPhone with Touch ID is 1 in 50,000, but with Face ID it is 1 in 1,000,000.

Code Signing

Code Signing prevents users from downloading and installing unauthorized applications on the device. Apple says:

"Code Signing is the process by which your compiled iOS application is sealed and identified as yours. Also, iOS devices won't run an application or load a library unless it is signed by a trusted party. To ensure that all apps come from a known and approved source and have not been tampered with, iOS requires that all executable code be signed using an Apple-issued certificate."

Sandboxing

Sandboxing mitigates post-code-execution exploitation by placing the application into a tightly restricted area. Applications installed on the iOS device are sandboxed, and one application cannot access the data stored by another. Essentially, a sandbox is a mechanism that enforces fine-grained controls that limit an application's access to files, network resources, hardware, and more.

Encryption

On iOS devices (starting with the iPhone 4), the entire filesystem is encrypted with a filesystem key, which is computed from the device's unique hardware key. This key is stored in effaceable storage, which exists between the OS and hardware level of the device. This is the reason that JTAG and chip-off methods are not useful acquisition methods, as the entire data dump will be encrypted.

Data protection

Data protection is designed to protect data at rest and to make offline attacks difficult. It allows applications to leverage the user's device passcode in concert with the device hardware encryption to generate a strong encryption key. Later, the strong encryption key is used to encrypt the data stored on the disk. This key prevents data from being accessed when the device is locked, ensuring that critical information is secured even if the device is compromised.

Address Space Layout Randomization

Address Space Layout Randomization (ASLR) is an exploit mitigation technique introduced with iOS 4.3. ASLR randomizes the application objects' location in the memory, making it difficult to exploit the memory corruption vulnerabilities.

Privilege separation

iOS runs with the principle of least privileges. It contains two user roles—**root** and **mobile**. The most important processes in the system run with root user privileges. All other applications that the user has direct access to, such as the browser and third-party applications, run with mobile user privileges.

Stack-smashing protection

Stack-smashing protection is an exploit mitigation technique. It protects against buffer overflow attacks by placing a random and known value (called stack canary) between a buffer and control data on the stack.

Data execution prevention

Data execution prevention (**DEP**) is an exploit mitigation technique mechanism in which a processor can distinguish the portions of memory that are executable code from data. For example, in code injection attacks, an attacker tries to inject his vector and execute it. But DEP prevents this because it recognizes the injected part as data and not code.

Data wipe

iOS provides the **Erase All Content and Settings** option to wipe the data on the iPhone. This type of data wipe erases user settings and information by removing the encryption keys that protect the data. As the encryption keys are erased from the device, it is not possible to recover the deleted data, not even during forensic investigations. Other wiping methods are available that overwrite the data in the device memory. More information on wiping can be found at `https://support.apple.com/en-in/HT201274`.

Activation Lock

Lock, introduced with iOS 7, is a theft deterrent that works by leveraging Find My iPhone. When Find My iPhone is enabled, it enables the Activation Lock, and your Apple ID and password will be required to turn off Find My iPhone, to erase your device, and to reactivate your device.

The App Store

The App Store is an application distribution platform for iOS, developed and maintained by Apple. It is a centralized online store where users can browse and download both free and paid apps. These apps expand the functionality of a mobile device. In January 2017, there were more than 2.2 million applications in the App Store.

Apps available in the App Store are generally written by third-party developers. Developers use XCode and the iPhone SDK to develop iOS applications. Later, they submit the app to Apple for approval. Apple follows an extensive review process to check the app against the company's guidelines. If Apple approves the app, it is published to the App Store, where users can download or buy it. The strict review process makes the App Store less prone to malware, but not 100% secure.

XCodeGhost, the Apple malware that infected 50 applications within the Apple App Store, was detected in September 2015. This malware was built into XCode, which made it harder to detect, and was reported to affect more than 500 million users worldwide. Once detected, Apple immediately removed the infected applications. Currently, users can access the App Store via iTunes and also from their iOS devices.

Jailbreaking

Jailbreaking is the process of removing limitations imposed by Apple's mobile operating system through the use of software and hardware exploits. Jailbreaking permits unsigned code to run and gain root access on the operating system. The most common reason for jailbreaking is to expand the limited feature set imposed by Apple's App Store and to install unapproved apps. Jailbreaking can aid in forensic acquisition, but will void the user's warranty, could *brick* the device, and may not support being restored to the factory settings.

 If you jailbreak a device, it's best to assume that it will forever be jailbroken and the warranty is no longer valid.

Many publicly available jailbreaking tools add an unofficial application installer to the device, such as Cydia, which allows users to install many third-party applications, tools, tweaks, and apps from an online file repository. The software downloaded from Cydia opens up endless possibilities on a device that a non-jailbroken device would never be able to do. The most popular jailbreaking tools are redsn0w, sn0wbreeze, evasi0n, Absinthe, seas0npass, Pangu, and TaiG. Not all iOS versions are jailbreakable. The following table will help you to choose the appropriate jailbreak tool according to the device you have and its iOS version:

| Name | Release date | Hardware | | | Firmware |
		iPad	iPhone	iPod Touch	
JailbreakMe 3.0	July 5, 2011	1, 2	3GS, 4	1	4.2.6 − 4.2.8, 4.3 − 4.3.3
redsn0w 0.9.15 beta 3	November 1, 2012	1	3GS, 4	1	4.1 − 6.1.6
Absinthe 2.0.4	May 30, 2012	1, 2, 3	3GS, 4, 4S	1	5.1.1
evasi0n	February 4, 2013	2, 3, 4, Mini 1	3GS, 4, 4S, 5	4, 5	6.0 − 6.1.2
evasi0n7	December 22, 2013	2, 3, 4, Air, Mini 1, Mini 2	4, 4S, 5, 5S, 5C	5	7.0 − 7.0.6
p0sixspwn	December 30, 2013	2, 3, 4, Mini 1	3GS, 4, 4S, 5	4, 5	6.1.3 − 6.1.6
Pangu	June 23, 2014	2, 3, 4, Air, Mini 1, Mini 2	4, 4S, 5, 5C, 5S	5	7.1 − 7.1.2
Pangu8	October 22, 2014	2, 3, 4, Air, Air 2, Mini 1, Mini 2, Mini 3	4S, 5, 5C, 5S, 6, 6 Plus	5	8.0 − 8.1
TaiG	November 29, 2014	2, 3, 4, Air, Air 2, Mini 1, Mini 2, Mini 3	4S, 5, 5C, 5S, 6, 6 Plus	5, 6	8.0 − 8.4
PPJailbreak	January 18, 2015	2, 3, 4, Air, Air 2, Mini 1, Mini 2, Mini 3	4S, 5, 5C, 5S, 6, 6 Plus	5, 6	8.0 − 8.4
Pangu9	October 14, 2015	2, 3, 4, Air, Air 2, Mini 1, Mini 2, Mini 3, Mini 4, Pro	4S, 5, 5C, 5S, 6, 6 Plus, 6S, 6S Plus	5, 6	9.0 − 9.1
PPJailbreak	July 24, 2016	Air, Air 2, Mini 2, Mini 3, Mini 4, Pro	5S, 6, 6 Plus, 6S, 6S Plus, SE	6	9.2 − 9.3.3
mach_portal + Yalu	December 22, 2016	Pro	6S, 6S Plus, 7, 7 Plus		10.0.1-10.1.1 (depends on device)
yalu102	January 26, 2017	Air 2, Mini 2, Mini 3, Pro	5S, 6, 6 Plus, 6S, 6S Plus, SE	6	10.0.1 − 10.2
Phoenix	August 6, 2017	2, 3, 4, Mini	4S, 5, 5C	5	9.3.5
Saigon	October 15, 2017	iPad Air 2, Mini 4	SE, 6S Plus, 6 Plus, 6S	6	10.2.1

In October 2012, the US Copyright Office declared that jailbreaking the iPad is illegal, while jailbreaking the iPhone is deemed legal. The governing law is reviewed every three years and has yet to be changed.

Summary

The first step in a forensic examination of an iOS device should be identifying the device model. The model of an iOS device can be used to help the examiner develop an understanding of the underlying components and capabilities of the device, which can be used to drive the methods for acquisition and examination. Legacy iOS devices should not be disregarded, because they may surface as part of an investigation. Examiners must be aware of all iOS devices, as old devices are sometimes still in use and may be tied to a criminal investigation. The next chapter will provide tools that will aid in obtaining data from iOS devices to later forensically examine. Not all tools are created equally, so it's important to understand the best tools to get the job done properly.

3
Data Acquisition from iOS Devices

An iOS device recovered from a crime scene can be a rich source of evidence. Think about how personal a smartphone is to a user; nothing else digital comes close. We rarely leave our homes or even walk around outside them without our smartphones within arm's reach. It is literally a glimpse of the most personal aspects of a human, almost like a diary of our everyday activity. According to several news references, Oscar Pistorius' iPads were examined by a mobile expert and presented during the murder trial to show internet activity hours before the murder of his girlfriend. When an iOS device can provide access to a so-called *smoking gun*, the examiner must ensure that they know how to properly handle, acquire, and analyze the device.

There are different ways to acquire forensic data from an iOS device. Though each method will have its positives and negatives, the fundamental principle of any acquisition method is to obtain a bit-by-bit or physical copy of the original data, where possible. With newer iOS devices, this is almost impossible.

In this chapter, we will cover the different methods of acquisition for iOS devices, including the following:

- iOS device operating modes
- Password protection and potential bypasses
- Logical acquisition
- Filesystem acquisition
- Physical acquisition

While the ultimate goal in a forensic examination is to obtain the physical image, this is not possible for all iOS devices, so we need to understand the next best option when our primary goal is not possible or supported by our tools.

Operating modes of iOS devices

Before we dive into the forensic techniques and acquisition methods, it is important to know the different operating modes of an iOS device. Many forensic tools and methods require you to place the device into one of the operating modes. Understanding the iOS device's operating modes is required in order to perform a particular action on the device.

While most commercial tools will demonstrate the proper steps to get the device into a particular mode, the examiner must understand what that mode represents. iOS devices are capable of running in different operating modes: the normal mode, the recovery mode, and the DFU mode. Some forensic tools require the examiner to know which mode the device is currently utilizing. We will define each mode in this section.

 Note that when the term *iPhone* is mentioned, it should be understood that the statement remains true for all iOS devices.

The normal mode

When an iPhone is switched on, it is booted to its operating system; this mode is known as the normal mode. Most regular activities (calling, texting, and so on) performed on an iPhone will be run in the normal mode.

When an iPhone is turned on, internally, it goes through a **secure boot chain**, as shown in the following figure. This does not occur for jailbroken devices. Each step in the boot-up process contains software components that are cryptographically signed by Apple to ensure integrity.

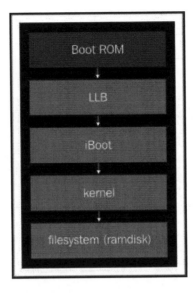

A secure boot chain of an iPhone in normal mode

The **Boot ROM**, known as the secure ROM, is **read-only memory (ROM)**, and is the first significant code that runs on an iPhone (`https://www.apple.com/business/docs/iOS_Security_Guide.pdf`). An explanation of the boot process for iOS devices is defined in the following steps:

1. The Boot ROM code contains the Apple root CA public key, which is used to verify the signature of the next stage before allowing it to load.
2. When the iPhone is started, the application processor executes the code from the Boot ROM.
3. The Boot ROM, in turn, verifies whether the **Low Level Bootloader (LLB)** is signed by Apple or not, and loads it.
4. When LLB finishes its tasks, it verifies and loads the second-stage boot loader (iBoot). iBoot verifies and loads the iOS kernel.
5. The iOS kernel, in turn, verifies and runs all the user applications, as shown in the preceding figure.
6. The secure boot chain ensures that iOS runs only on validated Apple devices.

When an iOS device is in this state, it is possible to gain a part that is accessible to the user through forensic acquisition. Most often, this includes a logical acquisition, which will be discussed later in this chapter.

The recovery mode

During the boot-up process, if one step is unable to load or verify the next step, then the boot-up is stopped and the iPhone displays a screen as shown in the following screenshot:

iOS device recovery mode

This mode is known as the **recovery mode**. The recovery mode is required to perform upgrades or to restore the iPhone. To enter the recovery mode, perform the following steps:

1. Turn off the device—press and hold down the **Sleep/Power** button located at the top of the iPhone until the red slider appears. Then, move the slider and wait for the device to turn off.

2. Hold down the iPhone **Home** button and connect the device to a computer via a USB cable. The device should turn on.

3. Continue holding the **Home** button until the **Connect to iTunes** screen appears. Then, you can release the **Home** button (on a jailbroken iOS device, this screen may appear with different icons). Most forensic tools and extraction methods will alert the examiner about the current state of the iOS device.

4. To exit the recovery mode, reboot the iPhone. This can be completed by holding down the **Home** and **Sleep/Power** button until the Apple logo appears.

On older iOS devices, the iTunes icon will be blue and the cable will reflect the original Apple cable.

You can read more about the iOS device recovery mode at `https://support.apple.com/en-in/HT201263`.

Normally, the process of rebooting returns the iPhone from recovery mode to normal mode. This same methodology applies to the Apple Watch. The examiner may experience a situation where the iPhone constantly reboots into the recovery mode. This is known as a **recovery loop**. A recovery loop may occur when the user or examiner attempts to jailbreak the iOS device and an error occurs. To get the device out of a recovery loop, the device must be connected to iTunes, and a backup is restored to the device.

This makes changes to the evidence, so ensure that you have validated your acquisition methods on a test device prior to attempting methods on real evidence.

For older devices, exiting a **recovery loop** was much easier on both Windows and Mac computers. For older devices, several open source methods exist to repair a recovery loop. The following steps show the **redsn0w tool** used on a Mac, which can be used to exit a recovery loop:

1. You can download the latest version of redsn0w at `https://sites.google.com/a/iphone-dev.com/files/`.

2. Then, navigate to **Extras | Recovery fix,** as shown in the following screenshot. An external method or tool may not be required. Sometimes, placing the device in DFU mode and connecting the device to iTunes will properly reboot the iPhone:

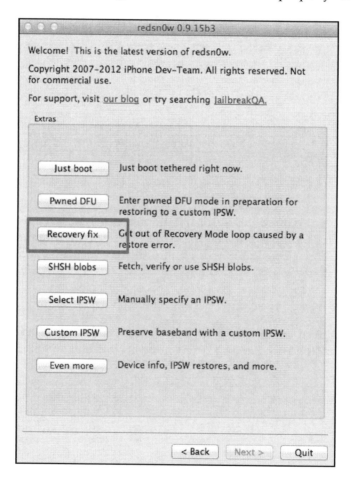

The redsn0w recovery fix

DFU mode

During the boot-up process, if the Boot ROM is not able to load or verify the LLB, then the iPhone displays a black screen. This mode is known as **Device Firmware Upgrade (DFU)** mode. DFU mode is a low-level diagnostic mode and is designed to perform firmware upgrades for the iPhone. During a firmware upgrade, the iPhone goes through a different boot sequence, as shown in the following figure. Most forensic tools use DFU mode to perform a physical acquisition on old iOS devices (iPhone 4 and older).

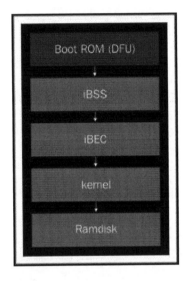

A secure boot chain of an iPhone in DFU mode

In DFU mode, the Boot ROM boots first, which, in turn, verifies and runs the second-stage boot loaders, iBSS and iBEC. iBSS is a modified version of iBoot that kicks off the iBEC loader, and verifies and loads the kernel (https://www.theiphonewiki.com/wiki/IBSS). The kernel verifies and loads the **ramdisk** into memory. Again, most forensic acquisition methods require the iOS device to successfully enter DFU mode.

As mentioned in Chapter 1, *Introduction to Mobile Forensics*, all steps must be well-documented by the examiner. The handling of the iOS device is no exception. DFU mode is a method recognized in mobile device forensics and is deemed to be a forensically sound action to prepare the device for forensic acquisition.

To enter DFU mode, perform the following steps:

1. Download and install iTunes on your forensic workstation from `https://www.apple.com/itunes/download/`. Make sure that you have the latest version and that it is forensically sterile to prevent cross-contamination across evidence plugged into the workstation. Connect your device to the forensic workstation via a USB cable.
2. Turn off the device.
3. Hold down the **Power** button for 3 seconds.
4. Hold down the **Home** button without releasing the **Power** button for exactly 10 seconds.
5. Release the **Power** button and continue to hold down the **Home** button until you are alerted by iTunes with the **iTunes has detected an iPhone in recovery mode. You must restore the iPhone before it can be used with iTunes** message.

At this point, the iPhone screen will be black and should not display anything. The iPhone is ready to be used in DFU mode. If you see the Apple logo or other signals that the device is booting, repeat steps 2 through 5 until iTunes displays that message.

Most forensic tools running on a Windows platform will provide these instructions, with graphics, as shown in the following screenshot. This figure shows UFED Physical Analyzer being used to physically acquire an iOS device:

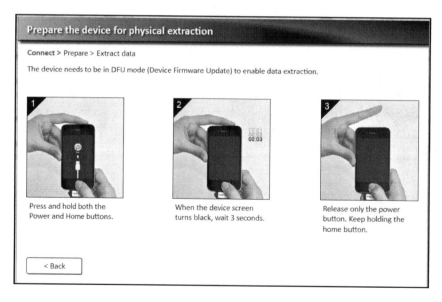

UFED Physical Analyzer explains how to place a device into DFU-mode

To verify whether the iPhone is in DFU mode on macOS X, launch **System Report** and go to the **USB** option. You should see a device similar to what is shown in the following screenshot:

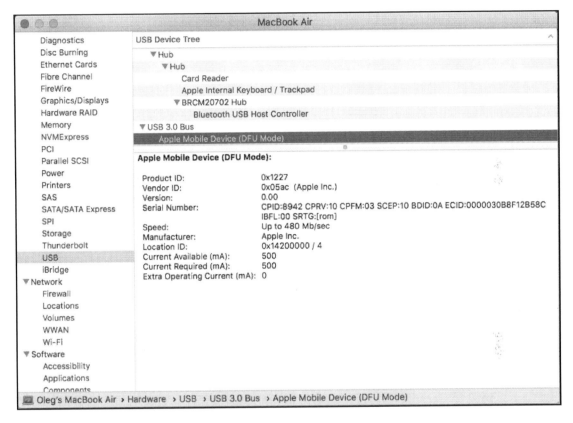

The MAC system information displaying a DFU-mode device

Just like in recovery mode, to exit DFU mode, hold down the **Home** button and the **Power** button until the Apple logo appears on the device.

 More information can be found on methods to verify DFU mode at `http:/ /www.zdziarski.com/blog/wp-content/uploads/2013/05/iOS-Forensic- Investigative-Methods.pdf`.

Pulling the cable during acquisition while the device is in DFU mode will not harm the device. Most tools will alert the examiner to not disconnect the device. However, in certain situations, such as covert or undercover operations, a device may have to be unplugged abruptly. If this is something you are faced with, rest assured that the device will not be damaged, but it is unlikely that you will obtain a forensic image that you can later examine.

Setting up the forensic environment

Nowadays we have a few tools that can be used by mobile forensic examiners to acquire and analyze iOS devices using both a Mac and a Windows system as the host. For example, **Elcomsoft iOS Forensic Toolkit** has both Mac and Windows versions; as for free and open source tools, the `libimobiledevice` library can be used not only on Mac and Windows forensic workstations, but even on Linux!

We are going to introduce you to these tools, with hands-on exercises, of course, including practical logical tools, filesystem and physical acquisitions, and even jailbreaking. But let's start with password protection and potential bypasses, as without the passcode we can hardly extract anything from the modern iOS device.

Password protection and potential bypasses

We want to start with the bad news: if you are examining an iPhone that runs iOS 8 or newer, and especially if it is a newer device, for example, the iPhone 6S, your chances to unlock it are not good at all.

Of course, there are some hardware-based solutions, for example **IP-BOX 3**, but all of them work only occasionally, and using one of them can even result in bricking the device. With iOS 11 this problem becomes even more severe—even if the device under examination is not passcode-protected, the examiner will need the passcode anyway as it must be entered to confirm the *trust* between the device and your workstation.

So, what should a mobile forensic examiner do? Use the **lockdown files**! The lockdown file, which is stored as a `plist` file on *trusted computers*, enables the examiner to trick the device into believing it is unlocked or *trusted* on the forensic workstation.

The lockdown files are located in:

- `/var/db/lockdown` on macOS X
- `C:\ProgramData\Apple\Lockdown` on Windows 7 and later releases

You must be aware that unlocking with a lockdown file only works if the device was unlocked with a passcode at least once after the last reboot.

There are some advanced techniques that exist. These include fingerprint molds to trick Touch ID, masks to trick Face ID, and NAND mirroring to bypass passcode entry limits.

The first technique was first demonstrated by Jason Chaikin. He showed how to bypass Touch ID by lifting another person's fingerprint with common molding materials, such as dental mold and Play-Doh.

The second technique was demonstrated as proof of concept by Vietnamese cyber security firm Bkav. They created a mask that can be used to trick the Face ID feature using a combination of 3D printing, makeup, and 2D images.

The last technique was demonstrated by Sergei Skorobogatov, senior research associate at the Cambridge Computer Laboratory's security group. This technique allows you to bypass passcode entry limits by soldering off the iPhone's flash memory chip and cloning it. This technique should work on any iOS device up to iPhone 6S Plus.

Logical acquisition

A logical acquisition captures a part of what is accessible to the user, in other words, what is included in an iTunes backup. It means we won't get any deleted files, but thanks to SQLite databases free lists and unallocated space, we can recover deleted records, including SMS and other chats, browsing history, and so on. We will discuss recovering SQLite data and deleted artifacts in `Chapter 5`, *iOS Data Analysis and Recovery.*

A logical acquisition is the simplest way to ascertain if the device is unlocked, as it simply uses the built-in backup mechanism. Most tools and methods that support logical acquisition of iOS devices will fail if the device is locked. Some think that if a physical image is captured, there is little to no need for a logical acquisition. However, not all data is parsed in a physical image, which is why having access to a logical image, resulting in readable data, will assist in digging deep into the physical image for artifacts to support your forensic investigation.

A logical acquisition is the fastest, easiest, and cheapest way to gain access to data stored on an iOS device. There are a variety of tools, ranging from commercial to free, that are capable of capturing logical images. Most of these tools require that the device be unlocked, or access to the `plist` file from the host machine be readily available.

Practical logical acquisition with libimobiledevice

Theory is good, but practice is much better. Let's create a logical image of an iPad running iOS 9.3.5 (we are going to use this iOS device for all types of acquisition) with `libimobiledevice`, which should already be installed on your workstation, as we already used it for device information gathering in the previous chapter.

Anyway, if you are using a Mac and still don't have it installed, follow the tutorial from the previous chapter, and if you are using a Windows workstation, download binaries here: https://github.com/rcmpayne/libimobiledevice-Compiled-Windows.

OK, let's start:

1. First of all, let's make our backups encrypted. Connect the iOS device to your workstation and start the Terminal (we are using a Mac workstation). Type the following command:

```
idevicebackup2 backup encryption on <your_password>
```

2. If you see the following—**Backup encryption has been enabled successfully**—you've done everything right and the backups will be encrypted. It will help you, the forensics examiner, to gain more info, including users' passwords.

3. It's time to create the backup—our iOS device logical image. To do it, type the following command:

```
idevicebackup2 backup --full
<the_folder_you_want_the_image_to_be_saved>
```

That's it. You can see the logical imaging process in the following figure:

```
● ● ●                   🏠 olegskulkin — -bash — 80×24
[Olegs-MacBook-Air:~ olegskulkin$ idevicebackup2 backup ---full /Users/olegskulkin]
/Desktop/backup
Backup directory is "/Users/olegskulkin/Desktop/backup"
Started "com.apple.mobilebackup2" service on port 49580.
Negotiated Protocol Version 2.1
Starting backup...
Enforcing full backup from device.
Backup will be encrypted.
Requesting backup from device...
Full backup mode.
[=                                          ]   1% Finished
Receiving files
[=                                          ]   0% (464 Bytes/7.1 MB)
[==========================================] 100% (7.1 MB/7.1 MB)
[==========================================] 100% (7.1 MB/7.1 MB)
[==========================================] 100% (7.1 MB/7.1 MB)
[==========================================] 100% (7.1 MB/7.1 MB)
[==========================================] 100% (7.1 MB/7.1 MB)
[==========================================] 100% (7.1 MB/7.1 MB)
[==========================================] 100% (7.1 MB/7.1 MB)
[==========================================] 100% (7.1 MB/7.1 MB)
[==========================================] 100% (7.1 MB/7.1 MB)
[==========================================] 100% (7.1 MB/7.1 MB)
[==========================================] 100% (7.1 MB/7.1 MB)
```

iPad logical imaging with libimobiledevice

Practical logical acquisition with Belkasoft Acquisition Tool

As logical acquisition is the most common option for modern iOS devices, we'll demonstrate how to use a few more free tools. The first one is Belkasoft Acquisition Tool. This tool could be used not only for iOS device acquisition, but also for hard drives, and even cloud data.

Let's acquire an iPhone running iOS 9.3.5 again, this time using Belkasoft Acquisition Tool.

1. Launch Belkasoft Acquisition Tool and choose the **Mobile device** option:

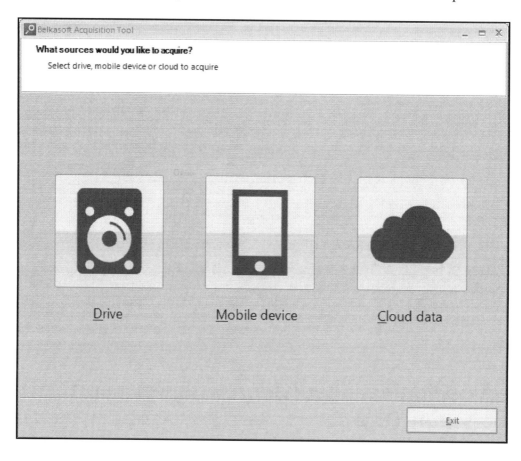

2. On the next window, choose the **Apple** option:

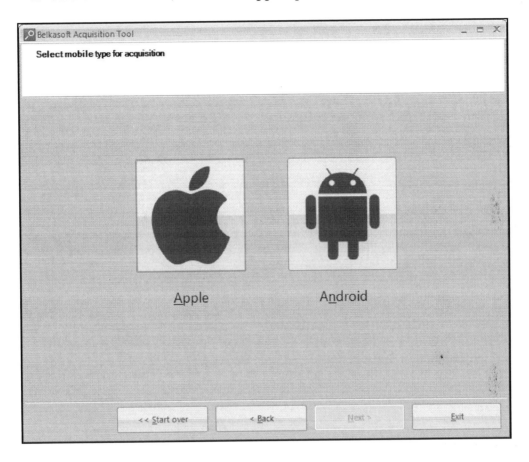

3. Now choose the device you want to acquire from the list, and the image path:

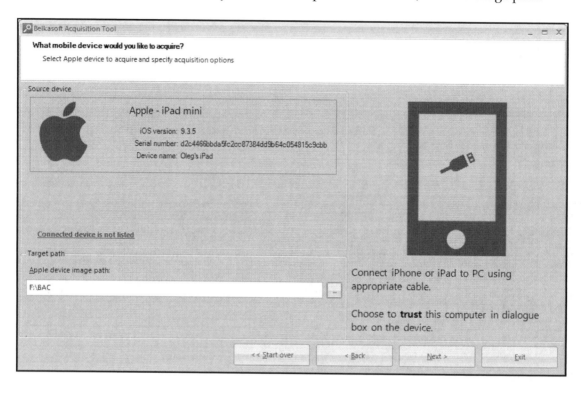

4. Wait for the task to be finished successfully, and you will find your device's logical image in the folder you chose in the previous step:

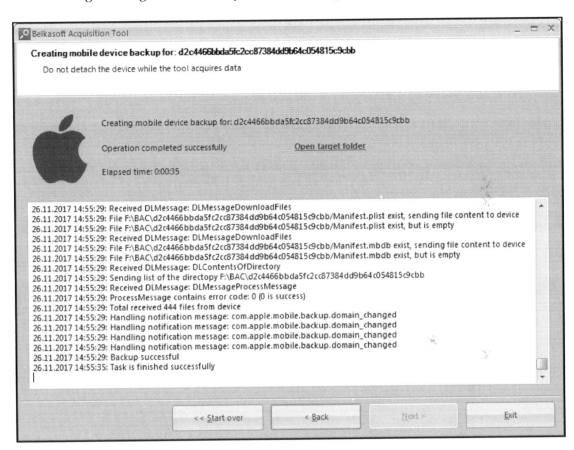

Practical logical acquisition with Magnet ACQUIRE

Another free tool capable of logical acquisition is ACQUIRE from Magnet Forensics. Let's perform a logical acquisition again; this time we will image an iPhone running the most recent iOS version 11.1.2 (at the time of writing).

1. Launch **Magnet ACQUIRE** and choose the device you want to image from the list:

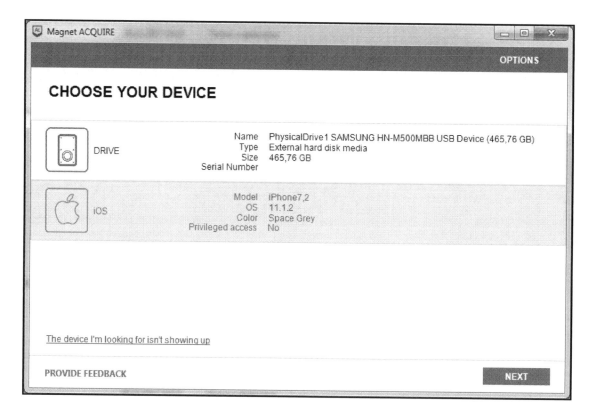

2. Choose the type of the image; we want to acquire a logical image and our device is not jailbroken, so we are choosing the **Quick** option:

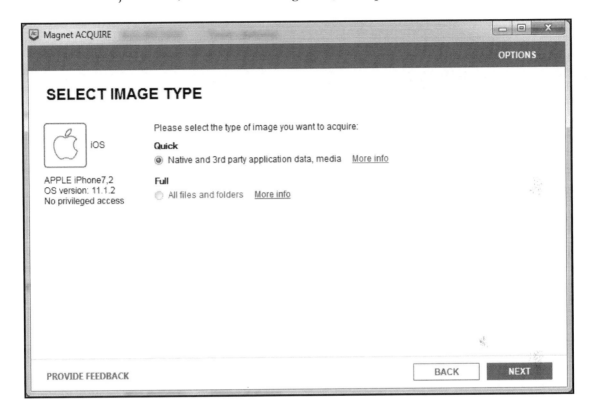

3. Fill in the fields available, and choose the folder where you want the image to be saved:

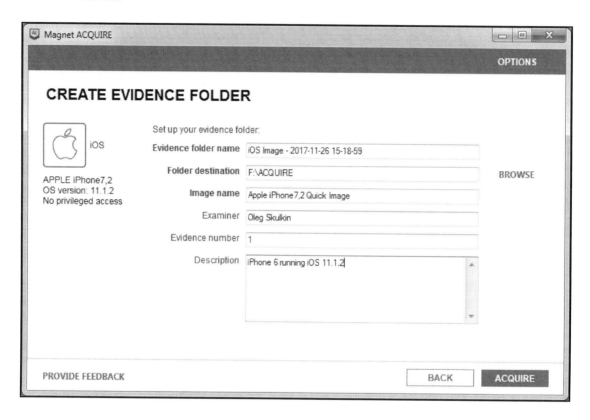

4. Wait for the tasks to be finished successfully, and you will find your device's logical image in the folder you chose in the previous step:

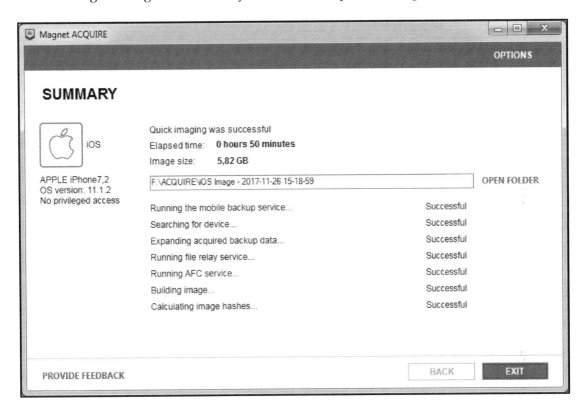

Filesystem acquisition

Secure Enclave has brought new challenges to iOS forensic examiners. Now, we can't extract encryption keys required to decrypt the device image, so physical acquisition is useless. But here comes the filesystem acquisition. Unfortunately, it requires the iOS device to be jailbroken. The next section will show you how to jailbreak our iPad running iOS 9.3.5 with Phoenix.

Practical jailbreaking

To perform filesystem and physical acquisitions, we need our iOS device to be jailbroken. Here are the steps to jailbreak a 32-bit iOS device running 9.3.5:

1. Download `Phoenix4.ipa` using the following link—`https://phoenixpwn.com/`.
2. Download Cydia Impactor using the following link—`http://www.cydiaimpactor.com/`.
3. Connect the iOS device, iPad in our case, to your forensic workstation.
4. Start Cydia Impactor. Drag and drop the IPA file you downloaded.
5. Enter the owner's Apple ID credentials. Make sure you are using a previously-created app-specific password. You can create one using the following link—`https://appleid.apple.com`. You will need the suspect's credentials!
6. On the device, go to **Settings | General | Device Management** to trust the certificate.
7. Run the Phoenix app on the device and tap on **Prepare For Jailbreak**.
8. Finally, tap on **Kickstart Jailbreak** in the app.

> For more jailbreaking techniques, refer to the *Jailbreaking* section in `Chapter 2`, *Understanding the Internals of iOS Devices*.

That's it. Now our iPad is jailbroken and we are almost ready for the filesystem acquisition.

The only thing left is OpenSSH installation via Cydia. Here is how to do it:

1. Open Cydia on the device you are examining.
2. Go to the **Search** tab, and type `OpenSSH` in the search bar.
3. Tap on the result and install OpenSSH.

Now we are ready for both filesystem and physical imaging of our iOS device.

Practical filesystem acquisition with Elcomsoft iOS Forensic Toolkit

It's time to perform a filesystem acquisition. We are going to use Elcomsoft iOS Forensic Toolkit to do it. Here is how to do it:

1. First of all, connect the device to your workstation (don't forget to tap **Trust** on the device) and start **Toolkit-JB.command** (Mac) or **Toolkit-JB.cmd** (Windows).
2. You will see a window with available options. As we are planning to perform filesystem acquisition now, we are interested in the **TAR FILES** option. This option enables the examiner to extract the filesystem from the user partition and save it in a TAR archive. This archive can be imported in most modern mobile forensics tools for processing. To choose this option, type 8.
3. Now, you should choose the image name and its location, otherwise the file will be saved in the current directory (Windows), or in the current user's home directory (macOS).
4. Once the imaging process is completed, you will get a TAR archive with the filesystem ready to be imported to the mobile forensics tool of your choice.

Physical acquisition

iOS devices have two types of memory—volatile (RAM) and non-volatile (NAND Flash). RAM is used to load and execute the key parts of the operating system or the application. The data stored in the RAM is lost after a device reboots. RAM usually contains very important application information, such as active applications, usernames, passwords, and encryption keys. Though the information stored in the RAM can be crucial in an investigation, currently there is no easy method or tool available to acquire the RAM memory from a live iPhone.

Unlike RAM, NAND is non-volatile memory and retains the data stored in it even after a device reboots. NAND flash is the main storage area, and contains the system files and user data (`http://nvlpubs.nist.gov/nistpubs/SpecialPublications/NIST.SP.800-101r1.pdf`). This document, written by NIST, not only covers memory storage in mobile devices, but mobile device forensic practices in general.

The goal of physical acquisition is to perform a bit-by-bit copy of the NAND memory, similar to the way in which a computer hard drive would be forensically acquired. While data storage seems similar, NAND differs from the magnetic media found in modern hard drives. NAND memory is cheaper, faster, and holds a great amount of data. Thus, NAND is the ideal storage for mobile devices, as mentioned in *Learning iOS Forensics, Mattia Epifani* and *Pasquale Stiparo, Packt Publishing*.

Physical acquisition has the greatest potential for recovering data from iOS devices; however, current and evolving security features (secure boot chain, storage encryption, and passcode) on these devices may hinder the accessibility of the data during forensic acquisition. Researchers and commercial forensic tool vendors are continually attempting new techniques to bypass the security features and perform physical acquisition on iOS devices, but for the latest model the only available option is jailbreaking, and even this won't help you to physically acquire devices with Secure Enclave, as has already been mentioned.

Practical physical acquisition with Elcomsoft iOS Forensic Toolkit

You've already used Elcomsoft iOS Forensic Toolkit for filesystem acquisition; now it's time to put your hands on physical acquisition with the help of this forensic tool.

Here are the steps:

1. Connect the device to your workstation and start **Toolkit-JB.command** (Mac) or **Toolkit-JB.cmd** (Windows).

2. Starting from the **GET KEYS** option, type 4. It will help you to get the device keys you need to decrypt the physical image.

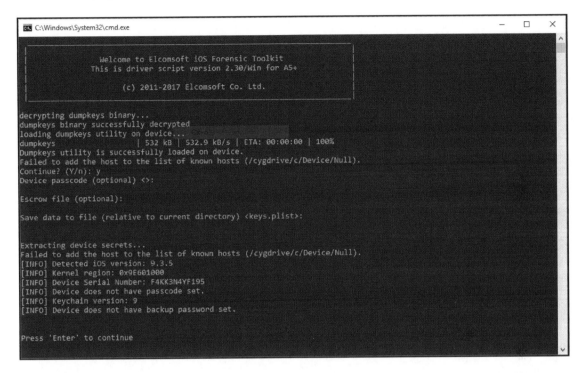

Extracting the device keys

3. We are ready to start imaging. Choose the **IMAGE DISK** option, and type 6. You will see two partitions, System (unencrypted) and User (encrypted). We are interested in the User partition, of course, so let's enter its number in the prompt.

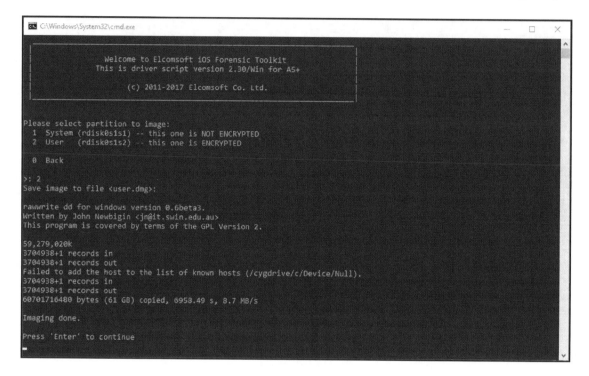

Imaging the User partition

4. Once the imaging process is completed, we are ready to decrypt the image using the device keys we extracted. To do this, use the **DECRYPT DISK** option, and type 7. As the result, you'll get a physical image ready to be imported into a mobile forensic tool of your choice.

Decrypting the image

Summary

The first step in iOS device forensic examination is to acquire the data from the device. There are several different ways to acquire data from an iOS device. This chapter covered logical, filesystem, and physical acquisition techniques, including techniques of acquiring jailbroken devices and methods to bypass passcodes. Physical acquisition is the preferred acquisition method as it recovers as close as we can get to a bit-by-bit copy of the data from the device; however, it is not possible to perform physical acquisition on all iOS devices.

While physical acquisition is the best method for forensically obtaining a majority of the data from iOS devices, backup files may exist or be the only method to extract data from the device.

The next chapter discusses iOS device backup files in detail, including user, forensic, encrypted, and iCloud backup files, and the methods to conduct your forensic examination.

4
Data Acquisition from iOS Backups

In the previous chapter, we covered techniques to acquire data from an iOS device. This chapter covers techniques to acquire a backup of files from the device onto a computer or iCloud using Apple's synchronization protocol.

The physical acquisition of an iOS device provides the most data in an investigation, but you can also find a wealth of information on iOS backups. iOS device users have several options to back up data present on their devices. Users can choose to back up data to their computer using the Apple iTunes software, or to the Apple cloud storage service known as iCloud. Every time an iPhone is synced with a computer or to iCloud, it creates a backup by copying the selected files from the device. The user can determine what is contained in the backup, so some may be more inclusive than others. Also, the user can back up to both a computer and iCloud, and the data derived from each location may differ. This often occurs due to the limitations of iCloud free storage. The user may simply back up photos and contacts to iCloud, but may take a complete backup of all data on their computer. As previously mentioned, physical acquisition provides the best access to all data on the iOS device; however, backups may be the only available source of digital evidence, especially if we are dealing with the most recent iOS devices.

In this chapter, we will cover the following topics:

- iTunes and iCloud backup files
- Creating and analyzing backup files
- How to handle encrypted backup files
- Backup file contents, file structure, and artifact recovery

iTunes backup

A wealth of information is stored on any computer that has been previously synced with an iOS device. These computers, commonly referred to as host computers, can have historical data and passcode-bypass certificates. In a criminal investigation, a search warrant can be obtained to seize a computer that belongs to a suspect to access the backup and lockdown certificates. For all other cases, consent or permissible access is required. iOS backup file forensics mainly involves analyzing an offline backup produced by an iPhone, iPad, iPod touch, and/or Apple Watch. The Apple Watch data will be contained within the iPhone backup to which it is synced.

The iTunes backup method is also useful in cases when physical, filesystem, and logical acquisition of an iOS device is not feasible. In this situation, examiners essentially create an iTunes backup of the device and analyze it using forensic software. Thus, it is important for an examiner to completely understand the backup process and the tools involved to ensure they are capable of creating a forensic backup without contaminating the devices with other data existing in iTunes.

iPhone backup files can be created using the iTunes software, which is available for the macOS and Windows platforms. iTunes is a free utility provided by Apple for data synchronization and management between iOS devices and the computer. iTunes uses Apple's proprietary synchronization protocol to copy data from the iOS device to a computer. For example, an iPhone can be synced with a computer using a cable or Wi-Fi. iTunes provides an option for encrypted backup, but by default, it creates an unencrypted backup whenever an iPhone is synced. Encrypted backups, when cracked, provide additional access to data stored on the iOS device. This will be discussed later in this chapter.

Users often create backup files to protect their data in the event that their device is damaged or lost. We either create a forensic backup to act as the best evidence or simply extract data from existing iOS backup files to search for legacy information. For example, if you are under investigation and you delete files or wipe your iPhone, your backup files on iCloud and your Mac still exist. Depending on whether iTunes or iCloud was used, multiple backups for the same device may exist. The examiner will have to forensically analyze each backup to uncover artifacts relating to the investigation.

iTunes is configured to automatically initiate the synchronization process once the iOS device is connected to the computer. To avoid unintended data exchange between the iOS device and the computer, disable the automatic synchronization process before connecting your evidence to the forensic workstation. The screenshot in step 2 illustrates the option that disables automatic syncing in iTunes version 12.7.1.14.

To disable auto-syncing in iTunes, perform the following steps:

1. Navigate to **iTunes | Preferences | Devices**.
2. Check **Prevent iPods, iPhones and iPads from syncing automatically** and click on the **OK** button:

Disabling automatic syncing in iTunes

3. As seen in the preceding screenshot, iOS backup files exist on the system. If this were a forensic workstation, these backup files would not exist or would be permanently removed to prevent cross-contamination.

4. Once you verify the synchronization settings, connect the iOS device to the computer using a USB cable. If the connected device is not protected with a passcode, iTunes immediately recognizes the device. This can be verified by the iPhone icon displayed on the left-hand side of the iTunes interface as shown in the following screenshot:

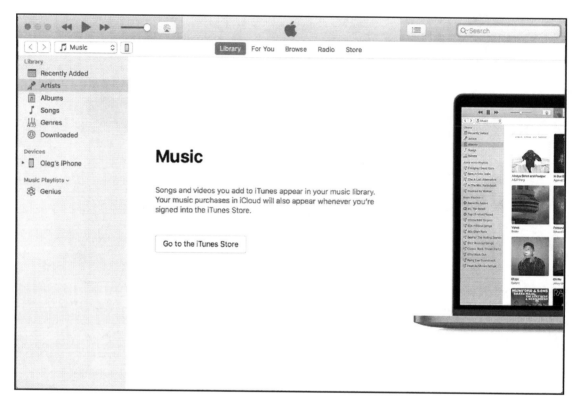

An iPhone recognized by iTunes

5. Before iTunes can access the iPhone, you must enable **Trust** between the computer and the phone. You will be prompted to press **Continue** on the computer and select **Trust** on the iPhone. With iOS 11, you must also enter the device's passcode:

iTunes prompts for access permissions

6. Once iTunes recognizes the device, a single click on the iPhone icon displays the iPhone summary, including the iPhone's name, capacity, firmware version, serial number, free space, and phone number. The iPhone **Summary** page also displays the options to create backups. Steps to create a backup will be discussed in the following section.

Creating backups with iTunes

In this section, we are going to walk you through backing up an iOS device with Apple iTunes. We are using iTunes version 12.7.1.14 and an iPhone running iOS version 11.1.2:

1. Connect the device and click on the iPhone icon displayed on the left-hand side of the iTunes interface.
2. Go to the **Backups** section, where you can choose the backup destination—local computer or iCloud, and also whether it's encrypted or not:

Encrypted iTunes backups contain data that unencrypted ones don't, including passwords, Wi-Fi settings, and web-browsing history, so make sure you are creating encrypted backups for forensic purposes.

iTunes Backups section

3. Click on the **Back Up Now** button and wait for the process to complete. Once it's complete, the latest backup will be changed.

   If you are using macOS, you can find the backup you created in the following location: `~/Library/Application Support/MobileSync/Backup/`.

   If you are using Windows, you can find the backup here: `C:\Users<user_name>\AppData\Roaming\Apple Computer\MobileSync\Backup\`.

If you want to use iTunes and save the backup to an external drive, follow these instructions (we are using iTunes version 12.7.1.14 and macOS 10.12.6):

1. Rename the original backup folder, and create a new one.
2. Connect the external drive, and create a backup folder on it.
3. Open Terminal, and type the following command:

   ```
   ln -s /Volumes/<volume_name>/Backup ~/Library/Application\
   Support/MobileSync/Backup
   ```

4. Now you can create a regular local backup, and it will be saved to your external drive.

Understanding the backup structure

When the iPhone is backed up to a computer, the backup files are stored in a backup directory, which exists as a 40-character hexadecimal string and corresponds to the **Unique Device Identifier** (**UDID**) of the device. The backup process may take a considerable amount of time depending on the size of the data stored on the iPhone during the first backup. The location of the backup directory in which your backup data is stored depends on the computer's operating system. The following table displays a list of the common operating systems and the default locations of the iTunes backup directory:

Operating system	Backup directory location
Windows XP	`\Documents and Settings\[user name]\Application Data\Apple Computer\MobileSync\Backup\`
Windows Vista/7/8+/10	`\Users\[user name]\AppData\Roaming\Apple Computer\MobileSync\Backup\`
macOS X	`~/Library/Application Support/MobileSync/Backup/` (~ represents the home folder)

During the first sync, iTunes creates a backup directory and takes a complete backup of the device. Currently, on subsequent syncs, iTunes only backs up the files that are modified on the device and updates the existing backup directory. This has not always been true as, in the past, a new backup was created every time the iOS device was backed up. Also, when a device is updated or restored, iTunes automatically initiates a backup and takes a **differential backup**. A differential backup has the same name as the backup directory, but is appended with a dash (-), the ISO date of the backup, a dash (-), and the time in a 24-hour format with seconds (`[UDID]+ '-' + [Date]+'-'+[Time stamp]`).

The iTunes backup may make a copy of everything on the device, including contacts, SMS, photos, the calendar, music, call logs, configuration files, documents, the keychain, network settings, offline web application cache, bookmarks, cookies, application data (if selected), and more. For example, email and passwords will not be extracted if the backup is not encrypted. The backup also contains device details such as the serial number, UDID, SIM details, and phone number. This information can also be used to prove a relationship between the backup and the mobile device.

The backup directory contains four standard files along with the individual files (up to iOS 9) or folders (iOS 10 and newer). Up to iOS 9, these four files were `info.plist`, `manifest.plist`, `status.plist`, and `manifest.mbdb`, but starting from iOS 10, we have the following standard files:

- `nfo.plist`
- `manifest.plist`
- `status.plist`
- `manifest.db`

These files store details about the backup and the device from which it was derived.

info.plist

The `info.plist` file stores details about the backed-up device and typically contains the following information:

- `Applications`: This is the list of applications installed on the device
- `Build version`: This is the iOS build version number
- `Device name and display name`: This is the name of the device, which typically includes the owner's name
- `GUID`: This is **Globally Unique Identifier (GUID)** of the device
- `ICCID`: This is the **Integrated Circuit Card Identifier (ICCID)**, which is the serial number of the SIM
- `IMEI`: This is the **International Mobile Equipment Identity (IMEI)**, which is used to uniquely identify the mobile phone
- `Last backup date`: This is the timestamp of the last successful backup
- `MEID`: This is the **Mobile Equipment Identifier** of the device
- `Phone Number`: This is the phone number of the device at the time of backup
- `Product Name`: This is the name of the device (for example, iPhone X)
- `Product type and product version`: This is the device's model and firmware version
- `Serial Number`: This is the serial number of the device
- `Target Identifier and Unique Identifier`: This is the UDID of the device
- `iTunes version`: This is the version of iTunes used to create the backup

manifest.plist

The `manifest.plist` file describes the contents of the backup and typically contains the following information:

- `Backup keybag`: The `Backup keybag` contains a set of data protection class keys that are different from the keys in the `System keybag`, and backed-up data is re-encrypted with the new class keys. Keys in the `Backup keybag` facilitate the storage of backups in a secure manner.
- `Date`: This is the timestamp of a backup created or last updated.
- `ManifestKey`: This is the key used to encrypt `Manifest.db` (wrapped with protection class four).
- `WasPasscodeSet`: This identifies whether a passcode was set on the device when it was last synced.
- `Lockdown`: This contains device details, the last backup computer's name, and other remote syncing profiles.
- `Applications`: This is a list of third-party applications installed on the backed-up device, their version numbers, and bundle identifiers.
- `IsEncrypted`: This identifies whether the backup is encrypted or not. For encrypted backups, the value is `True`, otherwise it is `False`.

status.plist

The `status.plist` file stores details about the backup status and typically contains the following information:

- `SnapshotState`: This identifies whether the backup process has successfully finished
- `IsFullBackup`: This identifies whether or not the backup was a full backup of the device
- `UUID`: This is the **Universally Unique Identifier (UUID)** of the device
- `Date`: This is the timestamp of the last time the backup was modified
- `BackupState`: This identifies whether the backup is a new backup or one that has been updated

manifest.db

`manifest.db` is a SQLite database, which contains a list of all the files and folders extracted from the iPhone via the backup mechanism. The `Files` table of the database includes the following columns:

- `fileID`: This is a SHA1 hash of the domain plus the symbol – and file or folder relative path. For example, `ae94e0607ca39a88c18aca095cb5b4f8471291a0` is the SHA1 hash for `CameraRollDomain-Media/PhotoData/Thumbnails/V2/DCIM/102APPLE`.

- `domain`: This is the domain the file or folder belongs to (all files in iOS are divided into multiple domains, for example, `CameraRollDomain` and `HomeDomain`).

- `relativePath`: This is the relative path to the file (including the filename) or folder.

- `flags`: These are the file flags.

- `file`: This is an embedded `.plist` file. These `.plist` files include the following important pieces of information, among others:
    - `LastModified`: This is the file's last modification timestamp in Unix format
    - `Birth`: This is the file creation timestamp in Unix format:

	fileID	domain	relativePath	flags	file
	Filter	Filter	Filter	Filter	Filter
3	e8281626dc6c...	AppDomainPlugin-com.a...	Library/Preferences	2	BLOB
4	d1b0eb5845a0...	AppDomainPlugin-com.a...	Documents	2	BLOB
5	be1f28f40e6e4...	CameraRollDomain		2	BLOB
6	735f4f65879e...	CameraRollDomain	Media	2	BLOB
7	f0a585e77da5...	CameraRollDomain	Media/PhotoData	2	BLOB
8	362cae198187...	CameraRollDomain	Media/PhotoData/iPhotoSandboxLibrary	2	BLOB
9	cacc5a1aca7bb...	CameraRollDomain	Media/PhotoData/Videos	2	BLOB
10	1e3b377ade50...	CameraRollDomain	Media/PhotoData/Thumbnails	2	BLOB
11	38cae1ba16df4...	CameraRollDomain	Media/PhotoData/Thumbnails/V2	2	BLOB
12	e4b86f7b2a58...	CameraRollDomain	Media/PhotoData/Thumbnails/V2/DCIM	2	BLOB
13	ae94e0607ca3...	CameraRollDomain	Media/PhotoData/Thumbnails/V2/DCIM/102APPLE	2	BLOB
14	73813e0c9e75...	CameraRollDomain	Media/PhotoData/Thumbnails/V2/DCIM/102APPLE...	2	BLOB
15	568f4d9a20e7f...	CameraRollDomain	Media/PhotoData/Thumbnails/V2/DCIM/102APPLE...	2	BLOB
16	9d0f5e50c9b4f...	CameraRollDomain	Media/PhotoData/Thumbnails/V2/DCIM/102APPLE...	2	BLOB

The manifest.db contents

You can easily export this embedded binary `.plist` using, for example, DB Browser for SQLite. To do this, follow these steps:

1. Open `manifest.db` using the **Open Database** button.
2. Go to the **Browse Data** tab.
3. Click on the the cell from the **file** column.
4. On the **Edit Database Cell** pane, use the **Export** button to save the data as a `.plist` file:

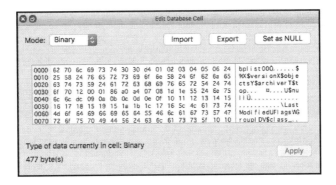

Exporting an embedded .plist file with DB Browser for SQLite

Since iOS 10, there are no more files named with a 40-character hexadecimal string. Instead, you will see a list of folders named with 2-character hexadecimal strings, which contain the files you used to see in previous versions:

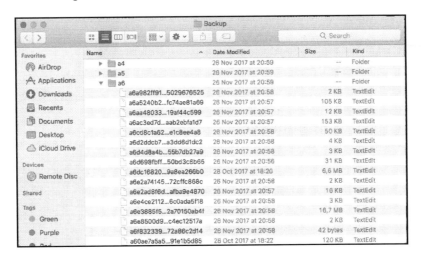

iPhone (running iOS 11.1.2) backup files

Extracting unencrypted backups

There are many free and commercial tools available to analyze data from unencrypted backups. These tools analyze the `manifest.db` database, restore the filenames, and create the file structure that users see on the iOS device. Some popular tools include the iBackup Viewer, iExplorer, and commercial tools such as BlackLight, AXIOM, Physical Analyzer, and more.

iBackup Viewer

iBackup Viewer is a free tool for both Windows and macOS, which can be downloaded from `http://www.imactools.com/iphonebackupviewer/`.

The tool expects the backup to be located in the default location, but you can change it to the location of your choice, for example, an external drive.

To extract the backup, follow these steps:

1. If the backup you want to analyze is not saved in the default location, click on the **Preferences** hyperlink on the main screen, and choose the right location:

Choosing the backup location

2. You will see the backups available in the location you chose. Click on the one you want to examine.

   You will see available potential evidence sources, including contacts, call history, messages, calendars, notes, voicemails, and browsing history:

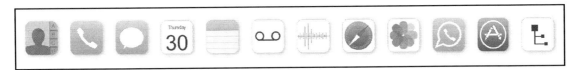

Potential evidence sources

3. It's important to note that you can browse the backup as a filesystem, using the Raw Data mode (the last icon on the previous illustration):

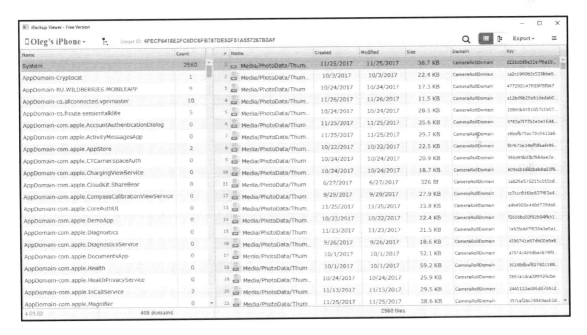

The Raw Data mode

iExplorer

iExplorer is a free tool for macOS X and Windows, which can be downloaded from `https://macroplant.com/iexplorer`. This tool supports both Windows and macOS, and is capable of browsing iTunes backups too. Here is how to use it:

1. Launch iExplorer, and click on **Browse iTunes Backups**.
2. To add a backup from a custom location, click on **Add / Modify Backup Location**.
3. Now click on the **Add Backup Location** button, and choose the path:

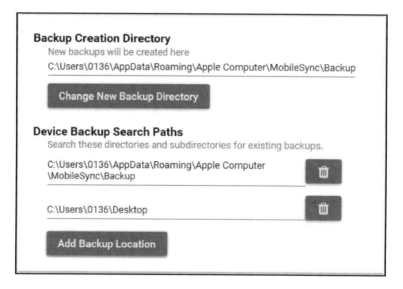

Adding a custom path

4. The backups from your custom location should now be available.

Also, there is an interesting option—iExplorer can gather SQLite databases for you. To do this, click on the **Raw Databases** button. You will learn more about SQLite forensics in the next chapter:

iExplorer Raw Databases option

You can browse the backup as a list of files and folders with the help of iExplorer too; use the left pane for this. Also, you can use the **Backup Explorer** button and use the main pane to browse the backup.

BlackLight

BlackLight is a commercial tool offered by BlackBag Technologies. This tool is one of the few that function on both Windows and macOS X, proving great support for all iOS acquisition types, even for encrypted backup files where the passcode is known or the lockdown file is available. BlackBag also provides free training in the use of the tool; visit `https://www.blackbagtech.com/training/courses/blacklight-tool-training.html` for more information.

To extract the backup, perform the following steps:

1. Launch the app and click **Add**—you will be prompted by an **Add Evidence** window.
2. Click **Add** again, and choose **Add Folder**.
3. Choose the backup you want to analyze, and click the **Select** button.
4. Now you should choose the method for extraction. The **All** option takes the longest, but parses the most artifacts for examination:

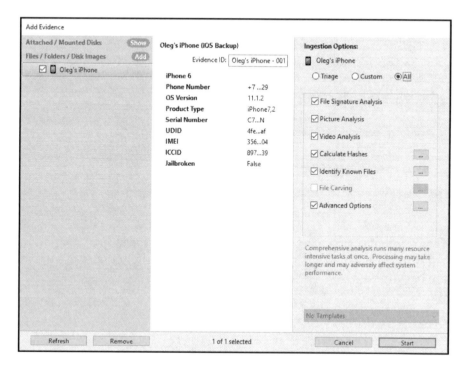

BlackLight Ingestion Options

5. Click **Start**. When processing has completed, an **Artifacts** summary can be viewed:

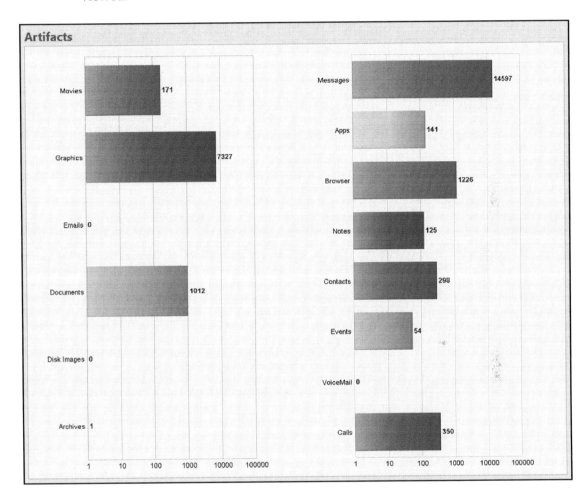

Artifacts summary

Encrypted backup

For encrypted backups, the backup files are encrypted using the AES256 algorithm in the CBC mode, with a unique key and a null **initialization vector (IV)**. The unique file keys are protected with a set of class keys from the `Backup keybag`. The class keys in the `Backup keybag` are protected with a key derived from the password set in iTunes through 10,000 iterations of **Password-Based Key Derivation Function 2 (PBKDF2)**. Both open source and commercial tools provide support for encrypted backup file parsing if the password is known. Some tools won't even prompt for a password, which makes them useless in a forensic investigation. Other tools will attempt to crack the password.

Elcomsoft Phone Breaker

Elcomsoft Phone Breaker is a GPU-accelerated commercial tool from Elcomsoft developed for the Windows platform. The tool can decrypt an encrypted backup file when the backup password is not available. The tool provides an option to launch a password brute-force attack on the encrypted backup if the backup password is not available. Elcomsoft Phone Breaker tries to recover the plain-text password that protects the encrypted backup using dictionary and brute-force attacks. Passwords that are relatively short and simple can be recovered in a reasonable time. But if the backup is protected with a strong and complex password, breaking it can take forever.

To brute-force the backup password, perform the following steps:

1. Launch the Elcomsoft Phone Breaker tool and the tool's main screen will appear, as shown in the following screenshot:

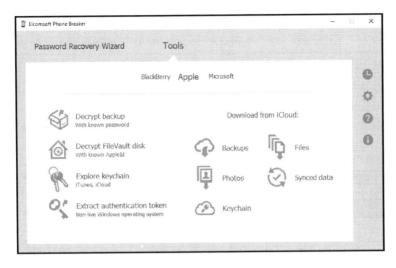

Elcomsoft Phone Breaker's main screen

2. Navigate to **Password Recovery Wizard | Choose source | iOS device backup**. Navigate to the backup file you want to crack and select the `Manifest.plist` file.

3. Configure the brute-force pattern in the **Attacks** section and click on the **Start** button to start the brute-force attack. If the brute-force attack is successful, the tool displays the password on the main screen:

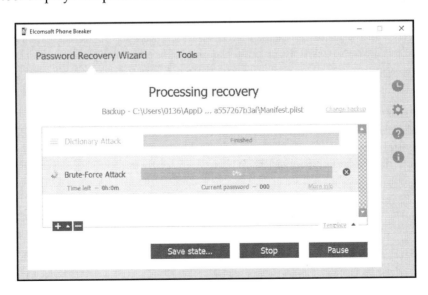

Password recovery process

If you have an iPhone running iOS 11 and its passcode, you can reset the actual password and make a backup with a new known password. Here is how to do it:

1. On the iPhone, go to **Settings** | **General** | **Reset**.
2. Choose **Reset All Settings** and enter the device's passcode. It's important to note that no data will be deleted.
3. Once the settings are reset, you can create a new backup with a password of your choice.

Working with iCloud backups

iCloud is a cloud storage and cloud computing service by Apple, launched in October 2011. The service allows users to keep data such as calendars, contacts, reminders, photos, documents, bookmarks, applications, notes, and more in sync across multiple compatible devices (iOS devices running with iOS 5 or later, computers with macOS X 10.7.2 or later, and Microsoft Windows), using a centralized iCloud account. The service also allows users to wirelessly and automatically back up their iOS devices to iCloud. iCloud also provides other services, such as **Find My iPhone** (to track a lost phone and wipe it remotely), **Find My Friends** (to share locations with friends and notify the user when a device arrives at a certain location), and more.

Signing up with iCloud is free and simple to do with an Apple ID. When you sign up for iCloud, Apple grants you access to 5 GB of free remote storage. If you need more storage, you can purchase the upgrade plan. To keep your data secure, Apple forces users to choose a strong password when creating an Apple ID to use with iCloud. The password must have a minimum of eight characters, a number, an uppercase letter, and a lowercase letter.

iOS devices running on iOS 5 and later allow users to back up the device settings and data to iCloud. Data backed up includes photos, videos, documents, application data, device settings, messages, contacts, calendar, email, keychain, and more. You can turn on iCloud backup on your device by navigating to **Settings** | **Accounts & Passwords** | **iCloud**, as shown in the following screenshot:

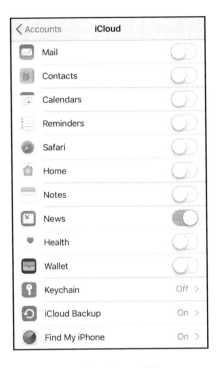

iCloud backup options on the iPhone

iCloud can automatically back up your data when your phone is plugged in, locked, and connected to Wi-Fi. That is to say, iCloud backups represent a fresh and near-real-time copy of information stored on the device, as long as space is available to create a current backup.

You can also initiate an iCloud backup from a computer by connecting the device to iTunes and choosing the iCloud option. iCloud backups are incremental; that is, once the initial iCloud backup is completed, all the subsequent backups only copy the files that are changed on the device. iCloud secures your data by encrypting it when it is transmitted over the internet, storing it in an encrypted format on the server, and using secure tokens for authentication.

Apple's built-in apps (for example, Email and Contacts) use a secure token to access iCloud services. Using secure tokens for authentication eliminates the need to store the iCloud password on devices and computers.

Extracting iCloud backups

Online backups stored on the iCloud are commonly retrieved when the original iOS device is damaged, upgraded, or lost. To extract a backup from iCloud, you must know the user's Apple ID and password. With the known Apple ID and password, you can log on to `https://www.icloud.com/` and get access to contacts, notes, email, calendar, photos, reminders, and more. To extract the complete backup from iCloud, you can use **Elcomsoft Phone Breaker**. As iCloud is not the fastest cloud storage service, downloading a large backup with Elcomsoft Phone Breaker can take hours and may not be successful. To speed up the investigation, the tool provides an option to download selected files.

To extract the iCloud backup, perform the following steps:

1. Launch Elcomsoft Phone Breaker.
2. Navigate to **Tools** | **Apple** | **Backups**. You are prompted to sign in with your Apple ID and password.
3. Successfully signing in with your Apple ID lists the available device backups that can be downloaded, as shown in the following screenshot:

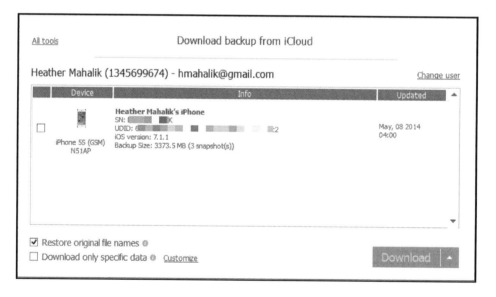

4. Select the backup you need and click on **Download**. You are prompted for a destination directory to save the extracted files into a number of domain directories by restoring the original filenames. The tool also provides an option to download the backup without restoring the original filenames so that you can use third-party software for analysis.

For iCloud backups, the keychain file contents are encrypted with a set of class keys in the `Backup keybag`. The `Backup keybag` itself is protected with a key (0x835) derived from the iPhone hardware key (UID key). You can follow the techniques explained in the preceding sections to decrypt the keychain from the extracted iCloud backup.

Summary

iOS device backups contain essential information that may be your only source of evidence. Information stored in iOS backups includes photos, videos, contacts, email, call logs, user accounts and passwords, applications, device settings, and more. This chapter covered techniques to create backup files and retrieve data from iTunes and iCloud backups, including encrypted backup files, wherever possible.

`Chapter 5`, *iOS Data Analysis and Recovery*, goes further into the forensic investigation by showing the examiner how to analyze the data recovered from the backup files. Areas containing data of potential evidentiary value will be explained in detail. `Chapter 5`, *iOS Data Analysis and Recovery*, will then teach you how to analyze the data pulled from `Chapter 3`, *Data Acquisition from iOS Devices*, and artifacts pulled from backup files as discussed in this chapter.

5
iOS Data Analysis and Recovery

A key aspect in iOS device forensics is to examine and analyze the data acquired to interpret the evidence. Data on most iOS devices is encrypted, and it is necessary to decrypt the data partition prior to an examination. In the previous chapters, you learned various techniques to acquire data from an iOS device. The raw disk image obtained during physical acquisition, the filesystem dump, or the logical or backup file, contains hundreds of data files that are often decrypted by the forensic tools described in earlier chapters. Even when the data is parsed and decrypted by the forensic tool, manual analysis may be required to uncover additional artifacts or to simply validate your findings. This chapter will help you understand how data is stored on iOS devices, and it will walk you through the key artifacts that should be examined in each investigation to recover the most data possible.

In this chapter, we will be covering the following topics:

- How iOS devices store data
- Key artifacts to examine in every investigation (databases and plists)
- The best tools and methods to extract key evidence
- How to recover deleted data from key database files

Timestamps

Before examining the data, it is important to understand the different timestamps that are used on iOS devices. Timestamps found on iOS devices are presented either in the Unix timestamp or **Mac absolute time** format. The examiner must ensure that the tools properly convert the timestamps for the files. Access to the raw SQLite files will allow the examiner to verify these timestamps manually. Further information on iOS timestamps can be found at `http://www.zdziarski.com/blog/wp-content/uploads/2013/05/iOS-Forensic-Investigative-Methods.pdf`.

Unix timestamps

A Unix timestamp is the number of seconds that offsets the Unix epoch time, which starts on January 1, 1970. A Unix timestamp can be converted easily using the date command on a Mac workstation or using an online Unix epoch converter; such as, `https://www.epochconverter.com/`.

The date command is as follows:

```
$ date -r 1512808725
Sat Dec  9 11:38:45 MSK 2017
```

You may also face Unix timestamps in millisecond or nanosecond format. This is not a big problem either; there are a number of online converters, such as, `http://currentmillis.com/`:

A Unix timestamp in milliseconds converted with http://currentmillis.com/

Mac absolute time

iOS devices adopted the use of Mac absolute time with iOS 5 for most of the data. Mac absolute time is the number of seconds that offsets the Mac epoch time, which starts on January 1, 2001. The difference between the Unix epoch time and the Mac time is exactly 978,307,200 seconds. It means you can easily convert the Mac time to the Unix epoch and use the same methods to finally convert it to a human-readable timestamp. Of course, there are a few online converters, such as, `https://www.epochconverter.com/coredata`:

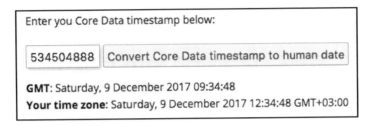

A Mac timestamp converted with https://www.epochconverter.com/coredata

WebKit/Chrome time

When analyzing iOS application data, especially web browsers such as Google Chrome, Safari, and Opera, you will face another timestamp format—**WebKit/Chrome time**. This is the number of microseconds since January 1, 1601. There is also an online converter for this: `https://www.epochconverter.com/webkit`.

If you don't like or don't want to use online converters for some reason, there is a free tool for you - Digital Detective's **DCode**. This tool can be used to convert timestamps in a number of different formats, including Unix time (both seconds and milliseconds), Mac time, and WebKit/Chrome time:

A WebKit/Chrome timestamp converted with DCode

SQLite databases

SQLite is an open source, in-process library that implements a self-contained, zero-configuration, transactional SQL database engine. This is a complete database with multiple tables, triggers, and views that are contained in a single cross-platform file. As SQLite is portable, reliable, and small, it is a popular database format that appears in many mobile platforms.

Apple iOS devices, like other smartphones, make heavy use of SQLite databases for data storage. Many of the built-in applications, such as phone, messages, mail, calendar, and notes, store data in SQLite databases. Apart from this, third-party applications installed on the device also leverage SQLite databases for data storage.

SQLite databases are created with or without a file extension. They typically have the `.sqlitedb` or `.db` file extensions, but some databases are given other extensions as well.

Data in SQLite files is broken up into tables that contain the actual data. To access the data stored in these files, a tool that can read them is needed. Most commercial forensic tools, such as Oxygen, SQLite Forensic Browser, and Physical Analyzer provide support for the examination of SQLite databases. If you don't own one of these tools, some good free tools are as follows:

- **DB browser for SQLite**: This can be downloaded from `http://sqlitebrowser.org/`.
- **SQLite command-line client**: This can be downloaded from `http://www.sqlite.org/`.
- **SQLite Professional** (`https://www.sqlitepro.com/`): This is a free **graphical user interface (GUI)** from Hankinsoft Development for macOS X users. You can download it from Apple's App Store.
- **SQLite Spy**: This is a free GUI tool for Windows. You can download it from `http://www.yunqa.de/delphi/doku.php/products/sqlitespy/index`.

macOS X includes the SQLite command-line utility (`sqlite3`) by default. This command-line utility can easily access individual files and issue SQL queries against a database. In the following sections, we will use both the `sqlite3` command-line utility and other SQLite tools and browsers to retrieve data from various SQLite databases. Before retrieving the data, the basic commands that you will need to learn are explained in the following sections.

Connecting to a database

Manual examination of iOS SQLite database files is possible with the use of free tools. The following is an example of how to examine a database using native Mac commands in Terminal. Make sure that your device image is mounted as read-only to prevent changes being made to the original evidence. To connect to a SQLite database from the command line, run the `sqlite3` command in the Terminal by entering your database file. This will give you a SQL prompt where you can issue SQL queries:

```
$ sqlite3 sms.db
SQLite version 3.19.3 2017-06-27 16:48:08
Enter ".help" for usage hints.
```

To disconnect, use the `.exit` command. This exits the SQLite client and returns to the Terminal prompt.

SQLite special commands

Once you connect to a database, there are a number of built-in SQLite commands, which are known as **dot commands** and can be used to obtain information from the database files.

You can obtain the list of special commands by issuing the `.help` command in the SQLite prompt. These are SQLite-specific commands, and they do not require a semicolon at the end of the command. The most commonly used dot commands include the following:

- `.tables`: This lists all of the tables within a database. The following example displays the list of tables found inside the `sms.db` database:

```
sqlite> .tables
_SqliteDatabaseProperties   kvtable
attachment                  message
chat                        message_attachment_join
chat_handle_join            message_processing_task
chat_message_join           sync_deleted_attachments
deleted_messages            sync_deleted_chats
handle                      sync_deleted_messages
```

- `.schema table-name`: This displays the SQL CREATE statement that was used to construct the table. The following example displays the schema for the `handle` table, which is found inside the `sms.db` database:

```
sqlite> .schema handle
CREATE TABLE handle ( ROWID INTEGER PRIMARY KEY AUTOINCREMENT UNIQUE, id TEXT NOT NULL,
country TEXT, service TEXT NOT NULL, uncanonicalized_id TEXT, UNIQUE (id, service) );
```

- `.dump table-name`: This dumps the entire content of a table into SQL statements. The following example displays the dump of the `handle` table, which is found inside the `sms.db` database:

```
sqlite> .dump deleted_messages
PRAGMA foreign_keys=OFF;
BEGIN TRANSACTION;
CREATE TABLE deleted_messages (ROWID INTEGER PRIMARY KEY AUTOINCREMENT UNIQUE,
 guid TEXT NOT NULL);
COMMIT;
```

- `.output file-name`: This redirects the output to a file on the disk instead of showing it on the screen.
- `.headers on`: This displays the column title whenever you issue a SELECT statement.
- `.help`: This displays the list of available SQLite dot commands.
- `.exit`: This disconnects from the database and exits the SQLite command shell.
- `.mode`: This sets the output mode, where MODE can be `.csv`, HTML, tabs, and so on.

Make sure that there is no space between the SQLite prompt and the dot command; otherwise, the entire command will be ignored.

Standard SQL queries

In addition to the SQLite dot commands, standard SQL queries, such as SELECT, INSERT, ALTER, DELETE, and more, can be issued to SQLite databases on the command line. Unlike the SQLite dot commands, standard SQL queries expect a semicolon at the end of the command.

Most of the databases that you will examine will contain only a reasonable number of records, so you can issue a SELECT statement, which outputs all of the data contained in the table. This will be covered in detail throughout this chapter.

Accessing a database using commercial tools

While manual examination of iOS SQLite database files is possible with the use of free tools, most examiners prefer commercial support prior to digging manually into the files for examination. The following is an example of how to examine a database using SQLite Forensic Browser—a Windows-based tool by Sanderson Forensics, which can be found at http://www.sandersonforensics.com/forum/content.php.

Launch SQLite Forensics Browser and navigate to **File | Open SQLite DB**:

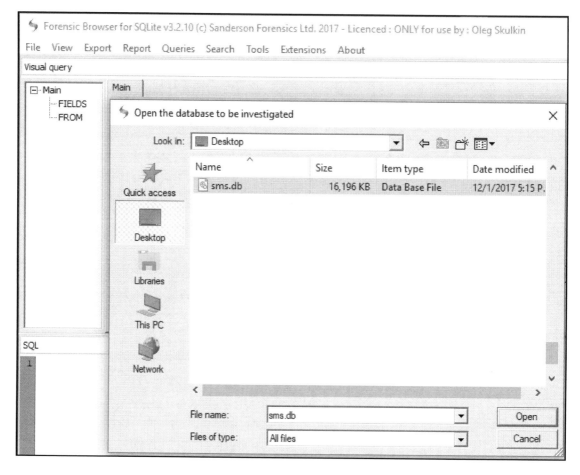

Opening a database in the Forensic Browser for SQLite

Once the SQLite DB file is opened, the examiner can access the various tables that are contained within the database, leverage the tool to convert date/timestamps, and visually look at the SQL queries being run behind the scenes to access the data.

Once loaded, tables can be selected for parsing. Note that the tool displays the queries that are being run behind the scenes to produce the output. These queries should be the same ones that will be displayed manually later in this chapter. These queries can be used on a Mac to validate your findings:

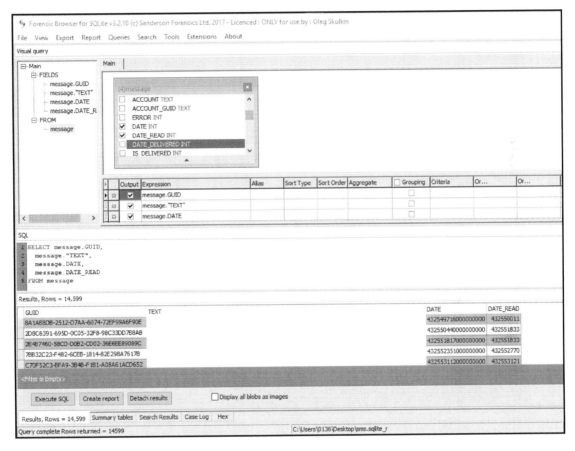

Examining the sms.db file in the Forensic Browser for SQLite

All of the columns can be formatted to show the best version of the data. For example, the date/timestamps highlighted in the preceding screenshot can be converted to Mac absolute time within the tool, as discussed earlier in this chapter. Simply right-click on it and select **View column as**:

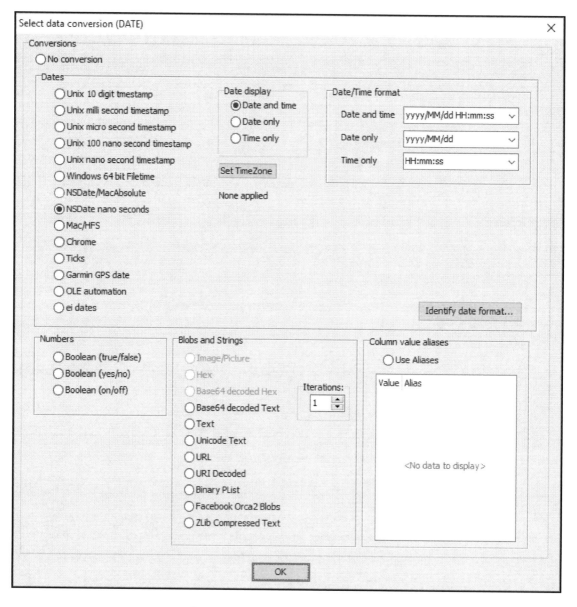

Data conversion selection in the Forensic Browser for SQLite

Once converted, the dates and time shown previously are converted to a format that is easier to examine:

DATE	DATE_READ	DATE_DELIVERED
2012/09/04 05:22:26	2012/09/04 05:22:26	2012/09/04 05:22:26
2012/09/04 05:22:47	2012/09/04 05:22:47	2012/09/04 05:22:47
2012/09/04 05:23:42	2012/09/04 05:23:42	2012/09/04 05:23:42
2012/09/04 14:04:34	2012/09/04 14:04:34	2012/09/04 14:04:34
2012/09/04 16:04:19	2012/09/04 16:04:19	2012/09/04 16:04:19
2012/09/04 16:05:37	2012/09/04 16:05:37	2012/09/04 16:05:37
2012/09/04 16:09:31	2012/09/04 16:09:31	2012/09/04 16:09:31
2012/09/04 16:15:11	2012/09/04 16:15:11	2012/09/04 16:15:11
2012/09/05 04:30:26	2012/09/05 04:30:26	2012/09/05 04:30:26
2012/09/05 08:45:37	2012/09/05 08:45:37	2012/09/05 08:45:37

Data conversion output in the Forensic Browser for SQLite

All of the database files that are described next can be loaded, examined, and reported using a tool such as SQLite Forensics Browser. In addition to this, the database files explained in the following sections can be exported from SQLite Forensics Browser by creating a report or exporting relevant files to include in your final forensic report.

Key artifacts – important iOS database files

Raw disk images, filesystems and logical dumps, and the backup that you extracted as per the instructions in *Chapter 3, Data Acquisition from iOS Devices* and *Chapter 4, Data Acquisition from iOS Backups*, should contain the following SQLite databases that may be important to your investigation. Should these files not be recovered, make sure that you acquired the iOS device correctly. The files that are shown in the following sections are extracted from an iOS 11 device. As Apple adds new features to the built-in applications with every iOS release, the format of the files may vary for different iOS versions. More information regarding important database files can be found at `https://digital-forensics.sans.org/media/for585-poster.pdf`.

Address book contacts

The address book contains a wealth of information about the owner's personal contacts. With the exception of third-party applications, the address book contains contact entries for all of the contacts that are stored on the device. The address book database is a `HomeDomain` file, and it can be found at `private/var/mobile/Library/AddressBook/AddressBook.sqlitedb`. The `AddressBook.sqlitedb` file contains several tables, of which the following three are of particular interest:

- `ABPerson`: This contains the name, organization, notes, and more for each contact.
- `ABMultiValue`: This contains phone numbers, email addresses, website URLs, and more for the entries in the `ABPerson` table. The `ABMultiValue` table uses a `record_id` file to associate the contact information with a `ROWID` from the `ABPerson` table.
- `ABMultiValueLabel`: This table contains labels to identify the kind of information stored in the `ABMultiValue` table.

Some of the data stored within the `AddressBook.sqlitedb` file could be from third-party applications. The examiner should manually examine the application file folders to ensure that all the contacts are accounted for and examined.

While all the following commands can be run natively on a Mac, we are going to use SQLPro for SQLite to examine the most common databases found on iOS devices and add some commercial tools, where relevant, to show a variety of examination options. This is a free tool that simplifies the process and provides a clear view of the data to the examiner. Once the database is loaded, you can draft queries to examine the data most relevant to you and the address book into a `.csv` file named `AddressBook.csv`:

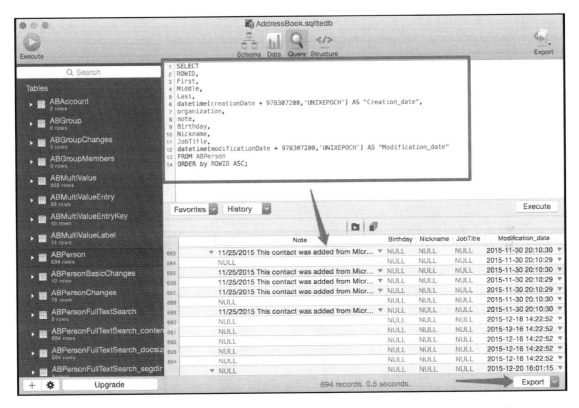

The AddressBook.sqlitedb file in SQLPro

In the preceding screenshot, you can see the suggested query to parse data from the ABPerson table. In later examples, table joins may be required to capture all of the information. The query also converts the Mac absolute time into a readable form using the SQLite datetime function. The results can be exported for insertion in your final forensic report:

ROWID	First	Middle	Last	Creation_date	Organization	Note	Nickname	Modification_date
2	Dad	<null>	<null>	2012-06-24 22:58:14	<null>	<HTCData><Favorite>actionid	<null>	2015-09-16 23:32:56
3	Andy	<null>	<null>	2012-06-24 22:58:14	SANS Singapore	<null>	<null>	2015-09-16 23:32:56
4	Heather	<null>	Mahalik	2012-06-24 22:58:14	<null>	<null>	Hank	2015-09-16 23:32:56
5	Lee	<null>	<null>	2012-06-24 22:58:14	<null>	<null>	<null>	2015-09-16 23:32:56
6	Hayes	<null>	<null>	2012-06-24 22:58:14	<null>	<null>	<null>	2015-09-16 23:32:56
7	Tabs	<null>	<null>	2012-06-24 22:58:14	<null>	<null>	<null>	2015-09-16 23:32:56
8	Jus	<null>	<null>	2012-06-24 22:58:12	<null>	<HTCData><Favorite>actionid	<null>	2015-09-16 23:32:56
9	Suresh	<null>	<null>	2012-06-24 22:58:14	<null>	<null>	<null>	2015-09-16 23:32:56
10	New	<null>	<null>	2012-06-24 22:58:14	<null>	<null>	<null>	2015-09-16 23:32:56
11	Crogs	<null>	<null>	2012-06-24 22:58:14	<null>	<HTCData><Favorite>actionid	<null>	2015-09-16 23:32:56
13	Rach	<null>	<null>	2012-06-25 15:55:31	<null>	<null>	<null>	2015-09-16 23:32:56
14	Hardcopy	<null>	<null>	2012-06-25 15:55:31	<null>	<null>	<null>	2015-09-16 23:32:56

SQLPro output from the AddressBook.sqlitedb file

Note that favorites are called out in the Note section. Thus, when a user marks a contact as a favorite, you may find this artifact. It is common for some columns to contain little to no data.

Address book images

In addition to the address book's data, each contact may contain an image associated with it. This image is displayed on the screen whenever the user receives an incoming call from a particular contact. These images can be created by third-party applications that have access to the contacts on the device. Often, the contact is linked to a third-party application profile photo. The address book images database is a HomeDomain file, and it can be found at /private/var/mobile/Library/AddressBook/AddressBookImages.sqlitedb.

The address book images can be parsed manually, but using commercial software makes this process much more practical. Most free and commercial tools will provide access to the address book images. However, some tools will not make the link between the graphic and the contact, which may require some manual rebuilding. Sometimes, the free solutions work best when parsing simple data from iOS devices. Next, we will examine the address book images in iExplorer, which was introduced in `Chapter 4`, *Data Acquisition from iOS Backups*. In this example, we simply loaded the iOS dataset into iExplorer and navigated to the `AddressBookImages.sqlitedb` file for examination:

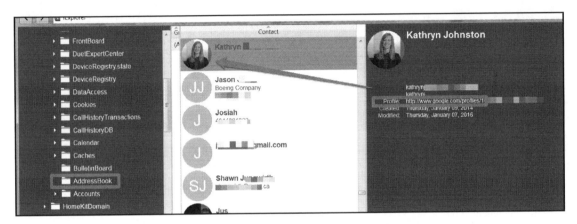

Examining AddressBookImages.sqlitedb in iExplorer

In this example, we can see that **Kathryn** is a contact on the phone, and her profile picture is being pulled from her Google account. Thus, the iPhone user in this example provided Google access to the contacts and the link was made. This happens often with common applications, such as Twitter, Facebook, Google, LinkedIn, and Instagram, to name a few.

When the user links a picture from their phone or takes a picture using the camera and assigns the photo as a contact, you will find no reference to a profile for the photo and the output will resemble what is shown in the following screenshot for the contact:

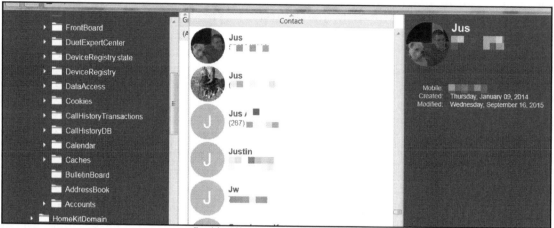

Examining AddressBookImages.sqlitedb in iExplorer

Call history

Phone or FaceTime calls placed, missed, and received by the user are logged in the call history along with other metadata, such as call duration, date/time, and more. The call history database is a `WirelessDomain` file, and it can be found at `/private/var/mobile/Library/CallHistoryDB/CallHistory.storedata`. The `CallHistory.storedata` file was introduced with iOS 8 and is currently in use at the time of writing (iOS 11). Keep in mind that most devices can be updated and will most likely have data in both locations, which means that you need to be aware of how the data is stored in each location and whether or not your tool is extracting data from each database. For this reason, we will examine both in this section.

The `ZCALLRECORD` table in the `CallHistory.storedata` file contains the call history. It's important to note that only a limited number of calls may be stored in the active database. Just because the database removes the oldest record when space is needed does not mean this data is deleted. It's simply in the free pages of the SQLite database file, and it can be recovered using forensic tools or manually. The most important columns in the `ZCALLRECORD` table are the following:

- `ZDATE`: This column contains the timestamps of calls in Mac absolute time format.
- `ZDURATION`: This column contains the duration of calls.

- ZLOCATION: This column contains the locations of phone numbers.
- ZADDRESS: This column contains the phone numbers.
- ZSERVICE_PROVIDER: This column contains the service providers; for example, Phone, WhatsApp, Telegram, and so on.

You can run the following queries in the DB Browser for SQLite to parse the call history. Afterwards, you can export it into a .csv file:

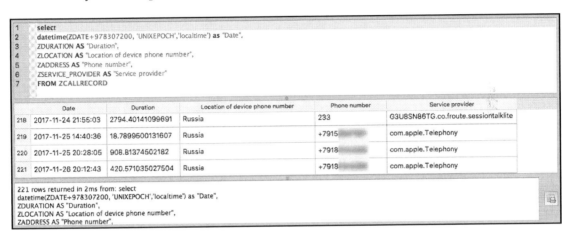

	Date	Duration	Location of device phone number	Phone number	Service provider
218	2017-11-24 21:55:03	2794.40141099691	Russia	233	G3U8SN86TG.co.froute.sessiontalklite
219	2017-11-25 14:40:36	18.7899500131607	Russia	+7915	com.apple.Telephony
220	2017-11-25 20:28:05	908.81374502182	Russia	+7918	com.apple.Telephony
221	2017-11-26 20:12:43	420.571035027504	Russia	+7918	com.apple.Telephony

221 rows returned in 2ms from: select
datetime(ZDATE+978307200, 'UNIXEPOCH','localtime') as "Date",
ZDURATION AS "Duration",
ZLOCATION AS "Location of device phone number",
ZADDRESS AS "Phone number",

Examining CallHistory.storedata in the DB Browser for SQLite

SMS messages

The **Short Message Service (SMS)** database contains text and multimedia messages that were sent from and received by the device along with the phone number of the remote party, date and time, and other carrier information. Starting with iOS 5, iMessages data is also stored in the SMS database. iMessage allows users to send SMS and MMS messages over a cellular or Wi-Fi network to other iOS or OS X users, thus providing an alternative to SMS. The SMS database is a HomeDomain file, and it can be found at /private/var/mobile/Library/SMS/sms.db. This location has not changed as iOS versions have been released.

You can run the following queries in the DB Browser for SQLite to parse the SMS messages. Afterwards, you can export it into a `.csv` file:

Examining sms.db in the DB Browser for SQLite

Calendar events

Calendar events that have been manually created by the user or synced using a mail application or other third-party applications are stored in the calendar database. The calendar database is a `HomeDomain` file and can be found at

`/private/var/mobile/Library/Calendar/Calendar.sqlitedb`.

The `CalendarItem` table in the `Calendar.sqlitedb` file contains the calendar events summary, description, start date, end date, and more. You can run the following queries in the DB Browser for SQLite to parse the calendar:

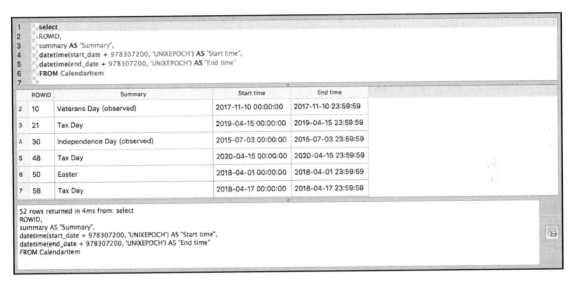

Examining calendar.sqlitedb in the DB Browser for SQLite

Notes

The `Notes` database contains the notes that are created by the user using the device's built-in *Notes* application. *Notes* is the simplest application, often containing the most sensitive and confidential information. The `Notes` database is a `HomeDomain` file and can be found at `/private/var/mobile/Library/Notes/notes.sqlite`.

The ZNOTE and ZNOTEBODY tables in the `notes.sqlite` file contain the `notes` title, content, creation date, modification date, and more. You can run the following queries to parse the `Notes` database:

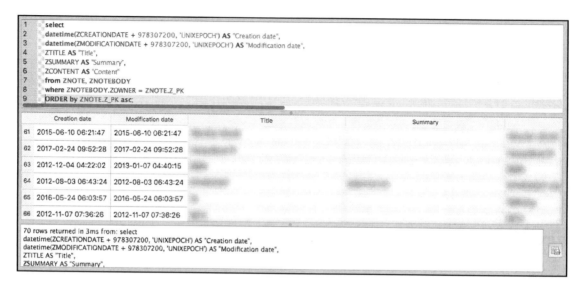

Examining notes in the DB Browser for SQLite

Safari bookmarks and cache

The Safari browser used on an Apple device allows users to bookmark their favorite websites. The bookmarks database is a `HomeDomain` file, and it can be found at `/private/var/mobile/Library/Safari/Bookmarks.db`. The Safari browser stores the recently downloaded and cached data in a database. The database is a `HomeDomain` file and can be found at `/private/var/mobile/Library/Caches/com.apple.mobilesafari/Cache.db`.

The file contains cached URLs and the web server's responses along with the timestamps. In addition to this, Safari stores information from various sites in the WebKit database that is located in the `/private/var/mobile/Library/WebKit/LocalStorage/` directory. The directory contains unique databases for each website, as shown in the following screenshot:

```
mbp-hmahalik:Webkit hmahalik$ cd /Users/
hmahalik/Desktop/Webkit/LocalStorage
mbp-hmahalik:LocalStorage hmahalik$ ls
StorageTracker.db
http_www.google.com_0.localstorage
http_m.youtube.com_0.localstorage
http_www.youtube.com_0.localstorage
http_www.bing.com_0.localstorage
https_m.facebook.com_0.localstorage
mbp-hmahalik:LocalStorage hmahalik$ █
```

The LocalStorage folder contents

All of the Safari files can be extracted using queries, as already demonstrated. In addition to Safari, other browsers can be used and can contain data on an iOS device. For this reason, we recommend using a tool built to parse internet history to ensure that data is not overlooked. Good forensic tools for solving this task are AXIOM or Internet Evidence Finder by Magnet Forensics, Evidence Center by Belkasoft, and some others.

Photo metadata

A manifestation of the photos in the device's photo album is stored in a database located at `/private/var/mobile/Media/PhotoData/Photos.sqlite`. The photo metadata database file is a member of `CameraRollDomain`.

You can run the following queries to view the photos stored in the database. From here, you can use the directory to locate the file path and the filename to track down the photo:

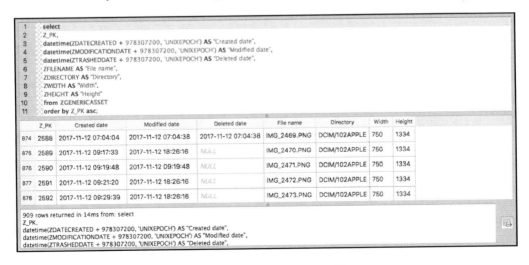

Examining photos.sqlite in the DB Browser for SQLite

Consolidated GPS cache

Geolocation history of cell towers and Wi-Fi on the device is stored in a database that is located at `/private/var/root/Caches/locationd/consolidated.db`. The database is a member of `RootDomain`. It contains location information for cell towers that the device came into close proximity with, as well as Wi-Fi networks that were available for the device to connect to. This database is often used to place a person near a specific location, as this data is cached to the database file without the user's consent.

The `CompassCalibration` table in the `consolidated.db` file contains the location information along with the timestamps. The file, when opened with the DB Browser for SQLite, displays the data, as shown in the following screenshot:

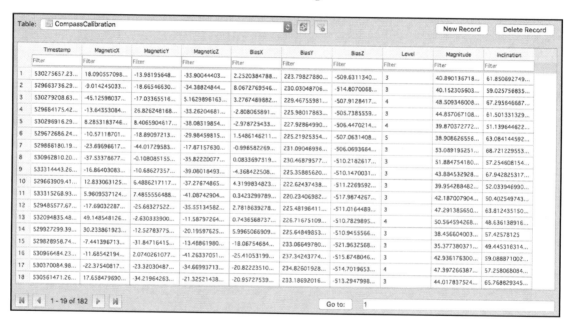

The Consolidated.db view with the DB Browser for SQLite

Voicemail

The Voicemail database contains metadata about each voicemail that is stored on the device that includes the sender's phone number, callback number, timestamp and message duration, and more. The voicemail recordings are stored as AMR audio files that can be played by any media player that supports the AMR codec (for example, **QuickTime Player**). The voicemail database is a HomeDomain file, and it can be found at /private/var/mobile/Library/Voicemail/voicemail.db, while the actual voicemail recordings are stored in the /private/var/mobile/Library/Voicemail/ directory.

Property lists

A property list, commonly referred to as a **plist**, is a structured data format used to store, organize, and access various types of data on an iOS device as well as a macOS device. Plists are binary-formatted files, and they can be viewed using a **Property List Editor**, which is capable of reading or converting the binary format to ASCII.

Plist files may or may not have a .plist file extension. To access the data stored in these files, you need a tool that can read them. Some of the good free tools include the following:

- Plist Editor for Windows, which can be downloaded from http://www.icopybot.com/plist-editor.htm
- The plutil command-line utility on macOS

You can also view the plist files using XCode. macOS includes the plutil command-line utility by default. The command-line utility can easily convert the binary-formatted files into human-readable files. In addition to this, most commercial forensic tools, such as Oxygen Forensics, include great support to parse plist files.

The following example displays the `com.Apple.maps.plist` file:

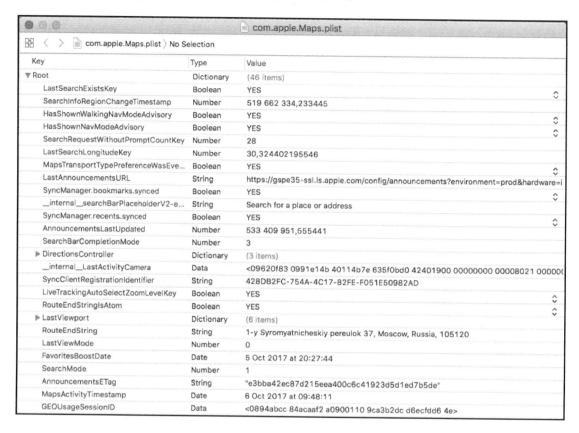

The com.Apple.maps.plist in XCode

Important plist files

Raw disk images or the backup that you extracted in `Chapter 3`, *Data Acquisition from iOS Devices* and `Chapter 4`, *Data Acquisition from iOS Backups* should contain the following plist files that are important for an investigation. The files displayed are extracted from an iOS 11 device. The file locations may vary for your iOS version.

The HomeDomain plist files

The following are the `HomeDomain` plist files, which contain data that may be relevant to your investigation:

- `/private/var/mobile/Library/Preferences/com.apple.mobilephone.plist`: This contains the last phone number entered into the keypad regardless of whether it was dialed or not
- `/private/var/mobile/Library/Preferences/com.apple.mobilephone.speeddial.plist`: This contains a list of the contacts that were added to the phone's favorites list
- `/private/var/mobile/Library/Preferences/com.apple.AppSupport.plist`: This contains the country code that was used for the App Store on the device
- `/private/var/mobile/Library/Preferences/com.apple.Maps.plist`: This contains the last latitude, longitude, and address pinned in the *Maps* application
- `/private/var/mobile/Library/Preferences/com.apple.mobiletimer.plist`: This contains a list of world clocks used
- `/private/var/mobile/Library/Preferences/com.apple.Preferences.plist`: This contains the keyboard language that was last used on the device
- `/private/var/mobile/Library/Preferences/com.apple.springboard.plist`: This contains a list of applications that are shown in the interface and iOS version
- `/private/var/mobile/Library/Preferences/com.apple.mobiletimer.plist`: This contains information about the current time zone, timers, alarms, and stopwatches
- `/private/var/mobile/Library/Preferences/com.apple.weather.plist`: This contains the cities for weather reports, date, and time of the last update
- `/private/var/mobile/Library/Preferences/com.apple.preferences.network.plist`: This contains the status of Bluetooth and Wi-Fi networks
- `/private/var/mobile/Library/Preferences/com.apple.locationd.plist`: This contains a list of application identifiers that use the location service on the device
- `/private/var/mobile/Library/Preferences/com.apple.assistant.backedup.plist`: This will help an examiner to determine whether cloud synchronization is enabled or not

- `/private/var/mobile/Library/Preferences/com.apple.commcenter.shared.plist`: This contains the owner's phone number
- `/private/var/mobile/Library/Preferences/com.apple.conference.plist`: This contains the owner's email address
- `/private/var/mobile/Library/Preferences/com.apple.facetime.plist`: This contains the last FaceTime number
- `/private/var/mobile/Library/Preferences/com.apple.icloud.findmydeviced.FMIPAccounts.plist`: This contains the history of iOS versions used on the device; if the device is restored from a backup, this may include items from the device the backup was originally created from
- `/private/var/mobile/Library/Preferences/com.apple.identityservices.idstatuscache.plist`: This contains the list of cached phone numbers
- `/private/var/mobile/Library/Preferences/com.apple.WebSheet.plist`: This contains the SSID of the last wireless network the device was connected to
- `/private/var/mobile/Library/Preferences/com.apple.youtube.dp.plist`: This contains the last YouTube search term and the ID of the last video watched
- `/private/var/mobile/Library/Safari/History.plist`: This contains the web-browsing history of Safari
- `/private/var/mobile/Library/Safari/SuspendState.plist`: This contains the web page title and the URL of all suspended web pages on Safari

The RootDomain plist files

The following `RootDomain` files listed should be examined for relevance to your investigation:

- `/private/var/root/Library/Preferences/com.apple.preferences.network.plist`: This contains information about whether airplane mode is presently enabled on the device
- `/private/var/root/Library/Preferences/com.apple.MobileBackup.plist`: This contains the timestamp of when the device was last restored from the backup, the device build version, and the backup build version
- `/private/var/root/Library/Caches/locationd/clients.plist`: This contains the location settings for applications and system services

The WirelessDomain plist files

The following `WirelessDomain` plist file contains useful information to identify the SIM card last used in the device and other information:

- `/private/wireless/Library/Preferences/com.apple.commcenter.plist`

The SystemPreferencesDomain plist files

The two plist files containing data of evidentiary value from the `SystemPreferencesDomain` files are as follows:

- `/private/var/preferences/SystemConfiguration/com.apple.network.identification.plist`: This contains networking information of the cached IP
- `/private/var/preferences/SystemConfiguration/com.apple.wifi.plist`: This contains a list of previously known Wi-Fi networks and the last time each one was connected to

Other important files

Apart from SQLite and plist files, several other locations may contain valuable information to an investigation.

The other sources include the following:

- Cookies
- Keyboard cache
- Photos
- Thumbnails
- Wallpaper
- Recordings
- Third-party applications

Cookies

Cookies can be recovered from
`/private/var/mobile/Library/Cookies/Cookies.binarycookies`. This file is a
standard binary file containing cookies that are saved when web pages are accessed on the
device. This information can be a good indication of what websites the user has been
actively visiting. Keep in mind that third-party applications may also contain this file.

To convert the binary cookie to human-readable format, run the `BinaryCookieReader.py`
Python script on the cookie file, as shown in the following command (the Python script can
be downloaded here: `https://gist.github.com/sh1n0b1/4bb8b737370bfe5f5ab8`):

```
● ● ●                             ⇧ olegskulkin — -bash — 118×24
Olegs-MacBook-Air:~ olegskulkin$ python BinaryCookieReader.py Cookies.binarycookies
#***********************************************************************#
# BinaryCookieReader: developed by Satishb3: http://www.securitylearn.net #
#***********************************************************************#
Cookie : __atuvc=1%7C21%2C0%7C22%2C0%7C23%2C1%7C24; domain=www.itkkit.ru; path=/; expires=Tue, 11 Jun 2019;
Cookie : rrrbt=; domain=www.itkkit.ru; path=/; expires=Thu, 28 Dec 2017;
Cookie : LocRegionAncestors_5=1%7C324%7C417; domain=.mobile.beeline.ru; path=/; expires=Thu, 27 Jan 2022;
Cookie : LocUserRegion_5=417%7Csochi; domain=.mobile.beeline.ru; path=/; expires=Thu, 27 Jan 2022;
Cookie : BX_USER_ID=e29ddd6d5320089beeee228723d43b54; domain=www.itkkit.com; path=/; expires=Wed, 21 Jul 2027;
Cookie : __atuvc=2%7C30; domain=www.itkkit.com; path=/; expires=Tue, 23 Jul 2019;
Cookie : rrrbt=; domain=www.itkkit.com; path=/; expires=Thu, 08 Feb 2018;
Cookie : __ar_v4=%7CTQSV74R4GVCSJITSZC2MCP%3A20160111%3A1%7CACPJ7LN56VBITNNAUDPDMG%3A20160111%3A1%7CDARDKNAFP5HS5ABHGM
36J3%3A20160111%3A1; domain=.www.darkreading.com; path=/; expires=Sun, 26 Sep 2021;
Cookie : WT_NVR=0=/:1=ru-ru:2=ru-ru/windows7|en-us/windows:3=ru-ru/windows7/products|ru-ru/windows/shop|en-us/windows/
help; domain=.windows.microsoft.com; path=/; expires=Sat, 02 Jul 2022;
Cookie : UniqueID=88d3d2890bf3c839d3ed62c7f4ca3b; domain=www.titus.de; path=/; expires=Sat, 17 Aug 2019; HttpOnly
Cookie : lsn_statp=Kc9DGhQAAABdPkbhrRC5Tw%3D%3D; domain=.linksynergy.com; path=/; expires=Mon, 26 Jan 2032;
Cookie : lsn_track=UmFuZG9tSVZtmaV36aREjwyVO8S1PYpdox6Hh14ZwzUfVqWkY2RO5ccWF4f8KzvDSlWwRh%2FSJVLU7ajjfnT6xQ%3D%3D; dom
ain=.linksynergy.com; path=/; expires=Fri, 28 Jan 2022;
Cookie : _sdsat_Internal/External=internal; domain=club.pokemon.com; path=/; expires=Mon, 01 Jul 2019;
Cookie : _sdsat_Language=en; domain=club.pokemon.com; path=/; expires=Mon, 01 Jul 2019;
Cookie : _sdsat_businessUnit=pcom; domain=club.pokemon.com; path=/; expires=Mon, 01 Jul 2019;
Cookie : django_language=en; domain=club.pokemon.com; path=/; expires=Sun, 01 Jul 2018;
Cookie : visid_incap_1155802=UZmozvjASyC0eVR5Ez90HjgXhlkAAAAAQUIPAAAAAAD4ul57XrhYrR+NSN1a+DpE; domain=.sans.org; path=
```

Parsing Cookies.binarycookies with BinaryCookieReader.py

Keyboard cache

The keyboard cache is captured and saved in the `dynamic-text.dat` file. This file is located at `/private/var/mobile/Library/Keyboard/dynamic-text.dat` and contains the keyboard cache, which is comprised of text entered by the user. This text is cached as part of the device's autocorrect feature, and it was designed to autocomplete the predictive common words as well as cache words typed by the user on the device. The file keeps a list of approximately 600 words per language that are used on the iOS device. Commonly, this file is the only source of the artifact should the data be inaccessible, encrypted, or permanently deleted from the iOS device.

The `dynamic-text.dat` is a binary file, and it can be viewed using a hex editor. This file may contain passwords that are cached by the iOS device, and they can be used to achieve brute force attacks on the device or an encrypted backup of the device. This is sometimes one of the best artifacts recovered from an iOS device.

Photos

Photos are stored in a directory located at `/private/var/mobile/Camera Roll/Media/DCIM/`, which contains the photos taken with the device's built-in camera, screenshots, selfies, photo stream, recently deleted photos, and accompanying thumbnails. Some third-party applications will also store photos taken in this directory. Every photo stored in the `DCIM` folder contains **Exchangeable Image File Format (EXIF)** data. EXIF data stored in the photo can be extracted using ExifTool, which can be downloaded from `https://sno.phy.queensu.ca/~phil/exiftool/`. EXIF data may also contain the geographical information when a photo is tagged with the user's geo location if the user has enabled location permissions on the iOS device.

Thumbnails

Another source of important artifacts related to photos is the ithmb files. You can find these files under /private/var/mobile/Camera Roll/Media/PhotoData/Thumbnails. These files contain thumbnails not only for actual photos on the device, but also for deleted ones. And, of course, there is a tool for parsing such files—**iThmb Converter**, which can be downloaded from http://www.ithmbconverter.com/en/download/:

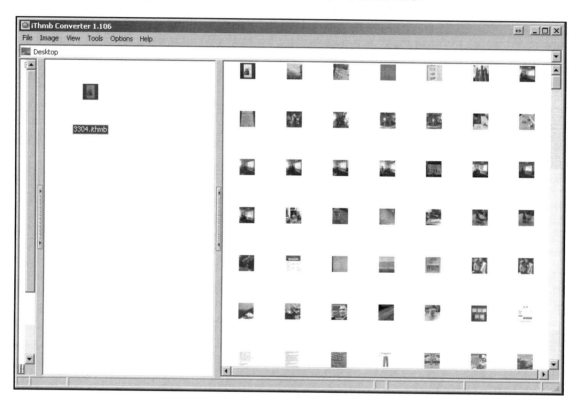

Examining 3304.ithmb with iThmb Converter

Wallpaper

The current background wallpaper set for the iOS device can be recovered from the LockBackgroundThumbnail.jpg file that is found in /private/var/mobile/Library/SpringBoard/LockBackgroundThumbnail.jpg.

This is complemented with a thumbnail named in the same directory. The wallpaper picture may contain identifying information about the user, which could help in a missing persons case or an iOS device recovered from a theft investigation.

Recordings

The iPhone allows a user to record voice memos very easily. The recorded voice memos are stored in the `/private/var/mobile/Media/Recordings/` directory. Recordings here could be used to identify a person, based on their voice, and they may also contain information, such as voice reminders, which won't be stored in the calendar database. Recordings provide a lot of information to the examiner as they are user-created and often not deleted.

Downloaded applications

Third-party applications, which are downloaded and installed from the App Store, including applications such as Facebook, WhatsApp, Viber, Threema, Tango, Skype, Gmail, and more, contain a wealth of information that is useful for an investigation. Some third-party applications use Base64 encoding, which needs to be converted for viewing purposes as well as encryption. Applications that encrypt the database file may prevent the examiner from accessing the data residing in the tables. Encryption varies among these applications based on the application and iOS versions.

A unique subdirectory GUI is created for each application that is installed on the device in the `/private/var/mobile/App/` directory. Most of the files stored in the application's directory are in the SQLite and plist format. Each file must be examined for relevance. We recommend using Oxygen Forensics and Magnet AXIOM when possible to extract these artifacts quickly before going back and manually running queries and parsing the data.

Apple Watch

Examining the Apple Watch is new and exciting. The good news is that the files found on the watch are similar, if not the same, as those found on the iPhone. We are going to see the data primarily existing in the SQLite database and plist files, and this is examined by creating or examining an iPhone backup file. Remember that an iPhone running iOS 8.2 or later is the only iOS device capable of being linked to an Apple Watch.

One unique aspect about the Apple Watch is that the data pertaining to the watch is stored in the `mobile/Library/DeviceRegistry` directory within the backup, which is shown in the following screenshot:

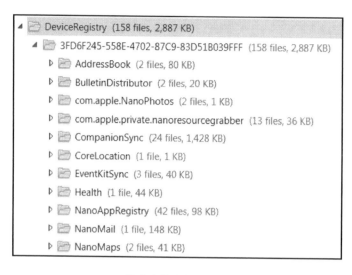

The Apple Watch data directory

Here, you will find exact copies of files found on the iPhone. If the case relies on determining what happened on the Apple Watch versus the iPhone, it may be impossible to solve. As of Watch 2.0, the files that are used by both the iPhone and the watch are exact copies of one another, and they do not contain status flags stating where the activity was initiated. This is one of the hardest topics to cover in all aspects of data synchronization. For example, if you examine my iPhone backup that contains my Apple Watch data, you will see map information in mobile `/Library/DeviceRegistry/NanoMaps/GeoHistory.Mapsdata` that occurred before the Apple Watch was released. This should be impossible, but it's simply because Apple is copying the iPhone maps database and placing a copy in the Apple Watch data location. The following is an example of what data in the `GeoHistory.Mapsdata` file looks like when being examined in UFED Physical Analyzer. While this tool is expensive, it is one of the best analytical platforms for manually carving and hunting artifacts that relate to your investigation. In this example, a keyword search was run for the term `current location` within the `GeoHistory.Mapsdata` file. From these results, we can ascertain that the user was at the address highlighted in the following screenshot when asking for or researching directions on the iPhone or the Apple Watch. Remember, this is an exact copy of the same file, so we currently cannot say whether this location was stamped by the Apple Watch or the iPhone:

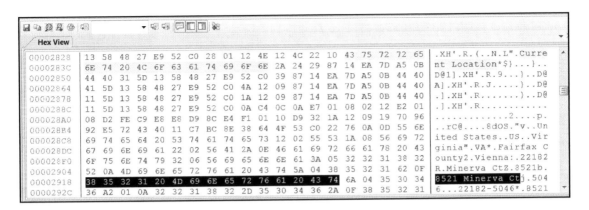

The GeoHistory.Mapsdata in Physical Analyzer

Some of the more common Apple Watch artifacts that can be recovered include the following:

- AddressBook
- GeoServices
- Health
- Mail
- Passes
- Preferences
- PairdSync
- Photos

This list is just a sample of the most popular items that we can recover data from on the Apple Watch. Again, these artifacts primarily exist as SQLite and plist files within the mobile /Library/DeviceRegistry/ directory. For Apple Watch identifiers, the binary plist file located at mobile /Library/DeviceRegistry.state/properties.bin can be examined to determine the watch name, make, model, OS, and GUID.

Recovering deleted SQLite records

SQLite databases store the deleted records within the database itself, so it is possible to recover deleted data, such as contacts, SMS, calendar, notes, email, voicemail, and more by parsing the corresponding SQLite database. If a SQLite database is vacuumed or defragmented, the likelihood of recovering the deleted data is minimal. The amount of cleanup that these databases require relies heavily on the iOS version, the device, and the user's settings on the device.

A SQLite database file comprises one or more fixed size pages, which are used just once. SQLite uses a **b-tree** layout of pages to store indices and table content. Detailed information on the b-tree layout can be found at `https://github.com/NotionalLabs/SQLiteZer/blob/master/_resources/Sqlite_carving_extractAndroidData.pdf`.

Commercial forensic tools provide support to recover deleted data from SQLite database files, but they don't always recover all of the data, nor do they support extracting data from all databases on an iOS device. It is recommended that each database containing key artifacts be examined for deleted data. The key artifacts, or databases, already discussed in this book, should be examined using free parses, hex viewers, or even your forensic tool to determine whether the user deleted artifacts that are relevant to the investigation.

To carve a SQLite database, you can examine the data in raw hex or use `sqliteparse.py`, a free Python script developed by Mari DeGrazia. The Python script can be downloaded from `https://github.com/mdegrazia/SQlite-Deleted-Records-Parser`.

The following example recovers the deleted records from the `notes.sqlitedb` file and dumps the output to the `output.txt` file. This script should work on all database files recovered from iOS devices. To validate your findings from running the script, simply examine the database in a hex viewer to ensure nothing is overlooked:

```
$python sqliteparse.py -f notes.sqlitedb -r -o output.txt
```

In addition to this, performing a strings dump of the database file can also reveal deleted records that may have been missed, as shown in the following command:

```
$strings notes.sqlitedb
```

Should you prefer a GUI, Mari DeGrazia kindly created one and placed it on her website at `http://az4n6.blogspot.in/`.

Another open source tool you can use for SQLite deleted records recovery is **Undark**. You can download it here: `http://pldaniels.com/undark/`. Here is how to use this tool:

```
./undark -i sms.db > sms_database.csv
```

It's important to note that Undark does not differentiate between current and deleted data, so you will get the whole set of data, both actual and deleted.

Summary

This chapter covered various data analysis techniques and specified the locations for common artifacts within the iOS device's filesystem. When writing this chapter, we aimed to cover the most popular artifacts that tie into most investigations. Clearly, it is impossible to cover them all. We hope that once you learn how to extract data from SQLite and plist files, intuition and persistence will assist you in parsing the artifacts that were not covered.

Keep in mind that most open source and commercial tools are able to pull active and deleted data from common database files, such as contacts, calls, SMS, and more, but they often overlook the third-party application database files. Our best advice is to know how to recover the data manually, just in case you need to validate your findings or testify to how your tool functions.

We covered techniques to recover deleted SQLite records that prove useful in most iOS device investigations. Again, the acquisition method, encoding, and encryption schemas can affect the amount of data that you can recover during your examination.

In the next chapter, *iOS Forensic Tools*, we will introduce you to the big four of the iOS forensics world—Cellebrite UFED Physical Analyzer, Magnet AXIOM, Oxygen Forensic Detective, and Belkasoft Evidence Center.

6
iOS Forensic Tools

An examiner must not only know how to use forensic tools, but must also understand the methods and acquisition techniques deployed by the tools they use in their investigations. Forensic tools not only save time, but also make the process a lot easier. However, each tool has its flaws, and the examiner must catch any mistakes and know how to correct them by leveraging another tool or technique. It's impossible for a tool to support all devices, and the examiner is responsible for learning and using the best tools to complete the job. As discussed in the previous chapters, the examiner must understand how data is stored on iOS devices, to ensure that the tool is capturing all accessible data. Without an expectation of what their forensic tool should extract, the examiner is limited and will be forced to rely solely on a tool.

Currently, there are a number of commercial tools, such as Elcomsoft iOS Forensic Toolkit, Cellebrite (UFED4PC, Touch, and Physical Analyzer), BlackLight, Oxygen Forensic Detective, AccessData MPE+, EnCase, Belkasoft Evidence Center, MSAB XRY, and many more, which are available for forensic acquisition and the analysis of iOS devices. For familiarity purposes, this chapter will walk you through the usage of a few of them and provide details of the steps required to perform acquisitions and analysis of iOS devices.

In this chapter, we will cover the following topics:

- Working with Cellebrite UFED Physical Analyzer
- Working with Magnet AXIOM
- Working with Oxygen Forensic Detective
- Working with Belkasoft Evidence Center

Working with Cellebrite UFED Physical Analyzer

As per the vendor, Cellebrite **Universal Forensic Extraction Device (UFED)** empowers law enforcement, antiterrorism, and security organizations to capture critical forensic evidence from mobile phones, smartphones, PDAs, and portable handset varieties, including updates for newly released models. The tool enables forensically sound data extraction, decoding, and analysis techniques to obtain existing and deleted data from different mobile devices. As of December 2017, UFED supports data extraction from more than 18,000 mobile devices.

Cellebrite UFED Physical Analyzer can be used to perform physical and advanced logical acquisitions of iOS devices. Advanced logical acquisitions are the same as filesystem acquisitions in which access to the filesystem data is provided. Physical acquisition on iOS devices using the A5-A11 chips (iPhone 4s and newer) is not possible using this tool. Thus, the advanced logical acquisition method is the best support and will pull the most data from these devices if they are unlocked (even if they are not jailbroken). If the device is jailbroken, additional data can be extracted. Cellebrite Physical Analyzer is available only for Windows platforms.

 For more information, visit `https://www.cellebrite.com/en/products/ufed-ultimate/`.

Features of Cellebrite UFED Physical Analyzer

The following are features of Cellebrite UFED Physical Analyzer:

- It supports physical and advanced logical acquisition (filesystem acquisition)
- It extracts device keys required to decrypt raw disk images as well as keychain items
- It decrypts raw disk images and keychain items
- It reveals device passwords (not available for all locked devices)
- It allows the examiner to open an encrypted raw disk image file with a known password

- It supports passcode recovery attacks
- It supports advanced analysis and decoding of extracted application data
- The platform provides access to physical and logical data extracted in the same user interface, making analysis easier
- It reports generation in several popular formats: Microsoft Excel, PDF, HTML, and more
- It has the ability to dump the raw filesystem partition to import and examine it in another forensic tool
- It creates a binary image file, in addition to the UFED shortcut file, for ease of importing into other forensic tools for verification

Advanced logical acquisition and analysis with Cellebrite UFED Physical Analyzer

As already mentioned, Physical Analyzer can be used not only for parsing different types of forensic artifacts from acquired images, but can also be used, for iOS devices, for performing both logical and physical types of extraction. Due to the fact that physical acquisition is actually only for older devices, the best option is an advanced logical acquisition.

We are going to acquire and analyze data from an iPhone running iOS 11.2.1:

1. Connect the device through the appropriate cable to your workstation, make sure it's trusted with it, and launch Physical Analyzer.

2. Go to **Extract | iOS Device Extraction**, and the **iOS Device Data Extraction Wizard** window will pop up:

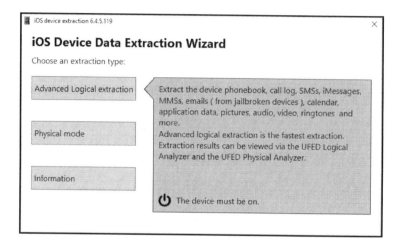

Choosing an extraction type

3. As we are dealing with a modern iOS device, let's choose **Advanced Logical extraction**. If the device is recognized, you'll see the device's name, its UDID, and also its iOS version:

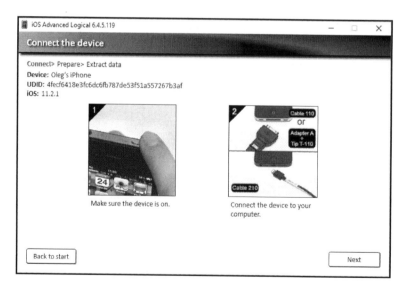

Connecting the device

4. In our case, the iPhone's iTunes backup is protected with a known password, so the best method is **Method 1**:

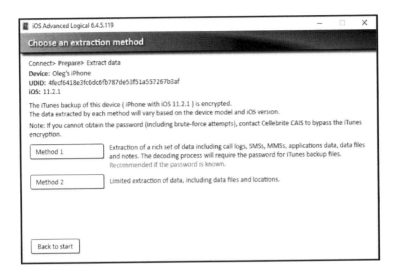

Choosing the extraction method

5. It's time to choose where the data will be saved; in our case, it's the root of the D:\ drive:

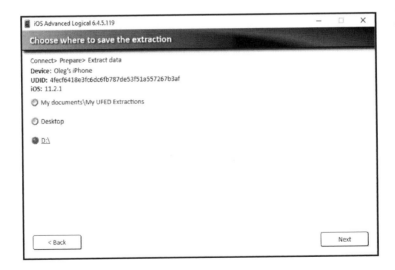

Choosing where to save the extraction

6. Now the acquisition process will be started. Make sure the device is connected until the end of the process:

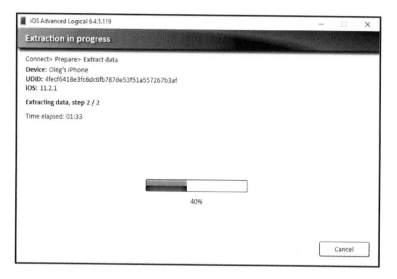

Extracting the data

Once the extraction process is finished, the extracted data will be parsed with powerful Physical Analyzer plugins. As a result, you will get a set of artifacts divided into a number of categories:

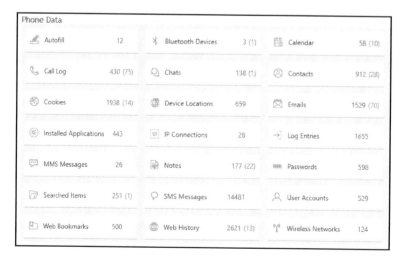

Phone data extracted and parsed by Physical Analyzer

The same can be said about the data files:

Data files extracted by Physical Analyzer

As you may have already noticed, there are red numbers in brackets—these are deleted records recovered by Physical Analyzer plugins. And it's not a miracle, as you already know, that deleted data can be recovered from SQLite databases, which are widely used in iOS.

Talking about SQLite databases again, there is another amazing feature of Physical Analyzer, which might be useful for adding custom artifacts to your mobile forensics reports and parsing unknown apps data—the SQLite wizard. You can find it under **Tools | SQLite wizard**.

Let's start by choosing a database. Of course, it's good to choose an app that isn't parsed by Physical Analyzer automatically; in our example, it's an app called **Scan**:

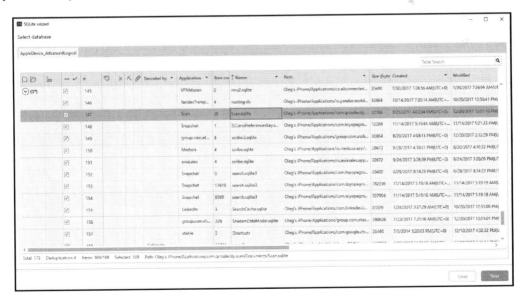

Selecting a database

Make sure you have selected the **Include deleted rows** option; this will help to recover data automatically but, of course, it will increase the number of false positive records:

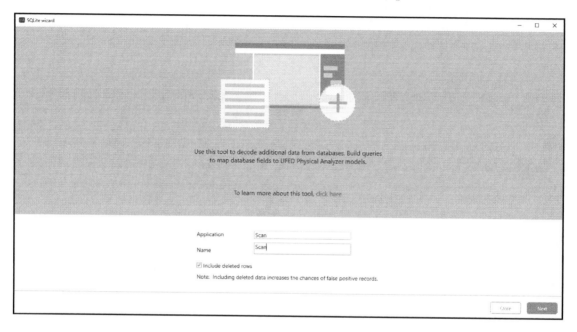

Starting the SQLite wizard

So, our app is used for scanning QR codes and contains four columns of interest—the scan date and time, latitude, longitude, and scan result. All of the rows are part of ZSCSCANEVENT:

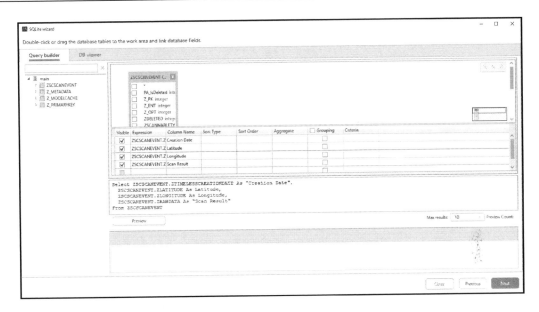

Choosing database tables and columns

You've already learned quite a bit about iOS timestamps and should recognize the format in ZTIMELESSCREATIONDATE, but even if you don't, SQLite wizard does it for you:

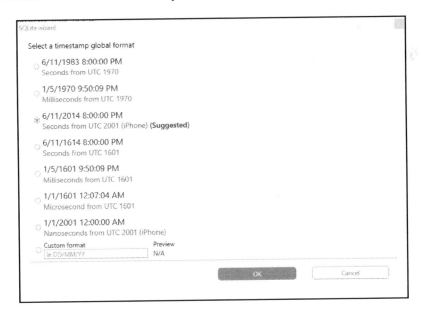

Selecting the timestamp format

The generic model will suit any database, but also there are some existing Physical Analyzer models that can be used for typical content, for example, *Chats* or *Contacts*. In our case, we are using the generic model:

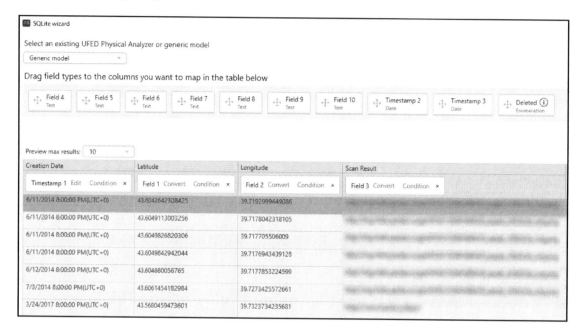

Choosing the model

Once you've chosen the model and field types for the column, you can run the query and add the new parsed artifacts to your extraction and, afterward, to your report.

Working with Magnet AXIOM

Magnet AXIOM is one of the most useful digital forensics tools on the market. It can be used both for computer and mobile forensics; the recent version of the suite introduced the newest feature—cloud forensics. As for iOS forensics, it can be used both for logical and filesystem acquisitions, and supports all iOS versions—from the oldest to the latest. Of course, it can be used for parsing iTunes backups and physical images created by third-party tools, for example, Elcomsoft iOS Forensic Toolkit.

One of the best features of Magnet AXIOM is its ability to start processing extraction data on the fly, so you don't have to wait for the acquisition process to be finished to start your forensic analysis.

Features of Magnet AXIOM

The following are features of Magnet AXIOM:

- It supports logical and filesystem (for jailbroken devices) acquisitions
- It supports both encrypted and unencrypted iTunes backups
- It recovers more than 500 artifact types
- It's designed to work with other popular mobile forensics tools, for example, Cellebrite UFED, XRY, and others
- It includes built-in SQLite and plist viewers
- It is able to create so-called **Portable Cases**, so an examiner can share the whole set of data to his or her teammates and third parties
- It allows an examiner to generate reports in several popular formats: Microsoft Excel, PDF, HTML, and more

Logical acquisition and analysis with Magnet AXIOM

As you remember, the most common acquisition for modern iOS devices is a logical type. Here is how to acquire an iOS device with Magnet AXIOM:

1. Start by creating a new case:

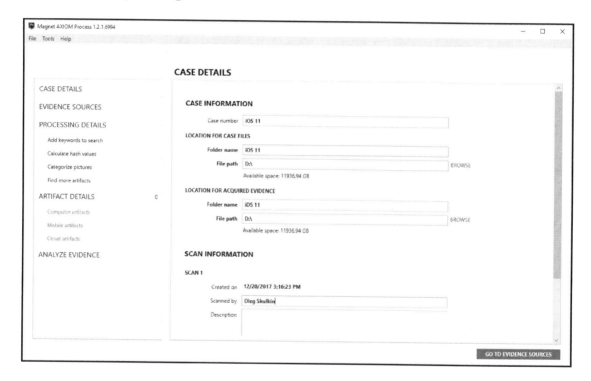

Creating a new case

2. As we are dealing with an iOS device, we will choose the **MOBILE** option:

Selecting the evidence source

3. There are a number of options, but in our case, the **IOS** option is the right one:

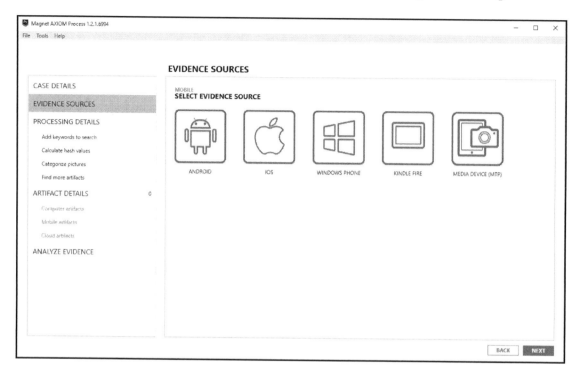

Selecting the evidence source

4. There are two options—we can choose an already-acquired image (for example, iTunes backup or a physical image acquired by a third-party tool), or extract data from the device. Let's choose the second option:

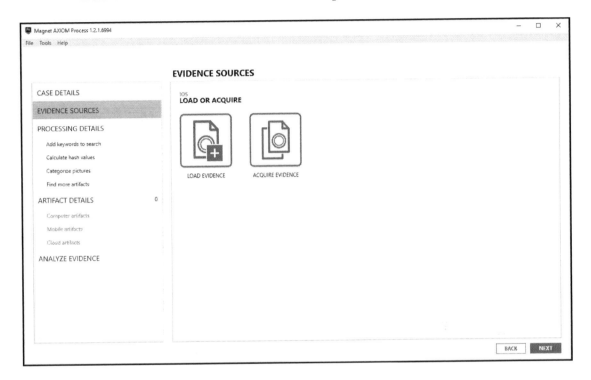

Choosing to acquire evidence

5. Our device is recognized and ready to be imaged. If you don't see your device, use the **UNKNOWN** option:

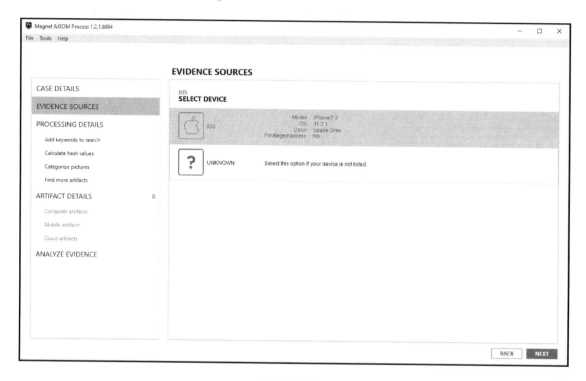

Selecting the device

6. There are two types of extraction—**Quick** and **Full**. The **Full** option is available only if the device you want to acquire is jailbroken; in our case, it's not:

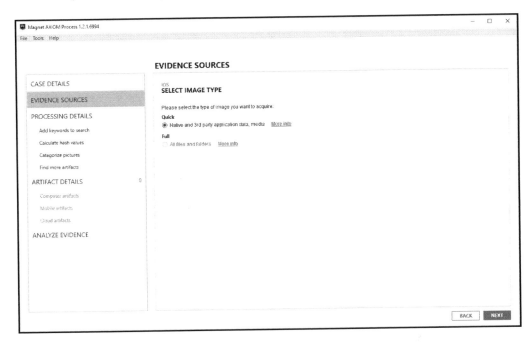

Choosing the image type

7. You will be prompted to enter the password for the backup; as you will remember, this way you can get more data, so it's highly recommended:

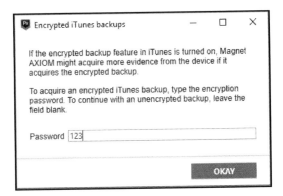

Encrypting the backup

8. Before the acquisition and processing are started, you can choose keywords of interest, import hashes for known-good files, and configure **Dynamic App Finder**:

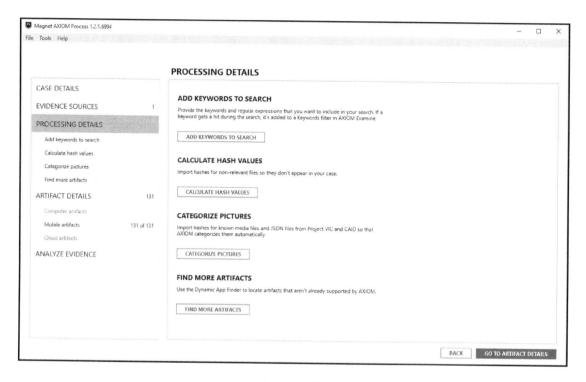

Processing details

Dynamic App Finder is a Magnet IEF and AXIOM feature capable of finding potential mobile chat app databases located on images. You can read more about this feature here: `https://www.magnetforensics.com/mobile-forensics/using-dynamic-app-finder-to-recover-more-mobile-artifacts/`.

9. You can customize **MOBILE ARTIFACTS**; for example, if you are interested only in chats, it's better to choose only these types of artifacts, as they will shorten the processing time:

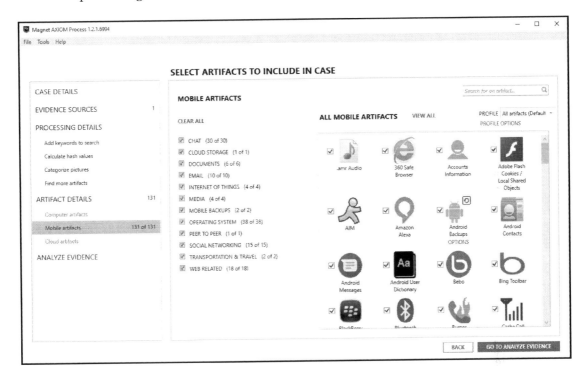

Selecting mobile artifacts

10. The **ANALYZE EVIDENCE** button will start the acquisition and analysis process:

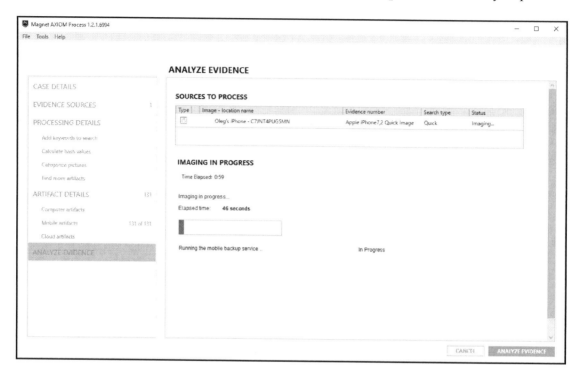

Imaging the evidence source

10. There are two windows of Magnet AXIOM—**Process** and **Examine**. The first can be used to monitor the process of acquiring and processing the evidence source, the second to analyze the extracted and parsed data. And as already mentioned, you can start the analysis before the processing phase is ended; all you need to do is click on **LOAD NEW RESULTS** in **Magnet Examine**:

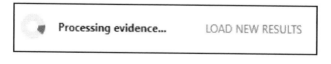

Loading new results

11. Once the processing stage is over, you can find the parsed data in the **MOBILE** section of **Magnet Examine**:

^ MOBILE	783
Calendar Events	50
iOS Call Logs	221
iOS Contacts	317
iOS Notes	70
iOS Wi-Fi Profiles	124
Owner Information	1

The MOBILE section

But, of course, it won't include everything; there are other valuable sections in which you can find evidence extracted from the iOS device, for example, **CHAT**, **MEDIA**, and **DOCUMENTS**.

Working with Belkasoft Evidence Center

Belkasoft Evidence Center is one more popular digital forensics tool capable of acquisition and analysis of iOS devices. Like AXIOM, it can be used for computer, mobile, and cloud forensics.

One of the best features of Belkasoft Evidence Center is its ability to deal with damaged iTunes backups. So if you have a backup none of your tools are able to process, try Belkasoft Evidence Center; according to our experience, it will process it successfully.

Features of Belkasoft Evidence Center

The following are features of Belkasoft Evidence Center:

- It supports logical and filesystem (for jailbroken devices) acquisitions
- It supports both encrypted and unencrypted iTunes backups
- It supports damaged iTunes backups

- It recovers more than 700 artifact types
- It's designed to work with other popular mobile forensics tools, for example, Cellebrite UFED, and XRY
- It includes built-in SQLite and plist viewers .
- It includes a free scripting module, BelkaScript, allowing examiners to write their own scripts to automate some common tasks
- It allows an examiner to generate reports in several popular formats: Microsoft Excel, PDF, HTML, and more

iTunes backup parsing and analysis with Belkasoft Evidence Center

As backup processing and analysis is one of the best features of Belkasoft Evidence Center, here we are going to walk you through this process:

1. Let's start by creating a new case:

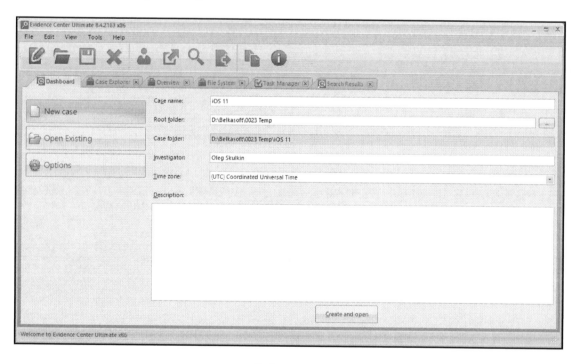

Creating a new case

2. There are multiple options here—you can process a previously acquired image, for example, iTunes backup, or choose to extract data from a device first. As we have decided to work with an iTunes backup, let's choose the **Mobile image** option:

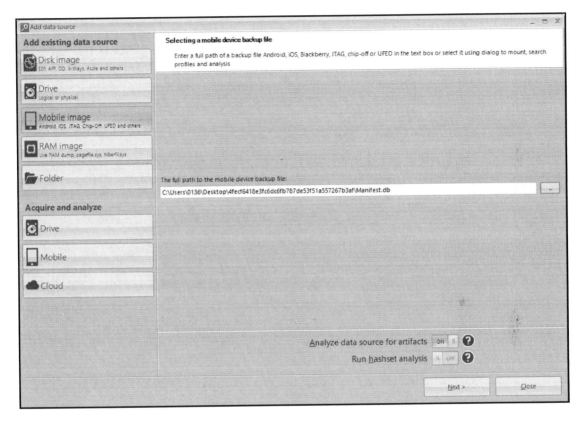

Choosing the data source

3. Make sure you choose only iOS-related artifacts; this will decrease the processing time:

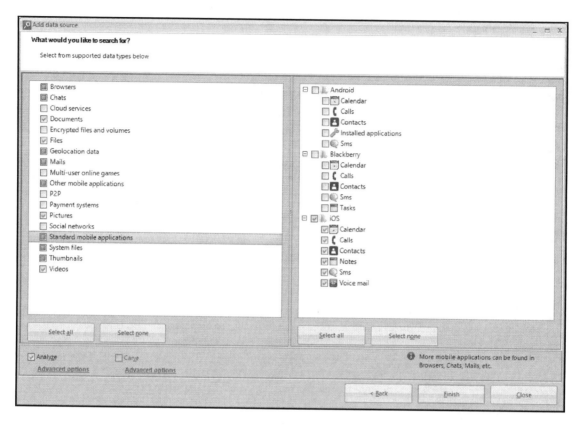

Choosing data types

4. Once processing is finished, extracted artifacts will be shown in the **Case Explorer** tab:

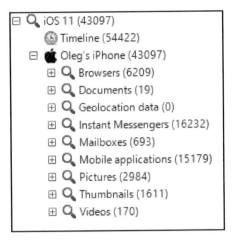

Case Explorer tab

5. The overview of extracted data is shown in the **Overview** tab:

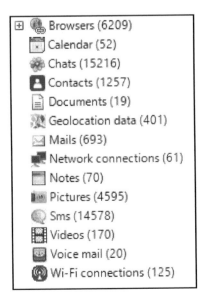

Overview tab

6. Finally, if you want to browse the filesystem of your forensic image, use the **Filesystem** tab:

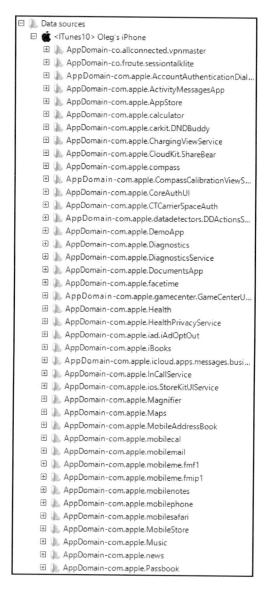

Filesystem tab

Other available tabs may be useful too—the **Dashboard** tab shows you all available info about the case you are currently working on, the **Process Monitor** tab allows you to monitor processing progress, and the **Search Results** tab shows you keyword search results.

Working with Oxygen Forensic Detective

Oxygen Forensic Detective is a piece of advanced forensic software capable of extracting and analyzing data from cell phones, smartphones, PDAs, and other mobile devices. The software provides not only acquisition support, but also advanced application parsing and analysis support. Currently, Oxygen Forensic Detective version 10 supports more than 17,000 different models of mobile devices.

Oxygen Forensic Detective uses proprietary low-level protocols to extract data from smartphones. Besides data extraction, Oxygen Forensic Detective also gives you the opportunity to import a backup or image file obtained using other forensic tools, such as Cellebrite, Elcomsoft, XRY, iTunes, and open source tools for data analysis. It also stores the database of all the analyzed devices so that you can always view the previously extracted data.

Features of Oxygen Forensic Detective

The following are the features of Oxygen Forensic Detective:

- It supports logical filesystem and physical acquisition. Logical acquisition recovers the active files on the device. Deleted data may be obtained if the SQLite database is recovered. Physical and filesystem acquisition provides access to the raw filesystem data of the iOS device.
- It supports password recovery from a keychain.
- It enables cloud data extraction and decryption.
- It reads backup or images obtained using other forensic tools.
- It provides rooting and jailbreaking assistance for devices.
- The timeline provides a single-place access to all the user's activities and movements, arranged by date and time.
- It supports aggregated contacts. This automatically combines accounts from different sources into one metacontact for each person.

Make sure that you know where the data is coming from! You should manually examine each file to ensure that nothing is overlooked and that the data is being reported correctly.

- It recovers deleted data automatically and provides the examiner with a tool to carve additional artifacts from SQLite databases.
- It provides access to raw files for manual analysis.

Note that these are the raw database files associated with each application, they are not always the raw filesystem partitions.

- It provides an intuitive and user-friendly UI to browse through the extracted data.
- It provides keyword lists and a regular expression library in order to search.
- It supports report generation in several popular formats—Microsoft Excel, PDF, HTML, and more.

Logical acquisition and analysis with Oxygen Forensic Detective

The acquisition of an iOS device is simple and straightforward with Oxygen Forensic Detective. The software helps you to connect a device in several mouse clicks, and downloads all the available device information in just a few minutes for a logical acquisition.

To perform the acquisition of an iOS device using Oxygen Forensic Extractor (the wizard that is used in Oxygen Forensic Detective), follow these steps:

1. Launch Oxygen Forensic Detective and click on the **Connect new device** button. You will be prompted to choose the connection mode, as shown in the following screenshot:

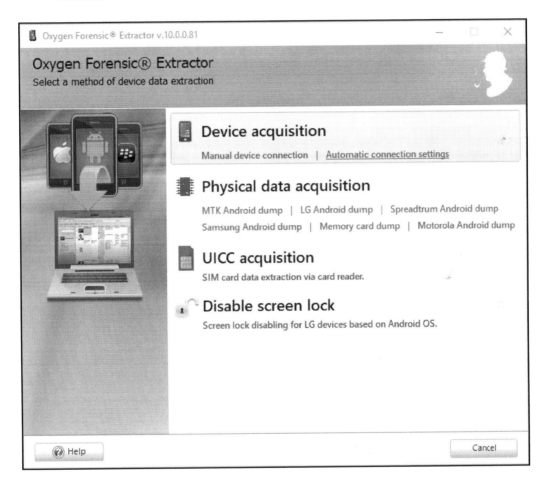

Oxygen Forensic Extractor

2. Connect the iOS device to the computer using a USB cable and choose **Automatic connection settings**. Oxygen Forensic Extractor detects the connected device and displays the device information, as shown in the following screenshot. You can also manually choose your device:

Connecting the device

3. Click on **Next**. It prompts you to fill in the information about the device and the case. Here you can also make your backup encrypted, and decide whether application data should be parsed (including deleted data) or you just want an forensic image:

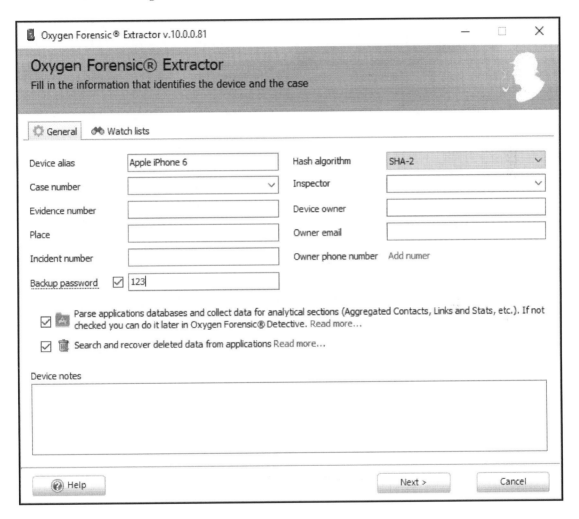

Filling in the device info

4. Now we are ready to start the extraction process. As you can see in the following screenshot, Oxygen Forensic Detective is using the iTunes backup service to create a logical image:

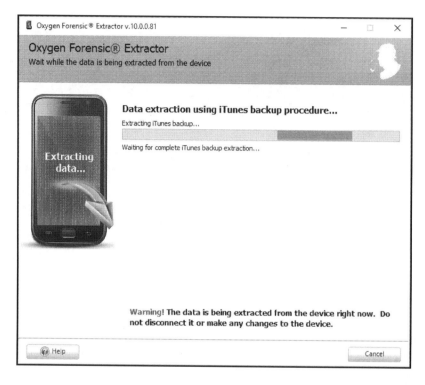

Data extraction process

Once the extraction process is finished and application data is processed and parsed, you will see a forensic artifacts overview:

Extracted data overview

Now the data is ready to be analyzed. You can use only automatically extracted artifacts to find evidence, or go for in-depth manual analysis with the help of filesystem browser, hex, SQLite, and plist viewers.

Summary

Forensic tools are helpful for an examiner as they not only save time, but also make the process a lot easier. However, not everyone has a budget large enough to purchase commercial tools to obtain iOS acquisition. While free tools exist for acquisition, support may be limited and multiple extractions may be required to obtain the same amount of data as a commercial tool.

For jailbroken devices, the iOS device could be connected to a Mac for live examination through SSH, which is how some of the tools acquire the data. However, this is not a method that is recommended for those new to digital forensics. For such purposes, this chapter introduced you to several available iOS forensic tools and included the steps to perform acquisition from an iOS device.

Examiners should take further steps to validate and understand each tool that might be used as part of an investigation. We recommend acquiring test devices with known data to ensure that nothing is overlooked, evidence is not altered, and the methods provide the examiner with access to the data of interest, where possible.

The next chapter introduces Android forensics and covers the fundamental concepts of the Android platform.

7
Understanding Android

In the previous chapters, we covered details about iOS devices, including the file system structure, key artifacts, backup files, and acquisition and analysis methods. Starting with this chapter, we will focus on the Android platform and how to perform forensics on Android devices. Having a good understanding of the Android ecosystem, security constraints, file systems, and other features proves useful during forensic investigation. Gaining knowledge of these fundamentals would help a forensic expert to make informed decisions while conducting an investigation.

We will cover the following topics in this chapter:

- The Android model
- Android security
- The Android file hierarchy
- The Android file system

The evolution of Android

Before we take a dive into the ocean of Android, let's first spend some time discussing the evolution of Android, or what we call *The Android Story*. Back in 2005, Google started investing money in start-up companies that it thought would be profitable in the future. Android Inc., founded in 2003 by Andy Rubin, Rich Miner, Nick Sears, and Chris White, was one such company acquired by Google that later turned out to be the best deal ever. During its first two years, Android Inc. operated under secrecy. It described itself as a company making software for mobile phones. Rubin later stayed with Google to pioneer Android as an operating system that revolutionized the way mobile handsets operate. With this acquisition, it was clear that Google was eyeing the mobile phone market. At Google, Rubin, along with his team, developed a powerful and flexible operating system built on a Linux kernel. There was speculation everywhere about what Google was trying to do. Some reported that Google was trying to incorporate search and other applications into mobile handsets. A few others reported that Google was developing its own mobile handset. Finally, in 2007, **Open Handset Alliance (OHA)**, a group of technology companies, device manufacturers, chipset makers, and wireless carriers, was formed with the main objective of proposing open standards for the mobile platform. Together, they developed **Android**—the first open and free mobile platform built on Linux kernel 2.6. Later, in 2008, HTC Dream was released, which was the first phone to run the Android operating system. After that, it was a dream run for Android, with its market share increasing exponentially over the next few years. At the time of writing this book, Android remains by far the most used OS throughout the world. According to IDC, in the first quarter of 2017, Android dominated the industry with an 85% market share. Since its release in 2007, Android has come up with various versions. The most recent major Android update is Android 8.0, dubbed **Oreo**, which was released in August 2017. Several versions of its Linux-based OS have been released in alphabetical order.

The following is an overview of Android version history:

Version	Version name	Release year
Android 1.0	Apple pie	2008
Android 1.1	Banana bread	2009
Android 1.5	Cupcake	2009
Android 1.6	Donut	2009
Android 2.0	Eclair	2009
Android 2.2	Froyo	2010

Android 2.3	Gingerbread	2010
Android 3.0	Honeycomb	2011
Android 4.0	Ice Cream Sandwich	2011
Android 4.1	Jelly Bean	2012
Android 4.4	KitKat	2013
Android 5.0	Lollipop	2014
Android 6.0	Marshmallow	2015
Android 7.0	Nougat	2016
Android 8.0	Oreo	2017

The Android model

To effectively understand the forensic concepts of Android, it would be helpful to have a basic understanding of the Android architecture. Just like a computer, any computing system that interacts with the user and performs complicated tasks requires an operating system to handle the tasks effectively. This operating system (whether it's a desktop operating system or a mobile phone operating system) takes the responsibility of managing the resources of the system and to provide a way for the applications to talk to the hardware or physical components to accomplish certain tasks. Android is currently the most popular mobile operating system designed to power mobile devices. You can find out more about this at: `https://developer.android.com/about/android.html`.

Android is open source and the code is released under the Apache license. Practically, this means anyone (especially device manufacturers) can access it, freely modify it, and use the software according to the requirements of any device. This is one of the primary reasons for its wide acceptance. Notable players that use Android include Samsung, HTC, Sony, and LG.

As with any other platform, Android consists of a stack of layers running one above the other. To understand the Android ecosystem, it's essential to have a basic understanding of what these layers are and what they do. The following figure summarizes the various layers involved in the Android software stack:

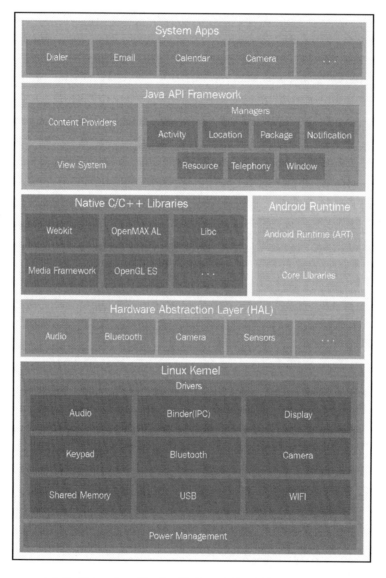

Android architecture referenced from: https://developer.android.com/guide/platform/index.html

[188]

Each of these layers performs several operations that support specific operating system functions. Each layer provides services to the layers lying on top of it.

The Linux kernel layer

Android OS is built on top of the Linux kernel, with some architectural changes made by Google. There are several reasons for choosing the Linux kernel. Most importantly, Linux is a portable platform that can be compiled easily on different hardware. The kernel acts as an abstraction layer between the software and hardware present on the device. Consider the case of a camera click. What happens when you take a photo using the camera button on your device? At some point, the hardware instruction (pressing a button) has to be converted to a software instruction (to take a picture and store it in the gallery). The kernel contains drivers to facilitate this process. When the user presses on the button, the instruction goes to the corresponding camera driver in the kernel, which sends the necessary commands to the camera hardware, similar to what occurs when a key is pressed on a keyboard. In simple words, the drivers in the kernel command control the underlying hardware. As shown in the preceding figure, the kernel contains drivers related to Wi-Fi, Bluetooth, USB, audio, display, and so on.

The Linux kernel is responsible for managing the core functionality of Android, such as process management, memory management, security, and networking. Linux is a proven platform when it comes to security and process management. Android has taken leverage of the existing Linux open source OS to build a solid foundation for its ecosystem. Each version of Android has a different version of the underlying Linux kernel. The Marshmallow Android version is known to use Linux kernel 3.18.10, whereas the Nougat version is known to use Linux kernel 4.4.1.

The Hardware Abstraction Layer

The device hardware capabilities are exposed to the high-level Java framework through the **Hardware Abstraction Layer (HAL)**. The HAL consists of several library modules that implement interfaces for a specific type of hardware component. This allows hardware vendors to implement functionality without changing the higher-level system.

Libraries

The next layer in the Android architecture consists of Android's native libraries. The libraries are written in the C or C++ language and help the device to handle different kinds of data. For example, the SQLite libraries are useful for storing and retrieving the data from a database. Other libraries include Media Framework, WebKit, Surface Manager, and SSL. The Media Framework library acts as the main interface to provide a service to the other underlying libraries. The WebKit library provides web pages in web browsers, and the surface manager maintains the graphics. In the same layer, we have Android Runtime and core libraries. The Android runtime is responsible for running applications on Android devices. The term **runtime** refers to the lapse in time from when an application is launched until it is shut down.

Dalvik virtual machine

All the applications that you install on the Android device are written in the Java programming language. When a Java program is compiled, we get bytecode. A virtual machine is an application that acts as an operating system, that is, it is possible to run a Windows OS on a Mac or vice versa using a virtual machine. JVM is one such virtual machine that can execute the previously mentioned bytecode. But, Android versions before use something called **Dalvik virtual machine (DVM)** to run their applications.

DVM runs Dalvik bytecode, which is Java bytecode converted by the Dex compiler. Thus, the .class files are converted to dex files using the dx tool. Dalvik bytecode, when compared with Java bytecode, is more suitable for low-memory and low-processing environments. Also, note that JVM's bytecode consists of one or more .class file depending on the number of Java files that are present in an application, but Dalvik bytecode is composed of only one dex file. Each Android application runs its own instance of DVM. This is a crucial aspect of Android security and will be addressed in detail in Chapter 8, *Android Forensic Setup and Pre-Data Extraction Techniques*.

The following figure provides an insight into how Android's DVM differs from Java's JVM:

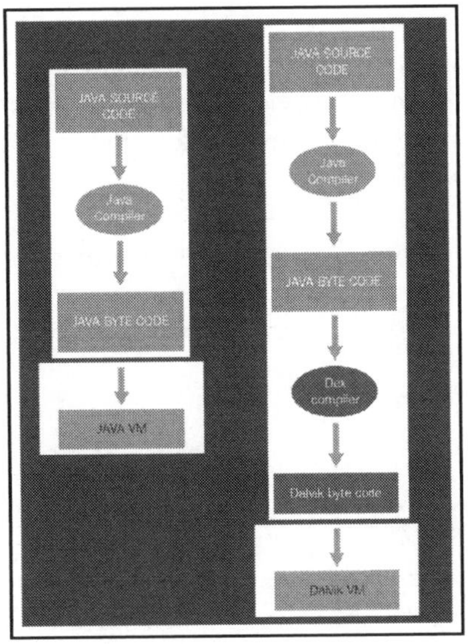

JVM versus DVM

Android Runtime (ART)

From Android 5.0 Lollipop version onward, Dalvik was replaced by **Android Runtime** (**ART**). As discussed previously, earlier versions of Android used trace-based **just-in-time** (**JIT**) compilation with Dalvik. In trace-based JIT, frequently executed operations are identified and dynamically compiled to native machine code. This native execution of these frequently used bytecodes, called traces, provides significant performance improvements. Unlike Dalvik, ART uses **ahead-of-time** (**AOT**) compilation, which compiles entire applications into native machine code upon their installation. This would automatically increase the install time for an application, but a major advantage is that this eliminates Dalvik's interpretation and trace-based JIT compilation, and thereby increases efficiency and reduces power consumption. ART uses a utility called **dex2oat** that accepts DEX files as input and generates a compiled app executable for the target device. With ART, the **optimised dex** (**.odex**) files are replaced with the **Executable and Linkable Format** (**ELF**) executables.

The Java API framework layer

The application framework is the layer responsible for handling the basic functioning of a phone, such as resource management, handling calls, and so on. This is the block with which the applications installed on the device directly talk to it. The following are some of the important blocks in the application framework layer:

- **Telephony manager**: This block manages all the voice calls
- **Content provider**: This block manages the sharing of data between different applications
- **Resource manager**: This block helps manage various resources used in applications

The system apps layer

This is the topmost layer where the user can interact directly with the device. There are two kinds of application—preinstalled applications and user-installed applications. Preinstalled applications, such as dialer, web browser, contacts, and more, come along with the device. User-installed applications can be downloaded from different places, such as Google Play Store, Amazon Marketplace, and so on. Everything that you see on your phone (contacts, mail, camera, and so on) is an application.

Android security

Android was designed with a specific focus on security. Android as a platform offers and enforces certain features that safeguard the user data present on the mobile through multi-layered security. There are certain safe defaults that will protect the user, and certain offerings that can be leveraged by the development community to build secure applications. The following are issues that are to be kept in mind while incorporating Android security controls:

- Protecting user-related data
- Safeguarding the system resources
- Making sure that one application cannot access the data of another application

The next few sections will help us understand more about Android's security features and offerings.

A detailed explanation on Android security can be found at: `https://source.android.com/security/`.

Secure kernel

Linux has evolved as a trusted platform over the years, and Android has leveraged this fact using it as its kernel. The user-based permission model of Linux has in fact worked well for Android. As mentioned earlier, there is a lot of specific code built into the Linux kernel. With each Android version release, the kernel version has also changed. The following table shows Android versions and their corresponding kernel versions:

Android version	Linux kernel version
1	2.6.25
1.5	2.6.27
1.6	2.6.29
2.2	2.6.32
2.3	2.6.35
3.0	2.6.36
4.0	3.0.1
4.1	3.0.31
4.2	3.4.0
4.2	3.4.39
4.4	3.8
5.0	3.16.1
6.0	3.18.1
7.0	4.4.1

The permission model

As shown in the following screenshot, any Android application must be granted permissions to access sensitive functionality, such as the internet, dialer, and so on, by the user. This provides an opportunity for the user to know in advance which functionality on the device is being accessed by the application. Simply put, it requires the user's permission to perform any kind of malicious activity (stealing data, compromising the system, and so on).

This model helps the user to prevent attacks, but if the user is unaware and gives away a lot of permissions, it leaves them in trouble (remember, when it comes to installing malware on any device, the weakest link is always the user).

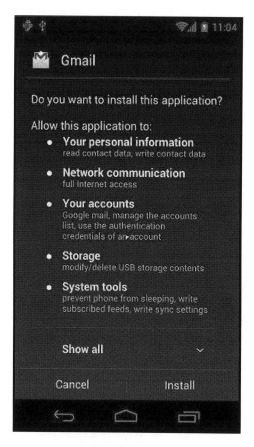

The permission model in Android

Until Android 6.0, users needed to grant the permissions during install time. Users had to either accept all the permissions or not install the application. But, starting from Android 6.0, users grant permissions to apps while the app is running. This new permission system also gives the user more control over the app's functionality by allowing the user to grant selective permissions. For example, a user can deny a particular app access to his location, but provide access to the internet. The user can revoke the permissions at any time by going to the app's **Settings** screen.

Application sandbox

In Linux systems, each user is assigned a **unique user ID (UID)**, and users are segregated so that one user cannot access the data of another user. However, all applications under a particular user are run with the same privileges. Similarly, in Android, each application runs as a unique user. In other words, a UID is assigned to each application and is run as a separate process. This concept ensures an application sandbox at the kernel level. The kernel manages the security restrictions between the applications by making use of existing Linux concepts, such as UID and GID. If an application attempts to do something malicious, say to read the data of another application, this is not permitted as the application does not have user privileges. Hence, the operating system protects an application from accessing the data of another application.

Secure inter-process communication

Android offers secure inter-process communication through which one's activity in an application can send messages to another activity in the same application or a different application. To achieve this, Android provides **inter-process communication (IPC)** mechanisms: intents, services, content providers, and so on.

Application signing

It is mandatory that all of the installed applications are digitally signed. Developers can place their applications in Google's Play Store only after signing the applications. The private key with which the application is signed is held by the developer. Using the same key, a developer can provide updates to their application, share data between the applications, and so on.

Security-Enhanced Linux

Security-Enhanced Linux (**SELinux**) is a security feature that was introduced in Android 4.3 and fully enforced in Android 5.0. Until this addition, Android security was based on **Discretionary Access Control** (**DAC**), which means applications can ask for permissions, and users can grant or deny those permissions. Thus, malware can create havoc on phones by gaining those permissions. But, SE Android uses **Mandatory Access Control** (**MAC**), which ensures that applications work in isolated environments. Hence, even if a user installs a malware app, the malware cannot access the OS and corrupt the device. SELinux is used to enforce MAC over all the processes, including the ones running with root privileges. SELinux operates on the principle of default denial: anything that is not explicitly allowed is denied. SELinux can operate in one of the two global modes: permissive mode, in which permission denials are logged but not enforced, and enforcing mode, in which denials are both logged and enforced. More details about SELinux can be found at: `https://source.android.com/security/selinux/concepts`.

Full Disk Encryption

With Android 6.0 Marshmallow, Google has mandated **Full Disk Encryption** (**FDE**) for most devices, provided that the hardware meets certain minimum standards. Encryption is the process of converting data into cipher text using a secret key. On Android devices, full disk encryption refers to the process of encrypting all user data using a secret key. This key is then encrypted by the lock screen PIN/pattern/password before being securely stored in a trusted location. Once a device is encrypted, all user-created data is automatically encrypted before writing it to disk, and all reads automatically decrypt data before returning it to the calling process. Full disk encryption in Android works only with an **Embedded Multimedia Card** (**eMMC**) and similar flash devices that present themselves to the kernel as block devices.

Staring from Android 7.x, Google decided to shift the encryption feature from **full-disk encryption** to **file-based encryption**. In file-based encryption, different files are encrypted with different keys. By doing so, those files can be unlocked independently without requiring an entire partition to be decrypted at once. As a result of this, the system can now decrypt and use files needed to boot the system, and open notifications without having to wait until the user unlocks the phone.

Trusted Execution Environment

Trusted Execution Environment (**TEE**) is an isolated area (typically a separate microprocessor) intended to guarantee security of data stored inside it, and also to execute code with integrity. The main processor on mobile devices is considered untrusted and cannot be used to store secret data (such as cryptographic keys). Hence, TEE is used specifically to perform such operations, and the software running on the main processor delegates any operations that require use of secret data to the TEE processor.

The Android file hierarchy

In order to perform forensic analysis on any system (desktop or mobile), it's important to understand the underlying file hierarchy. A basic understanding of how Android organizes its data in files and folders helps a forensic analyst narrow down their research to specific issues. Just like any other operating system, Android uses several partitions. This chapter provides an insight into some of the most significant partitions and the content stored in them.

It's worth mentioning again that Android uses the Linux kernel. Hence, if you are familiar with Unix-like systems, you will understand the file hierarchy in Android very well. For those who are not very well-acquainted with the Linux model, here is some basic information: in Linux, the file hierarchy is a single tree with the top of the tree being denoted as / (called the **root**). This is different from the concept of organizing files in drives (as with Windows). Whether the file system is local or remote, it will be present under the root. The Android file hierarchy is a customized version of this existing Linux hierarchy. Based on the device manufacturer and the underlying Linux version, the structure of this hierarchy may have a few insignificant changes. The following is a list of important folders that are common to most Android devices. Some of the folders listed are only visible through root access. Rooting is the process of gaining privileged access on an Android device. More details about rooting and executing the adb commands (which are shown in the following bullets) are covered in detail in Chapter 8, *Android Forensic Setup and Pre-Data Extraction Techniques*:

- /boot: As the name suggests, this partition has the information and files required for the phone to boot. It contains the kernel and RAM disk, so without this partition, the phone cannot start its processes. Data residing in RAM is rich in value and should be captured during a forensic acquisition.

- /system: This partition contains system-related files other than the kernel and RAM disk. This folder should never be deleted as that will make the device unbootable. The contents of this partition can be viewed using the following command:

```
root@android:/data # cd /system
root@android:/system # ls
CSCVersion.txt
SW_Configuration.xml
app
bin
build.prop
cameradata
csc
csc_contents
etc
fonts
framework
hdic
lib
media
sipdb
tts
usr
vendor
voicebargeindata
vsc
wakeupdata
wallpaper
xbin
```

- * /recovery: This is designed for backup purposes and allows the device to boot into recovery mode. In recovery mode, you can find tools to repair your phone installation.
- /data: This is the partition that contains the data of each application. Most of the data belonging to the user, such as the contacts, SMS, and dialed numbers, is stored in this folder. This folder has significant importance from a forensic point of view as it holds valuable data. The contents of the data folder can be viewed using the following command:

```
root@android:/ # cd /data
root@android:/data # ls
ISP_CV
TMAudioSocketClient
TMAudioSocketServer
anr
app
app-asec
app-private
backup
baro.dat
cfw
clipboard
dalvik-cache
data
dontpanic
drm
fota_test
gldata.sto
gps
hidden_volume.txt
lbsdata-000.sto
local
log
lost+found
media
misc
```

- * /cache: This is the folder used to store the frequently accessed data and some of the logs for faster retrieval. The /cache partition is also important to a forensic investigation as the data residing here may no longer be present in the /data partition.
- * /misc: As the name suggests, this folder contains information about miscellaneous settings. These settings mostly define the state of the device, that is, on/off. Information about hardware settings, USB settings, and so on, can be accessed from this folder.
- /sdcard: This is the partition that holds all the information present on the SD card. It is valuable as it can contain information such as pictures, videos, files, documents, and so on.

The Android file system

Understanding the file system is one essential part of forensic methodologies. Knowledge about properties and the structure of a file system proves to be useful during forensic analysis. The file system refers to the way data is stored, organized, and retrieved from a volume. A basic installation may be based on one volume split into several partitions; here, each partition can be managed by a different file system. As is true in Linux, Android utilizes mount points and not drives (that is, C: or E:). Each file system defines its own rules for managing the files in the volume. Depending on these rules, each file system offers a different speed for file retrieval, security, size, and so on. Linux uses several file systems, and so does Android. From a forensic point of view, it's important to understand which file systems are used by Android and to identify the file systems that are of significance to the investigation. For example, the file system that stores the user's data is of primary concern to us as opposed to a file system used to boot the device.

Viewing file systems on an Android device

The file systems supported by the Android kernel can be determined by checking the contents of the `filesystems` file in the `proc` folder. The content of this file can be viewed using the following command:

```
root@android:/ # cat /proc/filesystems
nodev   sysfs
nodev   rootfs
nodev   bdev
nodev   proc
nodev   cgroup
nodev   tmpfs
nodev   binfmt_misc
nodev   debugfs
nodev   sockfs
nodev   usbfs
nodev   pipefs
nodev   anon_inodefs
nodev   devpts
        ext2
        ext3
        ext4
nodev   ramfs
        vfat
        msdos
nodev   ecryptfs
nodev   fuse
        fuseblk
nodev   fusectl
        exfat
```

In the preceding output, the first column tells us whether the file system is mounted on the device. The ones with the `nodev` property are not mounted on the device. The second column lists all the file systems present on the device. A simple mount command displays different partitions available on the device, as follows:

```
root@android:/ # mount
rootfs / rootfs ro,relatime 0 0
tmpfs /dev tmpfs rw,nosuid,relatime,mode=755 0 0
devpts /dev/pts devpts rw,relatime,mode=600 0 0
proc /proc proc rw,relatime 0 0
sysfs /sys sysfs rw,relatime 0 0
none /acct cgroup rw,relatime,cpuacct 0 0
tmpfs /mnt/asec tmpfs rw,relatime,mode=755,gid=1000 0 0
tmpfs /mnt/obb tmpfs rw,relatime,mode=755,gid=1000 0 0
none /dev/cpuctl cgroup rw,relatime,cpu 0 0
/dev/block/mmcblk0p9 /system ext4 ro,noatime,barrier=1,data=ordered 0 0
/dev/block/mmcblk0p3 /efs ext4 rw,nosuid,nodev,noatime,barrier=1,journal_async_commit,data=ordered 0 0
/dev/block/mmcblk0p8 /cache ext4 rw,nosuid,nodev,noatime,errors=panic,barrier=1,journal_async_commit,data=ordered 0 0
/dev/block/mmcblk0p12 /data ext4 rw,nosuid,nodev,noatime,barrier=1,journal_async_commit,data=ordered,noauto_da_alloc,discard 0 0
/sys/kernel/debug /sys/kernel/debug debugfs rw,relatime 0 0
/dev/fuse /storage/sdcard0 fuse rw,nosuid,nodev,noexec,relatime,user_id=1023,group_id=1023,default_permissions,allow_other 0 0
```

The following is a brief overview of the important file systems:

- The root file system (`rootfs`) is one of the main components of Android and contains all the information required to boot the device. When the device starts the boot process, it needs access to many core files, and thus, it mounts the root file system. As shown in the preceding mount command-line output, this file system is mounted at / (`root` folder). Hence, this is the file system on which all the other file systems are slowly mounted. If this file system is corrupt, the device cannot be booted.
- The `sysfs` file system mounts the /`sys` folder, which contains information about the configuration of the device. The following output shows various folders under the `sys` directory in an Android device:

```
root@android:/ # cd /sys
root@android:/sys # ls
block
bus
class
dev
devices
firmware
fs
kernel
module
power
```

Since the data present in these folders is mostly related to configuration, this is not usually of much significance to a forensic investigator. But, there can be some circumstances where we might want to check whether a particular setting was enabled on the phone, and analyzing this folder could be useful under such conditions.

 Note that each folder consists of a large number of files. Capturing this data through forensic acquisition is the best method to ensure that this data is not changed during examination.

- The devpts file system presents an interface to the Terminal session on an Android device. It is mounted at /dev/pts. Whenever a Terminal connection is established, for instance, when an adb shell is connected to an Android device, a new node is created under /dev/pts. The following is the output showing this when the adb shell is connected to the device:

```
shell@Android:/ $ ls -l /dev/pts ls -l /dev/pts
crw------- shell shell 136, 0 2013-10-26 16:56 0
```

- The cgroup file system stands for control groups. Android devices use this file system to track their job. They are responsible for aggregating the tasks and keeping track of them. This data is generally not very useful during forensic analysis.
- The proc file system contains information about kernel data structures, processes, and other system-related information under the /proc directory. For instance, the /sys directory contains files related to kernel parameters. Similarly, /proc/filesystems displays the list of available file systems on the device. The following command shows all the information about the CPU of the device:

```
root@android:/ # cat /proc/cpuinfo
Processor       : ARMv7 Processor rev 0 (v7l)
processor       : 0
BogoMIPS        : 1592.52

processor       : 2
BogoMIPS        : 1990.65

processor       : 3
BogoMIPS        : 1990.65

Features        : swp half thumb fastmult vfp edsp neon vfpv3 tls
CPU implementer : 0x41
CPU architecture: 7
CPU variant     : 0x3
CPU part        : 0xc09
CPU revision    : 0

Chip revision   : 0011
Hardware        : SMDK4x12
Revision        : 000c
Serial          :
```

Similarly, there are many other useful files that provide valuable information when you traverse them.

- The `tmpfs` file system is a temporary storage facility on the device that stores the files in RAM (volatile memory). The main advantage of using RAM is faster access and retrieval. But, once the device is restarted or switched off, this data will not be accessible anymore. Hence, it's important for a forensic investigator to examine the data in RAM before a device reboot happens, or to extract the data via RAM acquisition methods.

Common file systems found on Android

The **Extended File System (EXT)**, which was introduced in 1992 specifically for the Linux kernel, was one of the first file systems, and it used a virtual file system. EXT2, EXT3, and EXT4 are the subsequent versions. Journaling is the main advantage of EXT3 over EXT2. With EXT3, in case of an unexpected shutdown, there is no need to verify the file system. The EXT4 file system, the fourth extended file system, has gained significance with mobile devices implementing dual-core processors. The YAFFS2 file system is known to have a bottleneck on dual-core systems. With the Gingerbread version of Android, the YAFFS file system was swapped for EXT4.

The following are the mount points that use EXT4 on the Samsung Galaxy mobile:

```
/dev/block/mmcblk0p9 /system ext4 ro,noatime,barrier=1,data=ordered 0     0
/dev/block/mmcblk0p3 /efs ext4
rw,nosuid,nodev,noatime,barrier=1,journal_async_commit,data=ordered 0 0
/dev/block/mmcblk0p8 /cache ext4
rw,nosuid,nodev,noatime,barrier=1,journal_async_commit,data=ordered 0 0
/dev/block/mmcblk0p12 /data ext4
rw,nosuid,nodev,noatime,barrier=1,journal_async_commit,data=ordered,n
oauto_da_alloc,discard 0 0
```

VFAT is an extension to the FAT16 and FAT32 file systems. Microsoft's FAT32 file system is supported by most Android devices. It is supported by almost all the major operating systems, including Windows, Linux, and macOS. This enables these systems to easily read, modify, and delete the files present on the FAT32 portion of the Android device. Most of the external SD cards are formatted using the FAT32 file system.

Observe the following output, which shows that the mount points /sdcard and /secure/asec use the VFAT file system:

```
root@android:/ # cd sdcard
root@android:/sdcard # mount
rootfs / rootfs ro,relatime 0 0
tmpfs /dev tmpfs rw,nosuid,relatime,mode=755 0 0
devpts /dev/pts devpts rw,relatime,mode=600 0 0
proc /proc proc rw,relatime 0 0
sysfs /sys sysfs rw,relatime 0 0
none /acct cgroup rw,relatime,cpuacct 0 0
tmpfs /mnt/asec tmpfs rw,relatime,mode=755,gid=1000 0 0
tmpfs /mnt/obb tmpfs rw,relatime,mode=755,gid=1000 0 0
none /dev/cpuctl cgroup rw,relatime,cpu 0 0
/dev/block/mmcblk0p9 /system ext4 ro,noatime,barrier=1,data=ordered 0 0
/dev/block/mmcblk0p3 /efs ext4 rw,nosuid,nodev,noatime,barrier=1,journal_async_commit,data=ordered 0 0
/dev/block/mmcblk0p8 /cache ext4 rw,nosuid,nodev,noatime,errors=panic,barrier=1,journal_async_commit,data=ordered 0 0
/dev/block/mmcblk0p12 /data ext4 rw,nosuid,nodev,noatime,barrier=1,journal_async_commit,data=ordered,noauto_da_alloc,discard 0 0
/sys/kernel/debug /sys/kernel/debug debugfs rw,relatime 0 0
/dev/fuse /storage/sdcard0 fuse rw,nosuid,nodev,noexec,relatime,user_id=1023,group_id=1023,default_permissions,allow_other 0 0
```

Yet Another Flash File System 2 (YAFFS2) is an open source, single-threaded file system released in 2002. It is mainly designed to be fast when dealing with the NAND flash. YAFFS2 utilizes **out of band (OOB)**, and this is often not captured or decoded correctly during forensic acquisition, which makes analysis difficult. We will discuss this further in Chapter 9, *Android Data Extraction Techniques*. YAFFS2 was the most popular release at one point and is still widely used in Android devices. YAFFS2 is a log-structured file system. Data integrity is guaranteed, even in the case of a sudden power outage. In 2010, there was an announcement stating that in releases after Gingerbread, devices were going to move from YAFFS2 to EXT4. Currently, YAFFS2 is not supported by newer kernel versions, but certain mobile manufacturers might still continue to support it.

Flash Friendly File System (F2FS) was released in February 2013 to support Samsung devices running the Linux 3.8 kernel. F2FS relies on log-structured methods that optimize the NAND flash memory. The offline support features are a highlight of this file system, though it is still transient and being updated.

Robust File System (RFS) supports NAND flash memory on Samsung devices. RFS can be summarized as a FAT16 (or FAT32) file system where journaling is enabled through a transaction log. Many users complain that Samsung should stick with EXT4. RFS has been known to have lag times that slow down the features of Android.

Summary

Understanding the underlying features, file systems, and capabilities of an Android device proves useful in a forensic investigation. Unlike iOS, several variants of Android exist as many devices run the Android operating system and each may have different file systems and unique features. The fact that Android is open and customizable also changes the playing field of digital forensics. A forensic examiner must be prepared to expect the unexpected when handling an Android device.

In the next chapter, we will discuss methods for accessing the data stored on Android devices.

8

Android Forensic Setup and Pre-Data Extraction Techniques

In the previous chapter, we covered the fundamentals of Android architecture, security features, filesystems, and other capabilities. Having an established forensic environment before the start of an examination is important, as it ensures that the data is protected while the examiner maintains control of the workstation. This chapter will explain the process of, and what to consider when, setting up a digital forensic examination environment. It is paramount that the examiner maintains control of the forensic environment at all times; this prevents the introduction of contaminants that could affect the forensic investigation.

We will cover the following topics in this chapter:

- Setting up a forensic environment
- Connecting the device and accessing it from a workstation
- Screen lock bypass techniques
- Gaining root access to the device

Setting up the forensic environment for Android

A forensic examiner may encounter a wide range of mobiles over the course of their investigation. Hence, it is necessary to have a basic environment set up, on top of which he can build based on the requirements. It is also very important that the forensic expert maintains complete control over the environment at all times, to avoid any unexpected situations. Setting up a proper lab environment is an essential part of the forensic process. The Android forensic setup usually involves the following steps:

- Start with a fresh or forensically sterile computer environment. This means that other data is either not present on the system or is contained in a manner that prevents it from contaminating the present investigation.
- Install the basic software necessary to connect to the device. Android forensic tools and methodologies will work on Windows, Linux, and OS X platforms.
- Obtain access to the device. An examiner must be able to enable settings or bypass them in order to allow the data to be extracted from the Android device.
- Issue commands to the device through the methods defined in this chapter and in Chapter 9, *Android Data Extraction Techniques*.

The following sections provide guidance on setting up a basic Android forensic workstation.

The Android Software Development Kit

The Android **Software Development Kit (SDK)** helps the development world to build, test, and debug applications to run on Android. This is achieved by providing the tools necessary to create the applications. However, along with this, it also provides valuable documentation and other tools that can be of great help during the investigation of an Android device.

A good understanding of the Android SDK will help you to get to grips with the particulars of a device and the data on the device.

> The Android SDK consists of software libraries, APIs, tools, emulators, and other reference material. It can be downloaded for free from: `https://developer.android.com/studio/index.html`

During a forensic investigation, the SDK helps connect to and access the data on the Android device. The Android SDK is updated very frequently, so it's important to verify that your workstation also remains up-to-date. The Android SDK can run on Windows, Linux, and OS X.

The Android SDK installation

A working installation of the Android SDK is a must during the investigation of a forensic device. Most websites recognize the operating system on the computer and will prompt you to download the correct Android SDK. Unlike Android Studio, the SDK tools package only includes the core SDK tools, which you can access from the command line.

The following is a step-by-step procedure to install the Android SDK on a Windows 7 machine:

1. Before you install the Android SDK, make sure that your system has Java Development Kit installed, because the Android SDK relies on **Java SE Development Kit (JDK)**.

> JDK can be downloaded from: `http://www.oracle.com/technetwork/java/javase/downloads/index.html`.

2. Download the latest version of the Android SDK from: `https://developer.android.com/studio/index.html`. The installer version of the SDK is recommended for this purpose.

3. Run the installer file, which we downloaded in the previous step. You will see a wizard window, as seen in the following screenshot. After this, run through the routine **Next** steps that you encounter:

Android SDK Tools setup wizard

4. The installation location is the user's choice and must be remembered for future access. In this example, we will install it in the C:\ folder. Click on the **Install** button and choose the location (say, C:\android-sdk). The necessary files will be extracted to this folder.

5. Open the directory (C:\android-sdk) and double-click on **SDK Manager.exe** to begin the update process. Make sure that you select Android SDK Platform tools and any one release platform version of Android, as shown in the following screenshot. Some of the items in the list are chosen by default. For instance, it is necessary to install the USB driver in order to work with Android devices in Windows. In our example, Google USB Driver is selected. Similarly, you can find other items under the **Extras** section. Accept the license and click on **Install**, as shown in the following screenshot:

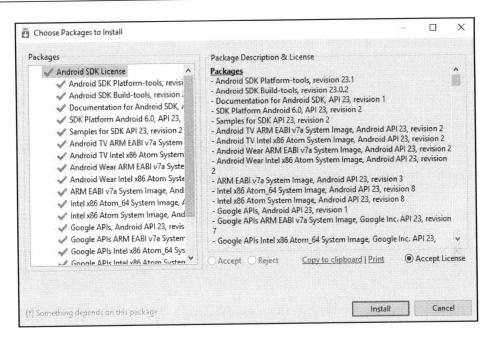

Android SDK license

This completes the Android SDK installation. You can also update the system's environment variables (path) by pointing to the executable files so that you can avoid navigating to the SDK folder every time you need to execute a command. This can be done by navigating to **Control Panel** | **System** | **Advanced Settings** | **Environment Variables** and then adding an SDK path to it.

 The installation of the Android SDK on OS X and Linux may vary. Make sure that you follow all the steps provided with the SDK download for full functionality.

An Android Virtual Device

Once the Android SDK is installed along with the release platform, you can create an **Android Virtual Device** (or **AVD,** also called an emulator), which is often used by developers when creating new applications. However, an emulator has significance from a forensic perspective, too. Emulators are useful when trying to understand how applications behave and execute on a device. This could be helpful in confirming certain findings that are unearthed during a forensic investigation.

Also, while working on a device which is running on an older platform, you can design an emulator with the same platform. Furthermore, before installing a forensic tool on a real device, the emulator can be used to find out how a forensic tool works and changes content on an Android device. To create a new AVD (on the Windows workstation), perform the following steps:

1. Open the command prompt (`cmd.exe`). Start the AVD manager from the command line by navigating to the path where the SDK is installed and call the Android tool with the `avd` option, as shown in the following command line. This will automatically open the AVD manager:

   ```
   C:\android-sdk\tools>android avd
   ```

Alternatively, the AVD manager can also be started using the graphical AVD manager. To start this, navigate to the location where the SDK is installed (`C:\android-sdk` in our example) and double-click on **AVD Manager**.

The **Android Virtual Device Manager** window is as shown in the following screenshot:

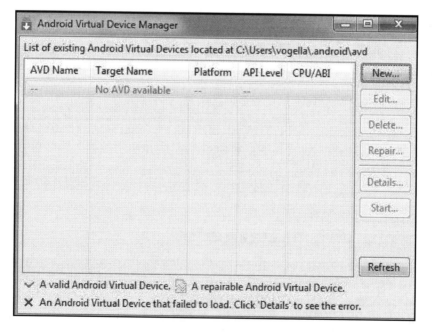

Android Virtual Device Manager

2. Click on **New...** in the AVD Manager window to create a new virtual device.
   Click on **Edit...** to change the configuration of an existing virtual device, as shown
   in the following screenshot:

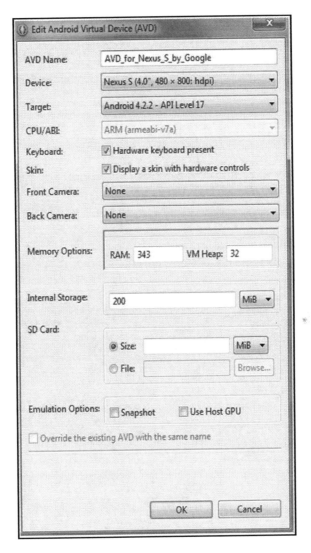

Virtual device configuration

3. Enter the following details:

   - **AVD Name**: This option is used to provide a name for the virtual device, for example, `ForensicsAVD`.
   - **Device**: This option is used to select any device from the available options based on the screen size.
   - **Target**: This option helps you select the platform of the device. Note that only the versions that were selected and installed during the SDK installation will be shown here to be selected.

   Similarly, you can select hardware features to customize the emulator, for example, the size of internal storage memory, SD card, and so on.

4. A confirmation message is shown once the device is successfully created. Now, select the AVD and click on **Start**. This will prompt you with the launch options. Select any option and click on **Launch**.

5. This should launch the emulator. Note that this could take a few minutes or even, longer depending on the workstation's CPU and RAM. The emulator does consume a significant amount of resources on the system. After a successful launch, the AVD will run, as shown in the following screenshot:

The Android emulator

From a forensic perspective, analysts and security researchers can leverage the functionality of an emulator to understand the filesystem, data storage, and so on. The data created when working on an emulator is stored in your home directory in a folder named android. For instance, in our example, the details about the ForensicsAVD emulator that we created earlier are stored under C:\Users\Rohit\.android\avd\ForensicsAVD.avd.

Among the various files present under this directory, the following are the files that are of interest for a forensic analyst:

- cache.img: This is the disk image of the /cache partition (remember that we discussed the /cache partition of an Android device in Chapter 7, *Understanding Android*).
- sdcard.img: This is the disk image of the SD card partition.
- Userdata-qemu.img: This is the disk image of the /data partition. The /data partition contains valuable information about the device user.

Connecting an Android device to a workstation

Forensic acquisition of an Android device using open source tools requires connecting the device to a forensic workstation. Forensic acquisition of any device should be conducted on a forensically sterile workstation. This means that the workstation is strictly used for forensics and not for personal use.

 Note that, any time a device is plugged into a computer, changes can be made to the device. The examiner must have full control of all interactions with the Android device at all times.

The following steps should be performed by the examiner in order to connect the device successfully to a workstation. Note that write protection may prevent the successful acquisition of the device, since commands may need to be pushed to the device in order to pull information. All the following steps should be validated on a test device prior to attempting them on real evidence.

Identifying the device cable

The physical USB interface of an Android device allows it to connect to a computer to share data, such as songs, videos, and photos. This USB interface might change from manufacturer to manufacturer and also from device to device. For example, some devices use mini-USB while some others use micro-USB and USB Type C. Apart from this, some manufacturers use their own proprietary formats, such as EXT-USB, EXT micro-USB, and so on. The first step in acquiring an Android device is to determine what kind of device cable is required.

There are different types such as mini-USB, micro-USB, and other proprietary formats. The following is a brief description of the most widely used connector types:

Connector type	Description
Mini - A USB	It is approximately 7 by 3 mm in size, with two of the corners on one long side lifted out.
Micro - B USB	It is approximately 6 by 1.5 mm in size, with two corners cut off to form a trapezoid.
Co-axial	It has a circular hole with a pin sticking up in the middle. There are different sizes under this varying from 2 to 5 mm in diameter. Widely used with Nokia models.
D Sub-miniature	It has the shape of a rectangle with two rounded corners. The length of the rectangle varies, but the height is always 1.5 to 2 mm. Used mostly by Samsung and LG devices.

Installing the device drivers

In order to identify the device properly, the computer may need certain drivers to be installed. Without necessary drivers, the computer may not identify and work with the connected device. The issue is that, since Android is allowed to be modified and customized by the manufacturers, there is no single generic driver that works for all Android devices. Each manufacturer writes its own proprietary drivers and distributes them over the internet. So, it's important to identify specific device drivers that need to be installed. Of course, some of the Android forensic toolkits (which we will discuss in the following chapters) do come with some generic drivers or a set of the most widely used drivers; they may not work with all models of Android phone. Some Windows operating systems are able to autodetect and install the drivers once the device is plugged in, but more often than not, it fails. The device drivers for each manufacturer can be found on their respective websites.

Accessing the connected device

If you haven't done so already, connect the unlocked Android device to the computer directly using the USB cable. The Android device will appear as a new drive and you will be able to access the files on the external storage. Some older Android devices may not be accessible unless the **Turn on USB storage** option is enabled on the phone, as shown in the following screenshot:

USB mass storage

In some Android phones (especially with HTC), the device may expose more than one functionality when connected with a USB cable. For instance, as shown in the following screenshot, when an HTC device is connected, it presents a menu with four options. The default selection is **Charge only**. When the **Disk drive** option is selected, it is mounted as a disk drive:

HTC mobile USB options

When the device is mounted as a disk drive, you will be able to access the SD card present on the device. From a forensic point of view, the SD card has significant value as it may contain files that are important to an investigation. However, the core application data stored under /data/data will remain on the device and cannot be accessed with these methods.

The Android Debug Bridge

Considered to be one of the most crucial components in Android forensics, the **Android Debug Bridge (ADB)** is a command-line tool that allows you to communicate with the Android device and control it. We will learn about the ADB in detail in the coming chapters; for now, we will focus on a basic introduction to ADB. You can access the ADB tool under <sdk>/platform-tools/.

Before we discuss anything about the ADB, we need to have an understanding of the **USB debugging** option.

USB debugging

The primary function of this option is to enable communication between the Android device and a workstation on which the Android SDK is installed. On a Samsung phone, you can access this under **Settings** | **Developer Options**, as shown in the following screenshot.

Other Android phones may have different environments and configuration features. The examiner may have to force the **Developer Options** option by accessing build mode:

The USB debugging option in Samsung mobiles

However, starting from Android 4.2, the **Developer Options** menu is hidden to make sure that users do not enable it by accident. To enable it, go to **Settings** | **About Phone** and then tap the **Build Number** field seven times. After this, **Developer Options** will be available in the **Settings** menu. Prior to Android 4.2.2, enabling this option was the only requirement for communicating with the device over ADB. However, starting from Android 4.2.2, Google has introduced the Secure USB debugging option. This feature only allows hosts that are explicitly authorized by the user to connect to the device using ADB. Thus, when you connect the device to a new workstation via USB in order to access ADB, you need to first unlock the device and authorize access by clicking on **OK** in the confirmation window, as shown in the following screenshot. If **Always allow from this computer is checked**, the device will not prompt for authorization in the future:

Secure USB debugging

When the **USB debugging** option is selected, the device will run the **adb daemon** (adbd) in the background and will continuously look for a USB connection. The daemon will usually run under a non-privileged shell user account and thus will not provide access to the complete data. However, on rooted phones, adbd will run under the root account and thus provide access to all the data. It is not recommended to root a device to gain full access unless all other forensic methods fail. Should the examiner elect to root an Android device, the methods must be well-documented and tested prior to attempting it on real evidence. Rooting will be discussed at the end of this chapter.

On the workstation where the Android SDK is installed, adbd will run as a background process. Also, on the same workstation, a client program, which can be invoked from a shell by issuing the adb command, will run. When the adb client is started, it first checks if an adb daemon is already running. If the response is negative, it initiates a new process to start the adb daemon. The adb client program communicates with local adbd over port 5037.

Accessing the device using adb

Once the environment setup is complete and the Android device is in **USB debugging mode**, connect the Android device the forensic workstation with a USB cable and start using adb.

Detecting connected devices

The following adb command provides a list of all the devices connected to the forensic workstation. This will also list the emulator if it is running at the time of issuing the command. Also remember that, if the necessary drivers are not installed, then the following command will show a blank message. If you encounter that situation, download the necessary drivers from the manufacturer and install them:

```
C:\android-sdk\platform-tools>adb.exe devices
List of devices attached
4df16ac3115e5f05        device
```

Killing the local adb server

The following command kills the local adb service:

```
C:\android-sdk\platform-tools>adb.exe kill-server
```

After killing the local adb service, issue the adb devices command and observe that the server is started, as shown in the following screenshot:

```
C:\android-sdk\platform-tools>adb.exe devices
List of devices attached
* daemon not running. starting it now on port 5037 *
* daemon started successfully *
4df16ac3115e5f05        device
```

Accessing the adb shell

This command allows forensic examiners to access the shell on an Android device and interact with the device.

The following is the command to access the adb shell and execute a basic ls command to see the contents of the current directory:

```
C:\android-sdk\platform-tools>adb.exe shell shell@android:/ $ ls
ls acct cache
config d
data default.prop dev
efs etc
factory fstab.smdk4x12 init
init.bt.rc init.goldfish.rc init.rc init.smdk4x12.rc init.smdk4x12.usb.rc
....
```

The Android emulator can be used by forensic examiners to execute and understand the adb commands before using them on the device. In Chapter 9, *Android Data Extraction Techniques*, we will explain more about leveraging adb to install applications, copy files and folders from the device, view device logs, and so on.

Basic Linux commands

We shall now take a quick look at some of the commonly used Linux commands and their usage with respect to Android device:

- ls: The ls command (with no option) lists files and directories present in the current directory. With the -l option, this command shows files and directories and also their size, modified date and time, the owner of file and its permission, and so on, as shown in the following command line output:

```
shell@android:/ $ ls -l
ls -l
drwxr-xr-x root      root               2015-01-17 10:13 acct
drwxrwx--- system    cache              2014-05-31 14:55 cache
dr-x------ root      root               2015-01-17 10:13 config
lrwxrwxrwx root      root               2015-01-17 10:13 d ->
/sys/kernel/debug
drwxrwx--x system    system             2015-01-17 10:13 data
-rw-r--r-- root      root           116 1970-01-01 05:30 default.prop
drwxr-xr-x root      root               2015-01-17 10:13 dev
drwxrwx--x radio     system             2013-08-13 09:34 efs
lrwxrwxrwx root      root               2015-01-17 10:13 etc ->
/system/etc
...
```

Similarly, the following are a few options that can be used along with `ls` command:

Option	Description
a	Lists hidden files
c	Displays files by timestamp
d	Displays only directories
n	Displays the long format listing, with GID and UID numbers.
R	Displays subdirectories as well
t	Displays files based on time stamp
u	Displays the file access time

Depending on the requirements, one or more of these options can be used by the investigator to view the details.

- cat: The `cat` command reads one or more files and prints them to standard output, as shown in the following command lines:

```
shell@android:/ $ cat default.prop
cat default.prop
#
# ADDITIONAL_DEFAULT_PROPERTIES
#
ro.secure=1
ro.allow.mock.location=0
ro.debuggable=0
persist.sys.usb.config=mtp
```

The operator > can be used to combine multiple files into one. The operator >> can be used to append to an existing file.

- cd: The `cd` command is used to change from one directory to another. This is more frequently used while navigating from one folder to another. The following example shows commands used to change to `system` folder:

```
shell@android:/ $ cd /system
cd /system
shell@android:/system $
```

- cp: The cp command can be used to copy a file from one location to another. The syntax for this command is as follows:

```
$ cp [options] <source><destination>
```

- chmod: The chmod command is used to change the access permissions to file system objects (files and directories). It may also alter special mode flags. The syntax for this command is as follows:

```
$ chmod [option] mode files
```

For example, chmod 777 on a file gives permission to everyone to read, write, and execute.

- dd: The dd command is used to copy a file, converting and formatting according to the operands. With Android, the dd command can be used to create a bit-by-bit image of the Android device. More details of imaging are covered in Chapter 4, *Data Acquisition from iOS Backups*. The following is the syntax that needs to be used with this command:

```
dd if=/test/file of=/sdcard/sample.image
```

- rm: The rm command can be used to delete files or directories. The following is the syntax for this command:

```
rm file_name
```

- grep: The grep command is used to search files or output for a particular pattern. The syntax for this command is as follows:

```
grep [options] pattern [files]
```

- pwd: The pwd command displays current working directory. For example, the following command line output shows that the current working directory is /system:

```
shell@android:/system $ pwd
pwd
/system
```

- `mkdir`: The `mkdir` command is used to create a new directory. The following is the syntax for this command:

  ```
  mkdir [options] directories
  ```

- `exit`: The `exit` command can be used to exit the shell you are in. Just type `exit` in the shell to exit from it.

Handling an Android device

Handling an Android device in a proper manner prior to the forensic investigation is a very important task. Care should be taken to make sure that our unintentional actions don't result in data modification or any other unwanted happenings. The following sections throw light on certain issues that need to be considered while handling the device in the initial stages of forensic investigation.

With the improvements in technology, the concept of **device locking** has effectively changed over the last few years. Most users now have a passcode locking mechanism enabled on their device due to the increase in general security awareness. Before we look at some of the techniques used to bypass locked Android devices, it is important not to miss an opportunity to disable the passcode when there is a chance.

When an Android device, which is to be analyzed, is first accessed, check whether the device is still active (unlocked). If so, change the settings of the device to enable greater access to the device. So, when the device is still active, consider performing the following tasks:

- **Enabling USB debugging**: Once the USB debugging option is enabled, it gives greater access to the device through the `adb` connection. This is of great significance when it comes to extracting data from the device. The location to enable USB debugging might change from device to device, but it's usually under **Developer Options** in **Settings**. Most methods for physically acquiring Android devices require USB debugging to be enabled.
- **Enabling the Stay awake setting**: If the **Stay awake** option is selected and the device is connected for charging, then the device never locks. Again, if the device locks, the acquisition can be halted.
- **Increasing screen timeout**: This is the time for which the device will be effectively active once it is unlocked. The location to access this setting varies depending upon the model of the device. On a Samsung Galaxy S3 phone, you can access the same by navigating to **Settings** | **Display** | **ScreenTimeout**.

Apart from this, as mentioned in `Chapter 1`, *Introduction to Mobile Forensics*, the device needs to be isolated from the network to make sure that remote wipe options do not work on the device. The Android Device Manager allows the phone to be remotely wiped or locked. This can be done by signing in to the Google account, which is configured on the mobile. More details about this are mentioned in the following section. If the Android device is not set up to allow remote wiping, the device can only be locked using the Android Device Manager. Also, there are several **Mobile Device Management** (**MDM**) software products available on the market, which allow users to remotely lock or wipe the Android device. Some of these may not require specific settings to be enabled on the device.

Using the available remote wipe software, it is possible to delete all the data, including e-mails, applications, photos, contacts, and other files including those found on the SD card. To isolate the device from the network, you can put the device in airplane mode and disable Wi-Fi as an extra precaution. Enabling airplane mode and disabling Wi-Fi works well, as the device will not be able to communicate over a cellular network and cannot be accessed via Wi-Fi. Removing the SIM card from the phone is also an option, but that does not effectively stop the device from communicating over Wi-Fi or some other cellular networks. To place the device in airplane mode, press and hold the Power Off button and select **Airplane mode**.

All these steps can be done when the Android device is not locked. However, during the investigation, we commonly encounter devices that are locked. Hence, it's important to understand how to bypass the lock code if it is enabled on an Android device.

Screen lock bypassing techniques

Due to the increase in user awareness and the ease of functionality, there has been an exponential increase in the usage of passcode options to lock Android devices. Hence, bypassing the device's screen lock during a forensic investigation becomes increasingly important. The applicability of the screen lock bypass techniques discussed so far is based on the situation. Note that some of these methods may result in making changes to the device. Make sure that you test and validate all the steps listed on non-evidentiary Android devices. The examiner must have authorization to make the required changes to the device, document all steps taken, and be able to describe the steps taken if a courtroom testimony is required.

Currently, there are three types of screen lock mechanisms offered by Android. Although there are some devices which have voice lock, face lock, and fingerprint lock options, we will limit our discussion to the following three options, since these are the most widely used on all Android devices:

- **Pattern lock**: The user sets a pattern or design on the phone and the same pattern must be drawn to unlock the device. Android was the first smartphone to introduce a pattern lock.
- **PIN code**: This is the most common lock option and is found on many mobile phones. The PIN code is a 4-digit number that needs to be entered to unlock the device.
- **Passcode**: This is an alphanumeric passcode. Unlike the PIN, which takes four digits, the alphanumeric passcode includes letters, as well as digits.

The following section details some of the techniques to bypass these Android lock mechanisms. Depending on the situation, these techniques might help an investigator to bypass the screen lock.

Using adb to bypass the screen lock

If USB debugging appears to be enabled on the Android device, it is wise to take advantage of it by connecting with adb using a USB connection, as discussed in the earlier sections of this chapter. The examiner should connect the device to the forensic workstation and issue the adb devices command. If the device shows up, it implies that USB debugging is enabled. If the Android device is locked, the examiner must attempt to bypass the screen lock. The following are the two methods that may allow the examiner to bypass the screen lock when USB debugging is enabled.

Deleting the gesture.key file

Deleting the gesture.key file will remove the pattern lock on the device. However, it's important to note that this will permanently change the device, as the pattern lock is gone. This should be considered if conducting cover operations. This is how the process is done:

1. Connect the device to the forensic workstation (a Windows machine in our example) using a USB cable.

2. Open the command prompt and execute the following instructions:

```
adb.exe shell
cd /data/system rm gesture.key
```

3. Reboot the device. If the pattern lock still appears, just draw any random design and the device should unlock without any trouble.

 This method works when the device is rooted. This method may not be successful on unrooted devices. Rooting an Android device should not be performed without proper authorization, as the device is altered.

Updating the settings.db file

To update the settings.db file, perform the following steps:

1. Connect the device to the forensic workstation using a USB cable.
2. Open the command prompt and execute the following instructions:

```
:/ $ cd /data/data/com.android.providers.settings/databases
sqlite3 settings.db
update system set value=0 where name='lock_pattern_autolock';
update secure set value=0 where name='lock_pattern_autolock';
/data/data/com.android.providers.settings/databases
update system set value=0 where name='lockscreen.lockedoutpermanently';
update secure set value=0 where name='lockscreen.lockedoutpermanently';
sqlite3 settings.db
.quit
exit
```

3. Exit and reboot the device.
4. The Android device should be unlocked. If not, attempt to remove gesture.key as explained earlier.

Checking for the modified recovery mode and adb connection

In Android, recovery refers to the dedicated partition where the recovery console is present. The two main functions of recovery are to delete all user data and install updates. For instance, when you factory reset your phone, recovery boots up and deletes all the data. Similarly, when updates are to be installed on the phone, it is done in recovery mode. There are many enthusiastic Android users who install custom ROM through a modified recovery module. This modified recovery module is mainly used to make the process of installing custom ROM easy. Recovery mode can be accessed in different ways, depending on the manufacturer of the device; information on which method is right for which manufacturer's devices is easily available on the internet. Usually, this is done by holding different keys together such as the Volume button and Power button. Once in recovery mode, connect the device to the workstation and try to access the adb connection. If the device has a recovery mode which is not modified, the examiner may not be able to access the adb connection. The modified recovery versions of the device present the user with different options and can easily be noticed, as shown in the following screenshot:

Flashing a new recovery partition

There are mechanisms available to flash the recovery partition of an Android device with a modified image. The fastboot utility would facilitate this process. The fastboot is a diagnostic protocol that comes with the SDK package, used primarily to modify the flash file system through a USB connection from a host computer. For this, you need to start the device in boot loader mode, in which only the most basic hardware initialization is performed.

Once the protocol is enabled on the device, it will accept a specific set of commands that are sent to it via the USB cable using a command line. Flashing or rewriting a partition with a binary image stored on the computer is one such command that is allowed. Once the recovery is flashed, boot the device in recovery mode, mount the /data and /system partitions, and use adb to remove the gesture.key file. Reboot the phone and you should be able to bypass the screen lock. However, this works only if the device bootloader is unlocked. Also, flashing permanently alters the device. Instead of flashing, you could use the fastboot boot command to boot to a recovery image temporarily to delete the key file without permanently changing the recovery partition.

Using automated tools

There are several automated solutions available in the market for unlocking Android devices. Commercial tools, such as Cellebrite and XRY, are capable of bypassing the screen locks, but most of them require USB debugging to be enabled. We will now examine how to unlock an Android device using the UFED user lock code recovery tool. Also, this tool only works on those devices that support USB OTG. This process also requires a UFED camera, Cable No. 500-Bypass lock, and Cable No. 501-Bypass lock. Once the tool is installed on the workstation, follow these steps to unlock an Android device:

1. Run the tool on the work station and press 1, as shown in the following screenshot:

```
UFED User Lock Code Recovery Tool

Disclaimer: All actions are subject to the full responsibility of the user, and
Cellebrite is not liable for any damage to the device.

Follow the instructions to recover the lock code.

Before you begin, check your computer's power options to make sure it won't go
into sleep mode. The process could take from a few minutes up to 21 hours. You
can still use the computer during this time.


What type of device is it?

[1] Android
[2] iOS (Apple)
[0] Exit
```

UFED user lock code recovery tool

2. Now, connect side A of Cable No. 500-Bypasslock to a USB port of the workstation. Also, connect side B of Cable No. 500-Bypasslock to Cable No. 501-OTG and then connect the other end to the device.

3. Once connected, the tool prompts you to select the recovery profile. Select `[1]` `Manually select the recovery profile.`.

4. Now, select the lock type used on the device and the recovery profile, and proceed by following the instructions on the screen.

5. After this, make sure that the keypad appears on the device screen and that it's ready to accept the PIN code.

6. Close any message windows that may appear. Press 1 and hit *Enter*. Now, make five incorrect login attempts by entering random input, and click on **Forgot pattern** at the bottom of the device.

7. Follow the instructions on the screen, wait for the camera window to open, and then click on the camera window.

8. Use the cursor to select any non-empty area on the device's screen by placing the green square over it. For example, select any number on the screen. This is used by the tool to detect if the device is unlocked. Press *Enter* to start the process.

9. The tool will try a number of combinations to unlock the device. Once unlocked, it would prompt you to end the process.

Using Android Device Manager

Most of the latest Android phones come with a service called Android Device Manager, which helps the owner of a device to locate their lost phone. This service can also be used to unlock a device; however, this is possible only when you know the Google account credentials that are configured on the device. If you have access to the account credentials, then follow these steps to unlock the device:

1. Visit `http://google.com/android/devicemanager` on your workstation.
2. Sign in using the Google account that is configured on the device.
3. Select the device you need to unlock and click on **Lock**, as shown in the following screenshot:

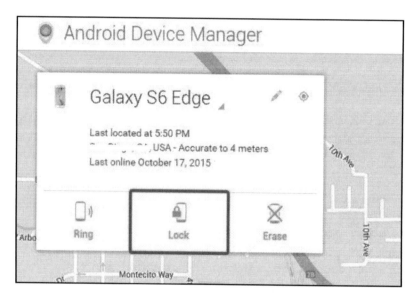

Android Device Manager

4. Enter a temporary password and click on **Lock** again.
5. Once it's successful, enter the temporary password on the device to unlock it.

It can be done without knowing the credentials of the computer where the login is saved (that is, the suspect's PC). Similarly, if you are dealing with a Samsung device, you can also try Samsung's *FindMyMobile* service, which enables you to set a temporary password to unlock the device.

Smudge attack

In rare cases, a smudge attack may be used to deduce the password of a touchscreen mobile device. This attack relies on identifying the smudges left behind by the user's fingers. While this may present a bypass method, it must be said that a smudge attack is unlikely since most Android devices are touchscreen and smudges will also be present from using the device. However, it has been demonstrated that, under proper lighting, the smudges that are left behind can easily be detected, as shown in the following screenshot. By analyzing the smudge marks, we can discern the pattern that is used to unlock the screen. This attack is more likely to work while discerning the pattern lock on the Android device. In some cases, PIN codes can also be recovered depending upon the cleanliness of the screen. So, during a forensic investigation, care should be taken when the device is first handled to make sure that the screen is not touched.

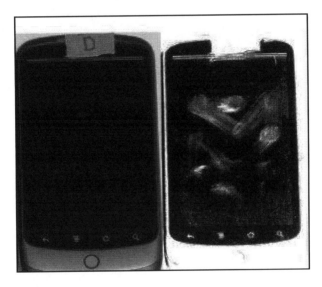

Smudges visible on a device under proper lighting (source: https://www.usenix.org/legacy/events/woot10/t ech/full_papers/Aviv.pdf)

Using the Forgot Password/Forgot Pattern option

If you know the username and password of the primary Gmail address that is configured on the device, you can change the PIN, password, or swipe on the device. After making a certain number of failed attempts to unlock the screen, Android provides an option named **Forgot Pattern** or **Forgot Password**, as shown in the following screenshot:

Forgot Pattern option on an Android device

Tap on that link and sign in using the Gmail username and password. This will allow you to create a new pattern lock or passcode for the device.

 Note that this works only on devices running Android 4.4 or earlier.

Bypassing third-party lock screens by booting into safe mode

If the screen lock is a third-party app, rather than the inbuilt lock, it can be bypassed by booting into safe mode and disabling it. To boot into safe mode on Android device 4.1 or later, long-press the power button until the power options menu appears. Then, long-press the Power Off option and you'll be asked if you want to reboot your Android device into safe mode. Tap the **OK** button, as shown in the following screenshot:

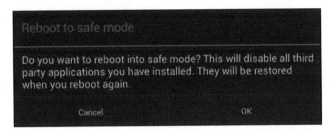

Safe mode in Android

Once you're in safe mode, you can disable the third-party lock screen app or uninstall it completely. After this, reboot the device and you should be able to access it without any lock screen.

Securing the USB debugging bypass using adb keys

As mentioned earlier, while using USB debugging, if the **Always allow from this computer** option is checked, the device will not prompt for authorization in future. This is done by storing certain keys, namely adbkey and adbkey.pub, on the computer. Any attempt to connect to adb from an untrusted computer is denied. In this case, the adbkey and the adbkey.pub files can be pulled from the suspect's computer and copied to the investigator's workstation. The device will then assume that it is communicating with a known, authorized computer. The adbkey and adbkey.pub files can be found at C:Users<username>.android on Windows machines.

Securing the USB debugging bypass in Android 4.4.2

As explained in the earlier sections, the secure USB debugging feature introduced in Android 4.4.2 allows only authorized workstations to connect to the device. However, there's a bug in this feature as reported at `https://labs.mwrinfosecurity.com/` which allows bypassing the Secure USB debugging feature and connecting the device to any workstation. Here are the steps to follow to bypass Secure USB debugging on an Android device:

1. On an unlocked device, attempt to use `adb` and observe that an error message is shown by the device.

2. Now, navigate to either the emergency dialer or the lock-screen camera and execute the following commands:

   ```
   $ adb kill-server
   $ adb shell
   ```

3. Observe that the confirmation dialog is now triggered and the workstation can be authorized without unlocking the device. The confirmation dialog box is displayed on the emergency dialer, as shown in the followings screenshot:

Bypassing Secure USB debugging in Android 4.2.2

4. Once connected to the device through `adb`, try to bypass the lock screen using the following command:

```
$ adb shell pm clear com.android.keyguard
```

Crashing the lock screen UI in Android 5.x

On devices running Android 5.0 to 5.1.1, the password lock screen (not the pin or pattern locks) can be bypassed by crashing the screen UI. This can be accomplished by following these steps, as explained at: `https://android.gadgethacks.com/`:

1. Click on the **Emergency Call** option on the lock screen and then enter any random input (for example, 10 asterisks) on the dialer screen.
2. Double-tap the field to highlight the entered text, as shown in the following screenshot, and choose **Copy**. Now, paste it into the same field:

Crashing lock screen UI

3. Repeat this process of copying and pasting to add more characters until double-tapping the field no longer highlights the characters.

4. Go back to the lock screen and open the camera shortcut. Now, pull down the notifications screen and tap the **Settings** icon. You will then be prompted to enter a password.

5. Long-press the input field and choose **Paste** and repeat this process several more times. After pasting enough characters into the field, the lock screen will crash and allow you to access the device.

Other techniques

All of the previously mentioned techniques and the commercial tools available prove to be useful to the forensic examiner trying to get access to the data on an Android device. However, there could be situations where none of these techniques work. To obtain a complete physical image of the device, techniques such as chip-off and JTAG may be required when commercial and open source solutions fail. A short description of these techniques is included here.

While the chip-off technique removes the memory chip from a circuit and tries to read it, the JTAG technique involves probing the JTAG **Test Access Ports** (**TAPs**) and soldering connectors to the JTAG ports in order to read data from the device memory. The chip-off technique is more destructive because, once the chip is removed from a device, it is difficult to restore the device to its original functional state. Also, expertise is needed to carefully remove the chip from the device by desoldering the chip from the circuit board. The heat required to remove the chip can also damage or destroy the data stored on that chip. Hence, this technique should be looked upon only when the data is not retrievable by open source or commercial tools or the device is damaged beyond repair. When using the JTAG technique, JTAG ports help an examiner to access the memory chip to retrieve a physical image of the data without needing to remove the chip. To turn off the screen lock on a device, an examiner can identify where the lock code is stored in the physical memory dump, turn off the locking, and copy that data back to the device. Commercial tools, such as Cellebrite Physical Analyzer, can accept the .bin files from chip-off and JTAG acquisitions and crack the lock code for the examiner. Once the code is either manually removed or cracked, the examiner can analyze the device using normal techniques.

 Both the chip-off and JTAG techniques require extensive research and experience to be attempted on a real device. A great resource for JTAG and chip-off on devices can be found at: http://forensicswiki.org/wiki/Main_Page.

Gaining root access

As a mobile device forensic examiner, it is essential to know everything that relates to twisting and tweaking the device. This would help you to understand the internal workings of the device in detail and comprehend many issues that you may face during your investigation. Rooting Android phones has become a common phenomenon and you can expect to encounter rooted phones during forensic examinations. The examiner, where applicable, may also need to root the device in order to acquire data for the forensic examination. Hence, it's important to know the ins and outs of rooted devices and how they are different from other phones. The following sections cover information about Android rooting and other related concepts.

What is rooting?

The default administrative account in Unix-like operating systems is called **root**. So, in Linux, the root user has the power to start/stop any system service, edit/delete any file, change the privileges of other users, and so on. We have already learned that Android uses the Linux kernel, and hence, most of the concepts present in Linux are applicable to Android as well. However, most of the Android phones do not let you log in as a root user by default.

 Rooting an Android phone is all about gaining access on the device to perform actions that are not normally allowed on the device. Manufacturers want the devices to function in a certain manner for normal users. Rooting a device may void a warranty, since root opens the system to vulnerabilities and provides the user with superuser capabilities.

Imagine a malicious application having access to an entire Android system with root access. Remember that, in Android, each application is treated as a separate user and issues a UID. Thus, the applications have access to limited resources and the concept of application isolation is enforced. Essentially, rooting an Android device allows superuser capabilities and provides open access to the Android device.

Rooting an Android device

Even though the hardware manufacturers try to put enough restrictions to restrict access to the root, hackers have always found different ways to get access to the root. The process of rooting varies depending on the underlying device manufacturer. However, rooting any device usually involves exploiting a security bug in the device's firmware and then copying the su (superuser) binary to a location in the current process's path (/system/xbin/su) and granting it executable permissions with the chmod command.

For the sake of simplicity, imagine that an Android device has three to four partitions, which run programs not entirely related to Android (Android being one among them).

The boot loader is present in the first partition and is the first program that runs when the phone is powered on. The primary job of this boot loader is to boot other partitions and load the Android partition, commonly referred to as ROM by default. To see the boot loader menu, a specific key combination is required such as holding the power button and pressing the volume up button. This menu provides options for you to boot into other partitions, such as the recovery partition.

The recovery partition deals with installing upgrades to the phone, which are written directly to the Android ROM partition. This is the mode that you see when you install any official update on the device. Device manufacturers make sure that only official updates are installed through the recovery partition. Thus, bypassing this restriction would allow you to install/flash any unlocked Android ROM. Modified recovery programs are those that not only allow an easier rooting process, but also provide various options that are not seen in the normal recovery mode. The following screenshot shows the normal recovery mode:

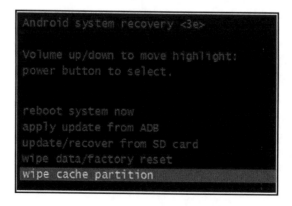

Normal Android system recovery mode

The following screenshot shows the modified recovery mode:

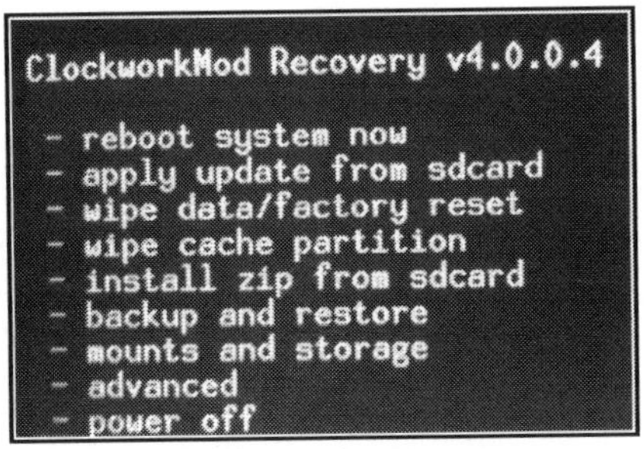

The modified recovery mode

The most commonly used recovery program in the Android world is the Clockwork recovery, also called **ClockworkMod**. Hence, most of the rooting methods begin by flashing a modified recovery to the recovery partition. After that, you can issue an update, which can root the device. However, you don't need to perform all the actions manually, as software is available for most of the models, which can root your phone with a single click.

Starting from Android 7.x, Google has started strictly enforcing *verified boot* on devices. Verified boot guarantees that the software on the device is not modified before booting into the normal mode. This is implemented in such a way that each stage verifies the integrity and authenticity of the next stage before executing it. If a particular partition or segment is modified, the integrity check fails and the mobile may not boot into normal mode. More information about verified boot can be found at `https://source.android.com/security/verifiedboot/verified-boot`.

This also means that rooting such Android devices is going to be extremely difficult, because rooting involves tweaking the Android OS. Marshmallow is the first Android version to provide alerts on the system integrity, but with Android 7.x, it is made mandatory.

Rooting a device has both advantages and disadvantages associated with it. The following are the advantages of rooting:

- Rooting allows modification of the software on the device to the deepest level. For example, you can overclock or underclock the device's CPU.
- It allows restrictions imposed on the device by carriers, manufacturers, and so on, to be bypassed.
- For extreme customization, new customized ROMs can be downloaded and installed.

The following are the disadvantages of rooting:

- Rooting a device must be done with extreme care as errors may result in irreparable damage to the software on the phone, turning the device into a useless brick.
- Rooting might void the warranty of a device.
- Rooting results in increased exposure to malware and other attacks. Malware with access to the entire Android system can create havoc.

Once the device is rooted, applications such as the **Superuser app** are available to provide and deny root privileges. This app helps you to grant and manage superuser rights on the device, as shown in the following screenshot:

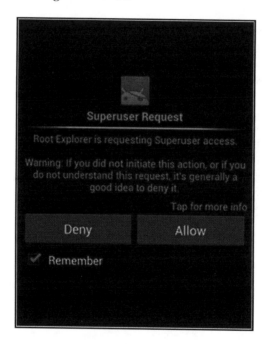

Application requesting root access

Root access - adb shell

A normal Android phone does not allow you to access certain directories and files on the device. For example, try to access the /data/data folder on an Android device that is not rooted. You will see the following message:

```
C:\android-sdk\platform-tools>adb.exe shell
shell@android:/ $ cd /data/data
shell@android:/data/data $ ls
opendir failed, Permission denied
255|shell@android:/data/data $
```

On a rooted phone, you can run the adb shell as a root by issuing the following command:

```
C:\android-sdk\platform-tools>adb.exe root
```

```
C:\android-sdk\platform-tools>adb.exe shell
root@android:/ # cd /data/data
root@android:/data/data # ls
android.googleSearch.googleSearchWidget
com.android.MtpApplication
com.android.Preconfig
com.android.apps.tag
com.android.backupconfirm
com.android.bluetooth
com.android.browser
```

Thus, rooting a phone enables you to access folders and data that are otherwise not accessible. Also, note that # symbolizes root or superuser access, while $ reflects a normal user, as shown in the preceding command lines.

Summary

A proper forensic workstation setup is required prior to conducting investigations on an Android device. Using open source methods to acquire and analyze Android devices requires the installation of specific software on the forensic workstation. If the method of forensic acquisition requires the Android device to be unlocked, the examiner needs to determine the best method by which to gain access to the device. The various screen lock bypass techniques explained in this chapter help an examiner to bypass the passcode under different circumstances. Depending on the forensic acquisition method and scope of the investigation, rooting the device should provide complete access to the files present on the device.

Now that the basic concepts of gaining access to an Android device have been covered, we will cover acquisition techniques and describe how data is pulled using each method in Chapter 9, *Android Data Extraction Techniques*.

9
Android Data Extraction Techniques

Using any of the screen lock bypass techniques explained in `Chapter 8`, *Android Forensic Setup and Pre-Data Extraction Techniques*, an examiner can try to access a locked device. Once the device is accessible, the next task is to extract the information present on the device. This can be achieved by applying various data extraction techniques to the Android device. This chapter will help you to identify the sensitive locations present on an Android device and explain various logical and physical techniques that can be applied to the device in order to extract the necessary information.

In this chapter, we will cover the following topics:

- Logical data extraction using ADB pull, ADB backup, ADB dumpsys, and content providers
- Physical extraction, which covers imaging an Android device and SD card, JTAG, and chip-off techniques

Data extraction techniques

Data residing on an Android device may be an integral part of civil, criminal, or internal investigations done as part of a corporate company's internal probe. While dealing with investigations involving Android devices, the forensic examiner needs to be mindful of the issues that need to be taken care of during the forensic process; this includes determining whether root access is permitted (via consent or legal authority) and what data can be extracted and analyzed during the investigation. For example, in a criminal case involving stalking, the court may only allow for SMS, call logs, and photos to be extracted and analyzed on the Android device belonging to the suspect. In this case, it may make the most sense to logically capture only those specific items. However, it is best to obtain full physical data extraction of the device and only examine the areas admissible by the court. You never know where your investigation may lead and it is best to obtain as much data from the device as possible immediately, rather than wishing you had a full image should the scope of consent change. The data extraction techniques on an Android device can be classified into three types:

- Manual data extraction
- Logical data extraction
- Physical data extraction

As described in Chapter 1, *Introduction to Mobile Forensics*, manual extraction involves browsing through the device normally and capturing any valuable information, while logical extraction deals with accessing the file system and physical extraction is about extracting a bit-by-bit image of the device. The extraction methods for each of these types will be described in detail in the following sections.

Some methods may require the device to be rooted in order to fully access the data. Each method has different implications and their success rates will depend on the tool and method used as well as the device's make and model.

Manual data extraction

This method of extraction involves the examiner utilizing the normal user interface of the mobile device to access content present in the memory. The examiner will browse through the device normally by accessing different menus to view the details such as call logs, text messages, and IM chats. The content of each screen is captured by taking pictures and can be presented as evidence. The main drawback with this type of examination is that only the files that are accessible via the operating system (in UI mode) can be investigated. Care must be taken when manually examining the device, as it's easy to press the wrong button and erase or add data. Manual extraction should be used as the last resort to verify findings extracted using one of the other methods. Certain circumstances may warrant the examiner to conduct manual examination as the first step. This may include cases of life or death situations or missing persons where a quick scan of the device may lead the police to the individual.

Logical data extraction

Logical data extraction techniques extract the data present on the device by interacting with the operating system and by accessing the file system. These techniques are significant, because they provide valuable data, work on most devices, and are easy to use. Once again, the concept of rooting comes into the picture while extracting the data. Logical techniques do not actually require root access for data extraction. However, having root access on a device allows you to access all the files present on a device. This means that some data may be extracted on a non-rooted device while root access will open the device and provide access to all the files present on the device. Hence, having root access to a device would greatly influence the amount and kind of data that could be extracted through logical techniques. The following sections explain various techniques that can be used to extract data logically from an Android device.

ADB pull data extraction

As seen earlier, adb is a command-line tool that helps you communicate with the device to retrieve information. Using adb, you can extract data from all the files on the device or just the relevant files in which you are interested.

To access an Android device through `adb`, it's necessary that the USB debugging option is enabled. From Android 4.2.2, due to secure USB debugging, the host connecting to the device should also be authorized. If the device is locked and USB debugging is not enabled, try to bypass the screen lock using the techniques explained in `Chapter 8`, *Android Forensic Setup and Pre-Data Extraction Techniques*.

As a forensic examiner, it's important to know how the data is stored on the Android device and to understand where important and sensitive information is stored so that the data can be extracted accordingly. Application data often contains a wealth of user data that may be relevant to the investigation. All files pertaining to applications of interest should be examined for relevance, as will be explained in `Chapter 10`, *Android Data Analysis and Recovery*. The application data can be stored in one of the following locations:

- **Shared preferences**: This stores data in key-value pairs in a lightweight XML format. Shared preference files are stored in the `shared_pref` folder of the application `/data` directory.
- **Internal storage**: This stores data that is private and is present in the device's internal memory. Files saved to the internal storage are private and cannot be accessed by other applications.
- **External storage**: This stores data that is public in the device's external memory, which does not usually enforce security mechanisms. This data is available in the `/sdcard` directory.
- **SQLite database**: This data is available in the `/data/data/PackageName/` database. It is usually stored with the `.db` file extension. The data present in a SQLite file can be viewed using a SQLite browser (`https://sourceforge.net/projects/sqlitebrowser/`) or by executing the necessary SQLite commands on the respective files.

Every Android application stores data on the device using one or more of the preceding data storage options. So, the Contacts application would store all the information about the contact details in the `/data/data` folder under its package name. Note that `/data/data` is a part of your device's internal storage, where all the apps are installed under normal circumstances. Some application data will reside on the SD card and in the /data/data partition. Using `adb`, we can pull the data present in this partition for further analysis using the `adb pull` command. Once again, it's important to note that this directory is only accessible on a rooted phone.

On a rooted phone, the `adb pull` command on the `databases` folder of the Dropbox app can be executed as follows:

```
C:\android-sdk\platform-tools>adb.exe pull /data/data/com.dropbox.android/databases C:\temp
pull: building file list...
pull: /data/data/com.dropbox.android/databases/prefs.db-journal -> C:\temp/prefs.db-journal
pull: /data/data/com.dropbox.android/databases/prefs.db -> C:\temp/prefs.db
pull: /data/data/com.dropbox.android/databases/db.db-journal -> C:\temp/db.db-journal
pull: /data/data/com.dropbox.android/databases/db.db -> C:\temp/db.db
4 files pulled. 0 files skipped.
1753 KB/s (140352 bytes in 0.078s)
```

Similarly, on a rooted phone, the entire `/data` folder can be pulled in this manner. As shown in the following screenshot, the complete `/data` directory on the Android device can be copied to the local directory on the machine. The entire `data` directory was extracted in 97 seconds. The extraction time will vary depending on the amount of data residing in `/data`:

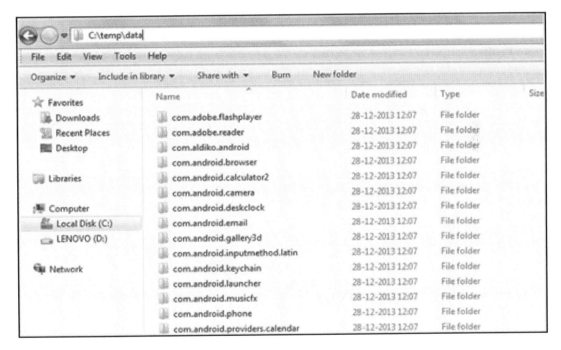

The /data directory extracted to a forensic workstation

On a non-rooted device, a `pull` command on the `/data` directory does not extract the files, as shown in the following output, since the shell user does not have permission to access those files:

```
C:\android-sdk\platform-tools>adb.exe pull /data C:\temp
pull: building file list...
0 files pulled. 0 files skipped.
```

The data copied from a rooted phone through the preceding process maintains its directory structure, thus allowing an investigator to browse through the necessary files to gain access to the information. By analyzing the data of the respective applications, a forensic expert can gather critical information that can influence the outcome of the investigation. Note that examining the folders natively on your forensic workstation will alter the dates and times of the content. The examiner should make a copy of the original output to use for a date/time comparison.

Using SQLite Browser to view the data

SQLite Browser is a tool that can help during the course of analyzing the extracted data. SQLite Browser allows you to explore the database files with the following extensions-- `qlite`, `.sqlite3`, `.sqlitedb`, `.db`, and `.db3`. The main advantage of using SQLite Browser is that it shows the data in a table form. Navigate to **File | Open Database** to open a `.db` file using SQLite Browser. As shown in the following screenshot, there are three tabs--**Database Structure**, **Browse Data**, and **Execute SQL**. The **Browse Data** tab allows you to see the information present in different tables within the `.db` files.

We will be mostly using this tab during our analysis. Alternately, Oxygen Forensic SQLite Database Viewer can also be used for the same purpose. Recovering deleted data from database files is possible and will be explained in `Chapter 10`, *Android Data Analysis and Recovery*:

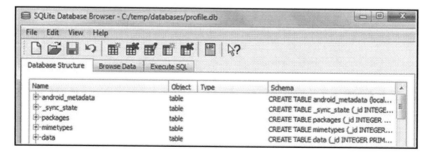

SQLite Browser

The following sections throw light on identifying important data and manually extracting various details from an Android phone.

Extracting device information

Knowing the details of your Android device, such as the model, version, and more, will aid your investigation. For example, when the device is physically damaged and this prohibits the examination of the device information, you can grab details about the device by viewing the `build.prop` file present in the `/system` folder, as follows:

```
root@android:/system # cat build.prop
# begin build properties
# autogenerated by buildinfo.sh
ro.build.id=JZO54K
ro.build.display.id=JZO54K.I        MH4
ro.build.version.incremental=I        MH4
ro.build.version.sdk=16
ro.build.version.codename=REL
ro.build.version.release=4.1.2
ro.build.date=Tue Sep 17 17:26:31 KST 2013
ro.build.date.utc=1379406391
ro.build.type=user
ro.build.user=dpi
ro.build.host=DELL224
ro.build.tags=release-keys
ro.product.model=GT-I9300
ro.product.brand=samsung
ro.product.name=m0xx
ro.product.device=m0
ro.product.board=smdk4x12
ro.product.cpu.abi=armeabi-v7a
ro.product.cpu.abi2=armeabi
ro.product_ship=true
ro.product.manufacturer=samsung
ro.product.locale.language=en
ro.product.locale.region=GB
ro.wifi.channels=
ro.board.platform=exynos4
```

Extracting call logs

Accessing the call logs of a phone is often required during the investigation to confirm certain events. The information about call logs is stored in the `contacts2.db` file located at `/data/data/com.android.providers.contacts/databases/`. As mentioned earlier, you can use SQLite Browser to see the data present in this file after extracting it to a local folder on the forensic workstation. As shown in the following screenshot, using the `adb pull` command, the necessary `.db` files can be extracted to a folder on the forensic workstation:

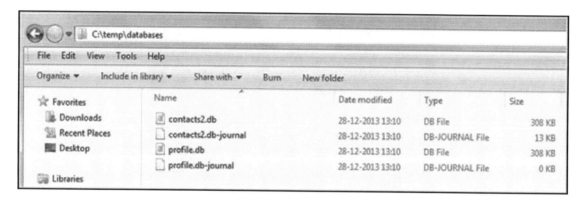

The contacts2.db file copied to a local folder

Note that applications used to make calls can store call log details in the respective application folder. All communication applications must be examined for call log details, as follows:

```
C:\android-sdk-windows\platform-tools>adb.exe pull
/data/data/com.android.providers.contacts C:temp
```

Now, open the `contacts2.db` file using SQLite Browser (by navigating to **File** | **Open Database**) and browse through the data present in different tables. The calls table present in the `contacts2.db` file provides information about the call history. The following screenshot highlights the call history along with the name, number, duration, and date:

id	number	date	duration	type	new	name
1	7777777777	1388206471836	11	2	0	Tom
2	8887775566	1388206593826	5	2	0	
3	4444444444	1388211842729	134	2	0	Robert
4	6666666666	1388211997835	4	2	0	Amy
5	9999999999	1388212023730	1	2	1	James

Extracting SMS/MMS

During the course of an investigation, a forensic examiner may be asked to retrieve the text messages that are sent by and delivered to a particular mobile device. Hence, it is important to understand where the details are stored and how to access the data. The `mmssms.db` file which is present under the `/data/data/com.android.providers.telephony/databases` location contains the necessary details. As with call logs, the examiner must ensure that applications capable of messaging are examined for relevant message logs, as follows:

```
C:\android-sdk\platform-tools>adb.exe pull /data/data/com.android.providers.telephony C:\temp
pull: building file list...
pull: /data/data/com.android.providers.telephony/databases/telephony.db-journal -> C:\temp/databases/telephony.db-journal
pull: /data/data/com.android.providers.telephony/databases/telephony.db -> C:\temp/databases/telephony.db
pull: /data/data/com.android.providers.telephony/databases/nwk_info.db-journal -> C:\temp/databases/nwk_info.db-journal
pull: /data/data/com.android.providers.telephony/databases/nwk_info.db -> C:\temp/databases/nwk_info.db
pull: /data/data/com.android.providers.telephony/databases/mmssms.db-shm -> C:\temp/databases/mmssms.db-shm
pull: /data/data/com.android.providers.telephony/databases/mmssms.db-wal -> C:\temp/databases/mmssms.db-wal
pull: /data/data/com.android.providers.telephony/databases/mmssms.db -> C:\temp/databases/mmssms.db
pull: /data/data/com.android.providers.telephony/shared_prefs/preferred-apn.xml -> C:\temp/shared_prefs/preferred-apn.xml
pull: /data/data/com.android.providers.telephony/optable.db -> C:\temp/optable.db
9 files pulled. 0 files skipped.
3096 KB/s (6193778 bytes in 1.953s)
```

The phone number can be seen under the address column and the corresponding text message can be seen under the body column, as shown in the following screenshot:

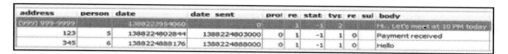

address	person	date	date sent	pro:	re	stat	tyr	re	su	body
(999) 999-9999		1388223054060		0	1	-1	2			Hi , Let's meet at 10 PM today
123	5	1388224802844	1388224803000	0	1	-1	1	0		Payment received
345	6	1388224888176	1388224888000	0	1	-1	1	0		Hello

The calls table in the contacts2.db file

Extracting browser history

Extracting browser history information is one task that is often required to be reconstructed by a forensic examiner. Apart from the default Android Browser, there are different browser applications that can be used on an Android phone, such as Firefox Mobile, Google Chrome, and so on. All of these browsers store their browser history in the SQLite .db format. For our example, we are extracting data from the default Android browser to our forensic workstation. This data is located at /data/data/com.android.browser. The file named browser2.db contains the browser history details. The following screenshot shows the browser data, as represented by **Oxygen Forensic SQLite Viewer**. Note that the trial version will hide certain information:

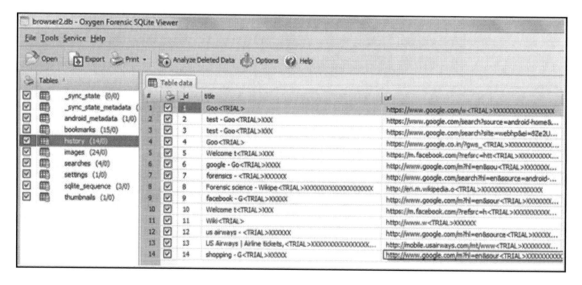

The browser2.db file in Oxygen Forensic SQLite Viewer

Analysis of social networking/IM chats

Social networking and IM chat applications such as Facebook, Twitter, and WhatsApp reveal sensitive data, which could be helpful during the investigation of any case. The analysis is pretty much the same as with any other Android applications. Download the data to a forensic workstation and analyze the `.db` files to find out if you can unearth any sensitive information. For example, let's look at the Facebook application and try to see what data can be extracted. First, we extract the `/data/data/com.facebook.katana` folder and navigate to the `databases` folder. The `fb.db` file present under this folder contains the information that is associated to the user's account. The `friends_data` table contains information about the friends' names along with their phone numbers, email IDs, and dates of birth, as shown in the following screenshot. Similarly, other files can be analyzed to find out if any sensitive information can be gathered:

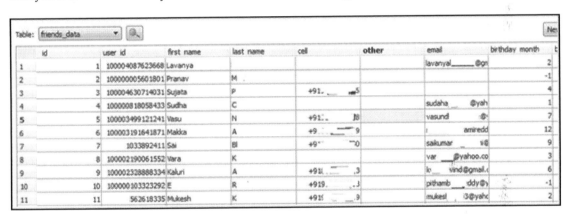

The fb.db file in SQLite browser

Similarly, by analyzing the data present in the `/data/data` folder, information about geo-location, calendar events, user notes, and more can be grabbed.

ADB backup extraction

Starting from Android 4.0, Google implemented the adb backup functionality, which allows users to back up application data to a computer using the adb tool. This process does not require root access and, hence, can be very useful during forensic examination. The main drawback is that it does not back up every application installed on the device. The backup feature is application dependent, as the owner of the application can choose to allow backups. Backups are allowed by default, but the developer can disable it if he wants to. Hence, most third-party apps have this enabled and thus, the adb backup command will work for them. Here is the syntax for the adb backup command:

```
adb backup [-f <file>] [-apk|-noapk] [-shared|-noshared] [-all] [-
system|nosystem] [<packages...>]
```

- -f: This is used to choose where the backup file will be stored. If not specified, it defaults to backup.ab in the present working directory.
- [-apk|noapk]: This is used to choose whether or not to back up the .apk file. The default is -noapk.
- [-obb|-noobb]: This is used to choose whether or not to back up the .obb (APK expansion) files. It defaults to -noobb.
- [-shared|-noshared]: This is used to choose whether or not to back up data from shared storage and the SD card. The default is -noshared.
- [-all]: This includes all applications for which backups are enabled.
- [-system|-nosystem]: This is used to choose whether or not to include system applications. It defaults to -system.
- [<packages>]: This is used to list a specific package name to be backed up.

Once the device is connected to the workstation and adb is able to access it, run the adb backup command, as shown in the following screenshot:

```
C:\android-sdk\platform-tools>adb.exe backup -shared -all
Now unlock your device and confirm the backup operation.
```

The adb backup command

Once the command is run, the user then needs to approve the permission on the device, as shown in the following screenshot. For this reason, if the device is screen locked, it's not possible to take a backup:

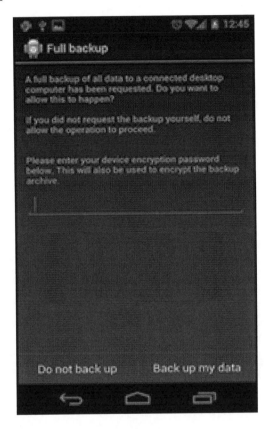

Backup permission on the device

An Android backup file is stored as an .ab file and, by default, it is stored in the platform-tools folder of the Android SDK. There are free tools, such as **Android Backup Extractor**, that can convert the .ab file into a .tar file, which can then be viewed. Android Backup Extractor can be downloaded from: https://sourceforge.net/projects/adbextractor/. This tool is a Java-based application, so ensure that Java is installed on the workstation before using the tool. To convert the backup file to .tar format, issue the following command:

```
java -jar abe.jar unpack backup.ab backup.tar
```

This will automatically create a file with the .tar extension, which can then be viewed easily using Archive tools such as WinRAR or 7Zip. However, note that if the password was entered on the device when the backup was created, the file would be encrypted and, therefore, the examiner needs to provide the password as an argument in the preceding command. The backup file contains two main folders—apps and shared. The apps folder contains all the information that is present under /data/data for the applications included in the backup. The shared folder contains all of the data present on the SD card.

ADB dumpsys extraction

The adb dumpsys command allows you to gather information about services and applications running on the system. The adb shell dumpsys command gives diagnostic output for all system services. The dumpsys command does not require root privileges to be executed and requires only USB debugging to be enabled as with any other adb command. As shown in the following screenshot, to see the list of all services that you can use with dumpsys, run the / command:

```
C:\android-sdk\platform-tools>adb.exe shell service list
Found 111 services:
0       SYSSCOPE: [com.sec.android.app.sysscope.service.ISysScopeService]
1       sip: [android.net.sip.ISipService]
2       phoneext: [com.android.internal.telephony.ITelephonyExt]
3       phone: [com.android.internal.telephony.ITelephony]
4       com.orange.authentication.simcard: [com.orange.authentication.simcard.ISimCardAuthenticationService]
5       iphonesubinfo: [com.android.internal.telephony.IPhoneSubInfo]
6       simphonebook: [com.android.internal.telephony.IIccPhoneBook]
7       isms: [com.android.internal.telephony.ISms]
8       nfc: [android.nfc.INfcAdapter]
9       FMPlayer: [com.samsung.media.fmradio.internal.IFMPlayer]
10      motion_recognition: [android.hardware.motion.IMotionRecognitionService]
11      samsung.facedetection_service: [com.sec.android.facedetection.IFaceDetectionService]
12      voip: [android.os.IVoIPInterface]
13      commontime_management: []
14      mini_mode_app_manager: [com.sec.android.app.minimode.manager.IMiniModeAppManager]
15      tvoutservice: [android.os.ITvoutService]
```

The dumpsys service list command

Analyzing certain dumpsys services, such as Wi-Fi, user, notification and so on, can be helpful in certain scenarios. Here are some of the interesting cases where running the dumpsys command could be helpful during forensic analysis:

The `dumpsys iphonesubinfo` service can be used to get information about device ID or the IMEI number, as shown in the following screenshot:

The dumpsys command showing the IMEI number

The `dumpsys wifi` service gives information about Wi-Fi points accessed by the user. It shows the SSIDs of the connections which have been saved. This information can be used to pin down the user to a particular location. Here is the `adb dumpsys` command, which gives this information:

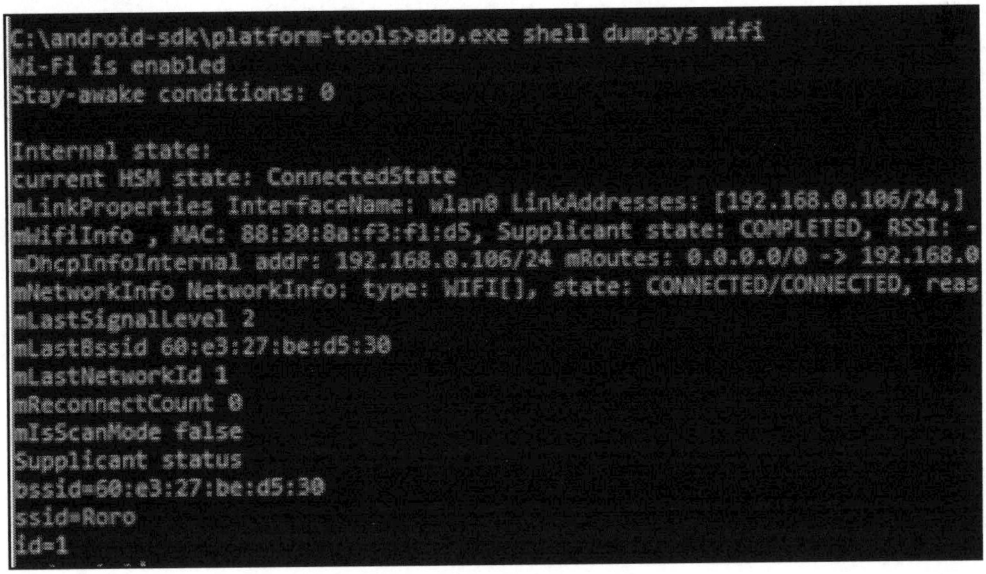

The dumpsys command showing last connected Wi-Fi details

The `dumpsys usagestats` service gives information about recently used applications, along with their date of usage. For example, the following screenshot shows that no apps were used on 02-01-2016, but on 01-31-2016, the Google Chrome browser was used and there was also an attempt to back up the phone data:

```
C:\android-sdk\platform-tools>adb.exe shell dumpsys usagestats
Date: 20160129 (old data version)
Date: 20160131
  android: 1 times, 7 ms
    com.android.server.ShutdownActivity: 1 starts
  com.android.chrome: 1 times, 172801 ms
    com.google.android.apps.chrome.Main: 1 starts
    org.chromium.chrome.browser.ChromeTabbedActivity: 1 starts, 500-750ms=1
  com.sec.android.app.launcher: 4 times, 509170 ms
    com.android.launcher2.Launcher: 4 starts, 2000-3000ms=1
  com.android.backupconfirm: 2 times, 77425 ms
    com.android.backupconfirm.BackupRestoreConfirmation: 2 starts, 500-750ms=1
Date: 20160201
  android: 0 times, 3052 ms
```

The dumpsys command showing recently used apps

Depending on the case being investigated, the forensic analyst needs to figure out if any of the `dumpsys` commands can be of use. Running a `dumpsys` command immediately after a device seizure can be extremely helpful later on. By running the `adb shell dumpsys` command, you can record all the `dumpsys` service information.

Using content providers

In Android, the data of one application cannot be accessed by another application under normal circumstances. However, Android provides a mechanism through which data can be shared with other applications. This is precisely achieved through the use of content providers. Content providers present data to external applications in the form of one or more tables. These tables are no different from the tables found in a relational database. They can be used by the applications to share data, usually through the URI addressing scheme. They are used by other applications that access the provider using a provider-client object. During the installation of an app, the user determines whether or not the app can gain access to the requested data (content providers). For instance, contacts, SMS/MMS, calendar, and so on, are examples of content providers.

Hence, by taking advantage of this, we can create an app that can grab all the information from all the available content providers. This is precisely how most commercial forensic tools work. The advantage of this method is that it can be used on both rooted and non-rooted devices. For our example, we use **AFLogical**, which takes advantage of the content provider mechanism to gain access to the information. This tool extracts the data and saves it to an SD card in CSV format. The following steps extract the information from an Android device using AFLogical Open Source Edition 1.5.2:

1. Download AFLogical OSE 1.5.2
   from: `https://github.com/nowsecure/android-forensics/downloads`.

 The AFLogical LE edition is capable of extracting a large amount of information and requires registration via forensics using an active law enforcement or government agency email. AFLogical OSE can pull all available MMSs, SMSs, contacts, and call logs.

2. Ensure that USB debugging mode is enabled and connect the device to the workstation.

3. Verify that the device is identified by issuing the following command:

```
C:\android-sdk\platform-tools>adb.exe devices
List of devices attached
4df16ac31               device
```

4. Save the AFLogical OSE app in the home directory and issue the following command to install it on the device:

```
C:\android-sdk\platform-tools>adb.exe install AFLogical-OSE_1.5.2.apk
1798 KB/s (28794 bytes in 0.015s)
        pkg: /data/local/tmp/AFLogical-OSE_1.5.2.apk
Success
```

5. Once the application is installed, you can run it directly from the device and click on the **Capture** button present at the bottom of the app, as shown in the following screenshot:

The AFLogical OSE app

6. The app starts extracting data from the respective content providers and, once the process is complete, a message will be displayed, as shown in the following screenshot:

Message displayed after the extraction is complete

7. The extracted data is saved to the SD card of the device in a directory named `forensics`. The extracted information is stored in CSV files, as shown in the following screenshot. The CSV files can be viewed using any editor:

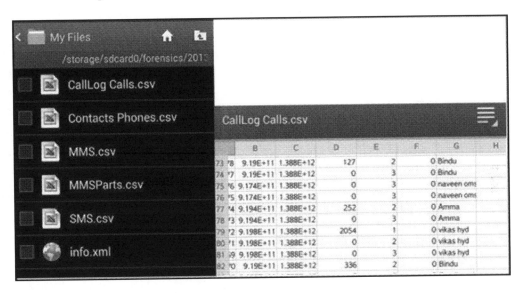

Files extracted using AFLogical OSE

8. The `info.xml` file present in the same directory provides information about the device including the IMEI number, IMSI number, Android version, information about installed applications, and so on.

However, note that third-party apps' installation should be allowed (by selecting the **Unknown Sources** option) on the device for this to work. Other tools that can help during investigation to logically extract data will be covered in `Chapter 11`, *Android App Analysis, Malware, and Reverse Engineering*.

Physical data extraction

Physical extraction refers to the process of obtaining an exact bit-by-bit image of the device. It is important to understand that a bit-by-bit image is not the same as copying and pasting the contents of the device. If we copy and paste the contents of a device, it will only copy the available files, such as visible files, hidden files, and system-related files. This method is considered as a logical image. With this method, deleted files and files that are not accessible are not copied by the copy command. Deleted files can be recovered (based on the circumstances) using certain techniques, which we will see in the following chapters. Unlike logical extraction, physical extraction is an exact copy of the device's memory and includes more information, such as the slack space, unallocated space, and so on.

Android data extraction through physical techniques is commonly performed using the dd command, while other advanced techniques such as JTAG and chip-off are also available, but are usually hard to implement and require great precision and experience to try them on real devices during the course of an investigation. JTAG and chip-off techniques are covered in detail in the following sections. However, extracting data through the dd command requires root access. The following sections provide an overview of various techniques which can be used to perform physical extraction.

Imaging an Android phone

Imaging a device is one of the most important steps in mobile device forensics. When possible, it's imperative to obtain a physical image of the Android device before performing any techniques to extract the data directly from the device. In forensics, this process of obtaining a physical acquisition is commonly called **imaging the device**. The terms physical image, forensic image, or raw image are often used to refer to the image captured through this process. Let's first revisit how imaging is done on a desktop computer as it helps us to correlate and realize the problems associated with imaging Android devices. Let's assume that a desktop computer, which is not powered on, is seized from a suspect and sent for forensic examination. In this case, a typical forensic examiner would remove the hard disk, connect it to a write blocker and obtain a bit-by-bit forensic image using any of the available tools. The original hard disk is then safely protected during the forensic imaging of the data.

With an Android device, all the areas that contain data cannot be easily removed. Also, if the device is active at the time of receiving it for examination, it is not possible to analyze the device without making any changes to it, because any interaction would change the state of the device.

An Android device may have two file storage areas: internal and external storage. Internal storage refers to the built-in non-volatile memory. External storage refers to the removable storage medium, such as a micro SD card. However, it's important to note that some devices do not have a removable storage medium such as an SD card, but they divide the available permanent storage space into internal and external storage. Hence, it's not always true that external storage is something that is removable. When a removable SD card is present, a forensic image of the memory card has to be obtained. As discussed in Chapter 7, *Understanding Android*, these removable cards are generally formatted with the FAT 32 file system. Some mobile device acquisition methods will acquire the SD card through the Android device. This process, while useful, will be slow due to the speed limitations of the USB phone cables.

Android, by default, does not provide access to the internal directories and system-related files. This restricted access is to ensure the security of the device. For instance, the /data/data folder is not accessible on a non-rooted device. This folder is especially of interest to us, because it stores most of the user-created data and many applications write valuable data into this folder. Hence, to obtain an image of the device, we need to root the Android device. Rooting a device gives us superuser privileges and access to all the data. It is important to realize that this book has been stressing that all the steps taken should be forensically sound and should not make changes to the device whenever possible. Rooting an Android device will make changes to it and should be tested on any device that the examiner has not previously investigated. Rooting is common for Android devices, but getting root access could alter the device in a manner that renders the data changed or worse yet-wiped. Some Android devices, such as the Nexus 4 and 5, may force the data partition to be wiped prior to allowing root access. This negates the need to root the device in order to gain access because all the user data is lost during the process. Just remember that, while rooting provides access to more data when successfully done, it can also wipe the data or destroy the phone. Hence, you must ensure that you have consent or legal rights to manipulate the Android device prior to proceeding with the root. As rooting techniques have been discussed in Chapter 8, *Android Forensic Setup and Pre-Data Extraction Techniques*, we will proceed with the example assuming that the device is rooted.

The following is a step-by-step process to obtain a forensic image of a rooted Android device:

1. Connect the Android device to the workstation and verify that the device is identified by issuing the adb devices command, as shown here:

2. Once the adb access is ready, the partitions can be acquired from the Android device using the following steps:

- **Using the dd command**: The dd command can be used to create a raw image of the device. This command helps us create a bit-by-bit image of the Android device by copying low-level data.

- **Inserting a new SD card**: Insert a new SD card into the device in order to copy the image file to this card. Make sure that this SD card is wiped and does not contain any other data.

- **Executing the command**: The file system of an Android device is stored in different locations within the /dev partition. A simple mount command on a Samsung Galaxy S3 phone returns the following output:

```
root@android:/ # mount
rootfs / rootfs ro,relatime 0 0
tmpfs /dev tmpfs rw,nosuid,relatime,mode=755 0 0
devpts /dev/pts devpts rw,relatime,mode=600 0 0
proc /proc proc rw,relatime 0 0
sysfs /sys sysfs rw,relatime 0 0
none /acct cgroup rw,relatime,cpuacct 0 0
tmpfs /mnt/asec tmpfs rw,relatime,mode=755,gid=1000 0 0
tmpfs /mnt/obb tmpfs rw,relatime,mode=755,gid=1000 0 0
none /dev/cpuctl cgroup rw,relatime,cpu 0 0
/dev/block/mmcblk0p9 /system ext4 ro,noatime,barrier=1,data=ordered 0 0
/dev/block/mmcblk0p3 /efs ext4 rw,nosuid,nodev,noatime,barrier=1,journal_asyn
/dev/block/mmcblk0p8 /cache ext4 rw,nosuid,nodev,noatime,errors=panic,barrier
/dev/block/mmcblk0p12 /data ext4 rw,nosuid,nodev,noatime,barrier=1,journal_as
/sys/kernel/debug /sys/kernel/debug debugfs rw,relatime 0 0
/dev/fuse /storage/sdcard0 fuse rw,nosuid,nodev,noexec,relatime,user_id=1023
```

3. From the preceding output, we can identify the blocks where the /system, /data, and /cache partitions are mounted. Although it's important to image all the files, most of the data is present in the /data and /system partitions. When time allows, all partitions should be acquired for completeness. Once this is done, execute the following command to image the device:

```
dd if=/dev/block/mmcblk0p12 of=/sdcard/tmp.image
```

In the preceding example, the data partition of a Samsung Galaxy S III was used (where if is the input file and of is the output file).

The preceding command will make a bit-by-bit image of the mmcblk0p12 file (data partition) and copy the image file to an SD card. Once this is done, the dd image file can be analyzed using the available forensic software.

The examiner must ensure that the SD card has enough storage space to contain the data partition image. Other methods are available to acquire data from the rooted devices.

If the image cannot be written to the SD card directly, the examiner can use `netcat` command to write the output directly to the machine. The `netcat` tool is a Linux-based tool used for transferring data over a network connection. Android devices do not usually come with `netcat` installed. To check, simply open the ADB shell and type `nc`. If it returns saying nc is not found, `netcat` will have to be installed manually on the device. You can download the `netcat` compiled for Android at: `https://sourceforge.net/projects/androidforensics-netcat/files/`. Push `netcat` on to the device using the following command on the examiner's computer:

```
adb push nc /dev/Case_Folder/nc
```

The command should have created the `Case_Folder` in `/dev` and `nc` should be in it. Now, we need to give it permission to execute from the ADB shell. This can be done as follows:

```
chomd +x /dev/Case_Folder/nc
```

Open two terminal windows with the ADB shell open in one of them. The other will be used to listen to the data being sent from the device. Now, we need to enable port forwarding over ADB from the examiner's computer:

```
adb forward tcp:9999 tcp:9999
```

`9999` is the port we chose to use for `netcat`; it can be any arbitrary port number between `1023` and `65535` on a Linux or Mac system (`1023` and below are reserved for system processes and require root permission to use). In the other terminal window, run the following:

```
nc 127.0.0.1 9999 > data_partition.img
```

The `data_partition.img` file should now be created in the current directory of the examiner's computer. When the data is finished transferring, `netcat` in both terminals will terminate and return to the command prompt. The process can take a significant amount of time depending on the size of the image.

Imaging a memory (SD) card

There are many tools available that can image a memory card. The following example uses **WinHex** to create a raw disk image of the SD card. The following is a step-by-step process with which to image a memory card using WinHex:

- **Connecting the memory card**: Remove the SD card from the memory slot and use a card reader to connect the memory card to the forensic workstation.

- **Write protect the card**: Open the disk using WinHex. Navigate to **Options | Edit Mode** and select **Read-only mode=(write-protected mode),** as shown in the following screenshot. This is to make sure that the device is write protected and no data can be written on it:

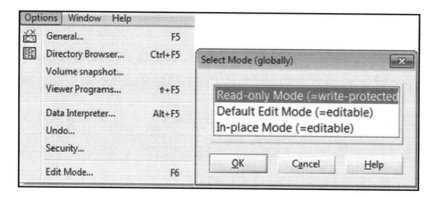

WinHex view of Edit Mode (left) and WinHex Read-only Mode enabled (right)

- **Calculating the hash value**: Calculate the hash value of the memory card to make sure that no changes are made at any point during the investigation. Navigate to **Tools | Compute hash** and choose any hashing algorithm.

- **Creating the image of the disk**: Navigate to **File** | **Create Disk Image**, as shown in the following screenshot. Select the raw image option (.dd) to create an image. This completes the imaging of the memory card:

The WinHex disk image option

Once a forensic image is obtained using any of the methods described previously, it needs to be analyzed to extract the relevant information. There are several commercial tools, such as Cellebrite, XRY, and so on, that can analyze the image files. Analyzing Android images is covered in detail in `Chapter 10`, *Android Data Analysis and Recovery*.

Joint Test Action Group

Joint Test Action Group (**JTAG**) involves using advanced data acquisition methods, which involve connecting to specific ports on the device and instructing the processor to transfer the data stored on the device. Using this method, a full physical image of a device can be acquired. It is always recommended to first try out the other techniques mentioned earlier, as they are easy to implement and require less effort. Examiners must have proper training and experience prior to attempting JTAG, as the device may be damaged if handled improperly.

The JTAG process usually involves the following forensic steps:

- In JTAG, the device **Test Access Ports** (**TAPs**) are used to access the CPU of the device. Identifying the TAPs is the primary and most important step. TAPs are identified and the connection is traced to the CPU to find out which pad is responsible for each function. Although device manufacturers document resources about the JTAG schematics of a particular device, they are not released for general viewing. A good site for JTAG on an Android device is: `http://www.forensicswiki.org/wiki/JTAG_Forensics`.

- Wire leads are then soldered to appropriate connector pins and the other end is connected to the device that can control the CPU, as shown in the following image (published by `http://www.binaryintel.com/`). JTAG jigs can be used to forgo soldering for certain devices. The use of a jig or JTAG adapter negates the need to solder, as it connects the TAPs to the CPU:

The JTAG setup

- Once the preceding steps are complete, power must be applied to boot the CPU. The voltage that must be applied depends on the specifications released by the hardware manufacturer. Do not apply a voltage beyond the number given in the specification.
- After applying the power, a full binary memory dump of the NAND flash can be extracted.
- Analyze the extracted data using the forensic techniques and tools learned in this book. A raw .bin file will be obtained during the acquisition; most forensic tools support ingestion and analysis of this image format.

JTAG may sound complicated (perhaps it is), but it serves many useful purposes and three advantages are listed here:

- The main advantage with this technique is that it works even if the device is not powered on
- It does not require root, ADB, or USB debugging
- It can be used to recover device PINs/passwords and so can image the entire flash memory and recover/crack password files

It is also important to understand that the JTAG technique should not result in the loss of functionality of the device. If reassembled properly, the device should function without any problems. Although the JTAG technique is effective in extracting the data, only experienced and qualified personnel should attempt it. Any error in soldering the JTAG pads or applying the wrong voltage could severely damage the device.

Chip-off

Chip-off, as the name suggests, is a technique where the NAND flash chips are removed from the device and examined to extract the information. Hence, this technique will work even when the device is passcode-protected and USB debugging is not enabled. Unlike the JTAG technique, where the device functions normally after examination, the chip-off technique usually results in destruction of the device, that is, it is more difficult to reattach the NAND flash to the device after examination. The process of reattaching the NAND flash to the device is called **re-balling** and requires training and practice.

Chip-off techniques usually involve the following forensic steps:

- All of the chips on the device must be researched to determine which chip contains user data.
- Once determined, the NAND flash is physically removed from the device. This can be done by applying heat to desolder the chip (published by `http://www.binaryintel.com/`).
- This is a very delicate process and must be done with great care, as it may result in damaging the NAND flash.
- The chip is then cleaned and repaired to make sure that the connectors are present and functioning.

- Using specialized hardware device adapters, the chip can now be read. This is done by inserting the chip into the hardware device, which supports the specific NAND flash chip. In this process, raw data is acquired from the chip, resulting in a `.bin` file.

- The data acquired can now be analyzed using forensic techniques and the tools described earlier.

The chip-off technique is most helpful when the device is damaged severely, locked, or otherwise inaccessible. However, the application of this technique requires not only expertise, but also costly equipment and tools. There is always a risk of damaging the NAND flash while removing it and, hence, it is recommended to try out the logical techniques first to extract any data.

While root access is a must to perform any of the techniques discussed earlier, it must be noted here that at the time of writing this book, none of these techniques would work on devices which have **Full Disk Encryption (FDE)** enabled. As discussed in `Chapter 7`, *Understanding Android*, Google has mandated the use of FDE for most devices starting from Android 6.0. Although some techniques were demonstrated and published for decrypting full disk encryption, they are device-specific and are not widely applicable.

Summary

Extracting data from an Android device is one of the crucial steps during the course of an investigation. Once the device is accessible, an examiner can extract the data using manual, logical, or physical data extraction techniques. Logical techniques extract the data by interacting with the device using tools such as ADB. Physical techniques, on the other hand, access a larger set of data; they are complex and require a great deal of expertise to perform. Imaging a device produces a bit-by-bit image of the device, which is later analyzed using tools. Imaging a device is one of the primary steps to ensure that the data on the device is not modified.

In the next chapter, we will see how to extract relevant data such as call logs, text messages, browsing history, and so on from an image file. We will also cover data recovery techniques, using which we can recover the data deleted from a device.

10
Android Data Analysis and Recovery

In the previous chapter, we covered various logical and physical extraction techniques. In physical extraction, a bit-by-bit image of the Android device is obtained, which contains valuable information. In this chapter, we will learn how to analyze and extract relevant data, such as call logs, text messages, and so on, from an image file. While the data extraction and analysis techniques provide information about various details, not all techniques can provide information about the deleted data. Data recovery is a crucial aspect of mobile forensics, as it helps to unearth the deleted items. This chapter aims at covering various techniques, which can be used by a forensic analyst to recover the data from an Android device.

In this chapter, we will cover the following two major topics:

- Analyzing and extracting data from Android image files using the open source tool, **Autopsy**
- Various techniques to recover deleted files from the SD card and internal memory

Analyzing an Android image

The term **Android image** refers to the physical image (also called forensic image or raw image) that is obtained by performing any of the physical data extraction techniques. Using the techniques explained in `Chapter 9`, *Android Data Extraction Techniques*, you can image the entire `/data/data` block, or any particular block that is of relevance to the investigation. Once the image is obtained, an investigator can manually go through the contents of the file or take advantage of the available tools to parse through the contents. Commercial tools, such as Cellebrite, XRY, and so on, can drill into the data and present a comprehensive picture of the contents. Autopsy is one of the very widely used open source tools in the forensics world that performs an excellent job of analyzing an Android image.

Autopsy

Autopsy is a forensic platform and acts as a GUI for the Sleuth Kit. It is available for free; you can download it at: `http://www.sleuthkit.org/`. The Sleuth Kit is a collection of UNIX and Windows-based tools and utilities, which are used to perform forensic analysis. Autopsy displays the results by forensically analyzing a given volume, and thereby helps investigators focus on relevant sections of the data. Autopsy is free, extensible, and has several modules that can be plugged in. Autopsy can be used to load and analyze an Android image that is obtained after physical extraction.

Adding an image to Autopsy

Once you have downloaded and installed Autopsy, follow these steps to add an image to Autopsy:

1. Open the Autopsy tool and select the **Create New Case** option, as shown in following screenshot:

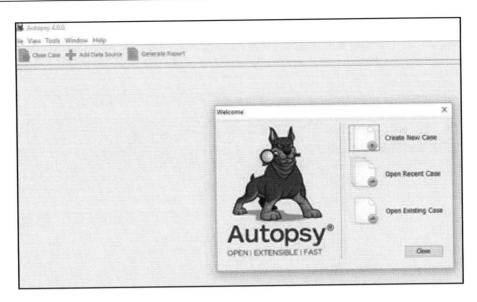

Creating new case in Autopsy

2. Enter all the necessary case details, including the name of the case, the location where data needs to be stored, and so on, as shown in the following screenshot:

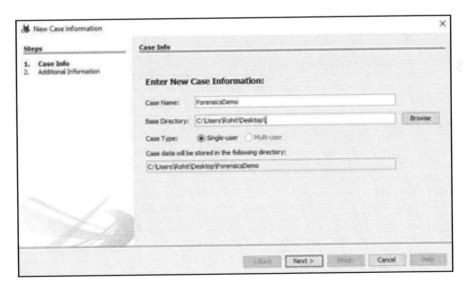

Entering case information in Autopsy

3. Enter the case number and examiner details, and click on **Finish**.

4. Now, click on the **Add Data Source** button, add the image file to be analyzed, and click on **Next**:

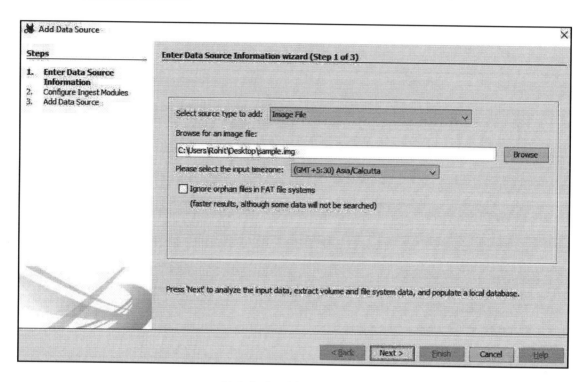

Entering Data Source information in Autopsy

5. On the next screen, you can configure what modules have to be run on the images, as shown in the following screenshot. It is recommended to select the **Recent Activity**, **Exif Parser**, **Keyword Search**, and **Android Analyzer** modules. In the next step, click on **Finish**:

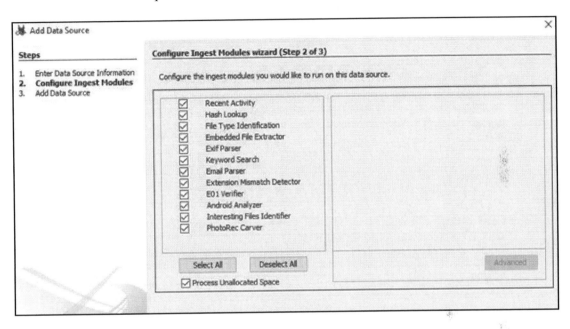

Configuring modules in Autopsy

Once this is done, the tool usually takes a few minutes to parse through the image depending on its size. During this time, you might see some errors or warning messages if any are encountered by the tool. However, Autopsy provides the fastest access to the artifacts and the file system when compared to other tools.

Analyzing an image using Autopsy

Once the image is loaded, expand the file present under **Data Sources** to see data present in the image. For example, the following screenshot shows the contents of the /data/data folder:

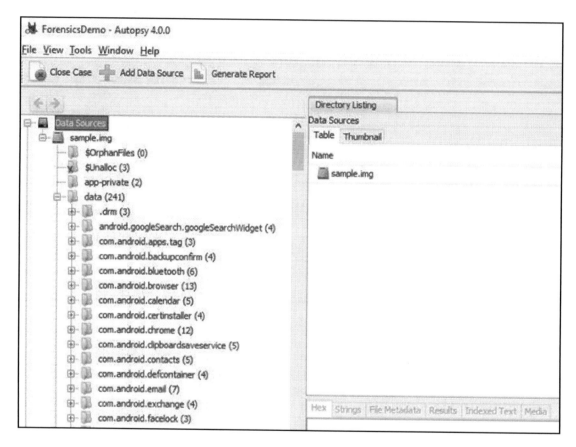

Analyzing an image in Autopsy

In the preceding example, only the /data portion of the device has been imaged. If the entire device is imaged, then the tool would show more volumes. Depending on the underlying details of the investigation, relevant portions need to be analyzed. In the following example, by examining the folders present under com.android.browser, we can extract the list of various sites visited by the user along with their dates:

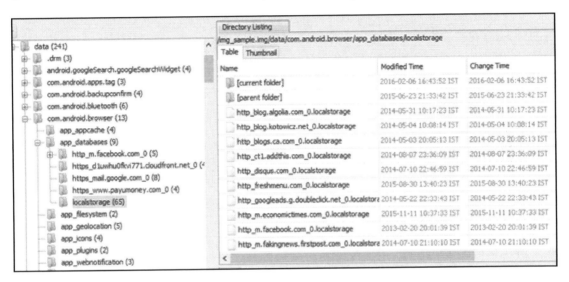

Analyzing browsing details in Autopsy

Valuable data, such as text messages, browsing history, chats, call history, pictures, videos, location details, and so on, could be unearthed by analyzing the data present under various sections.

Android data recovery

Data recovery is one of the most significant and powerful aspects of forensic analysis. The ability to recover deleted data can be crucial to crack many civil and criminal cases. From a normal user's point of view, recovering data that has been deleted would usually refer to the operating system's built-in solutions, such as the Recycle Bin in Windows. While it's true that data can be recovered from these locations, due to an increase in user awareness, these options don't often work. For instance, on a desktop computer, people now use *Shift + Delete* as a way to delete a file completely from their desktop.

Data recovery is the process of retrieving deleted data from a device when it cannot be accessed normally. Consider the scenario where a mobile phone has been seized from a terrorist. Wouldn't it be of the greatest importance to know which items were deleted by the terrorist? Access to any deleted SMS messages, pictures, dialed numbers, application data, and more can be of critical importance, as they often reveal sensitive information. With Android, it is possible to recover most of the deleted data if the device files are properly acquired. However, if proper care is not taken while handling the device, the deleted data could be lost forever. To ensure that the deleted data is not overwritten, it is recommended to keep the following points in mind:

- Do not use the phone for any activity after seizing it. The deleted data exists on the device until the space is needed by some other incoming data. Hence, the phone must not be used for any sort of activity to prevent the data from being overwritten.
- Even when the phone is not used, without any intervention from our end, data can be overwritten. For instance, an incoming SMS would automatically occupy space, which could overwrite the data marked for deletion. To prevent occurrence of such events, the examiner should follow the forensic handling methods described in the previous chapters. The easiest solution is to place the device in airplane mode or disable all connectivity options on the device. This prevents the delivery of any new messages.

All Android file systems have metadata that contains information about the hierarchy of files, filenames, and so on. Deletion will not really erase this data but remove the file system metadata. When text messages or any other files are deleted from the device, they are just made invisible to the user, but the files are still present on the device. Essentially, the files are simply marked for deletion, but they reside on the file system until being overwritten. Recovering deleted data from an Android device involves two scenarios: recovering data that is deleted from the SD card, such as pictures, videos, application data, and more, and recovering data that is deleted from the internal memory of the device. The following sections cover the techniques that can be used to recover deleted data from both the SD card and the internal memory of the Android device.

Recovering deleted data from an external SD card

Data present on SD cards can reveal a lot of information to forensic investigators. SD cards are capable of storing pictures and videos taken by the phone's camera, voice recordings, application data, cached files, and more. Essentially, anything that can be stored on a computer hard drive can be stored on an SD card as much as the available space allows.

Recovering the deleted data from an external SD card is a straightforward process. SD cards can be mounted as an external mass storage device and forensically acquired using standard digital forensic methods, as discussed in Chapter 9, *Android Data Extraction Techniques*. As mentioned in the previous chapters, SD cards in Android devices often use the FAT32 file system. The main reason for this is that the FAT32 file system is widely supported in most operating systems, including Windows, Linux, and macOS X. The maximum file size on a FAT32 formatted drive is around 4 GB. With increasingly high-resolution formats now available, this limit is commonly reached. Apart from this, FAT32 can be used on partitions that are less than 32 GB in size. Hence, the exFAT file system, which overcomes these problems, is now being used in some of the devices.

Recovering the deleted data from an external SD card can be easily accomplished if it can be mounted as a drive. Hence, if the SD card is removable, connect it to a workstation using a write blocker for acquisition. However, the latest Android devices do not usually mount as a mass storage. This is because these devices use MTP or PTP protocols instead of USB mass storage. The problem with USB mass storage is that the computer would need exclusive access to the storage. In other words, the external storage needs to be completely disconnected from the Android OS when it is connected to a workstation. This has led to several other complications with respect to mobile apps. When an Android device uses MTP, it appears to the computer as a media device and not as **Removable Storage**, as shown in the following screenshot:

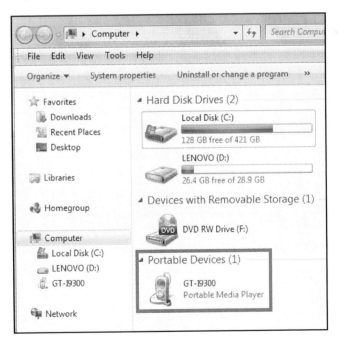

But, the normal data recovery tools would need a mount drive in order to perform a scan. Hence, most of the latest devices which use MTP/PTP are not treated as a mount drive, and so the traditional data recovery tools which work for computers do not work on them.

For this reason, when the device uses MTP/PTP and is not mounted as a drive, the recovery can be done by certain Android-specific data recovery tools which need USB debugging option to be turned on. Almost all the Android data recovery tools in the market need you to enable USB debugging so that your device and the SD card can be recognized before starting Android data recovery.

Examiners must understand that Android devices might use space on the SD card to cache application data; therefore, it is important to make sure that as much data as possible is obtained from the device prior to removing the SD card. Some older devices automatically mount the device as a drive when connected through USB. It is a sound forensic practice to not work directly on the device for the purpose of data extraction, data recovery, and so on. Hence, a physical image of the SD card needs to be taken and all required analysis is performed on the image itself. It is recommended to acquire the SD card through the device as well as separately to ensure that all data is obtained. To achieve the SD card image, dd through adb can be used while the device is running to obtain an image of the SD card of the device if the device cannot be powered off due to possible evidence running in the memory. If the SD card is removed and connected to the workstation through a card reader, it appears as external mass storage which can then be imaged using the standard forensic techniques described in earlier chapters.

Once the image is obtained, it can be analyzed using any standard forensic tools, such as FTK Imager. FTK Imager is a simple tool that can be used to create and analyze disk images.

It is available for download
at: https://accessdata.com/product-download/ftk-imager-version-3.2.0.

The following is a step-by-step process to recover the deleted files from an SD card image using FTK Imager:

1. Start FTK Imager and click on **File**, then click on **Add Evidence Item...** in the menu:

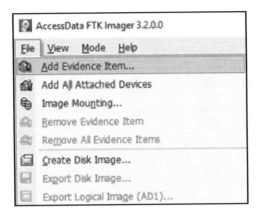

Adding evidence in FTK Imager

2. Select **Image File** as the evidence type in the **Select Source** dialog, and click on **Next**:

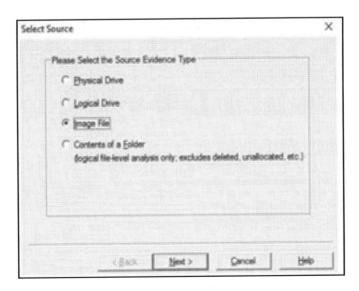

Selecting File Type in FTK Imager

3. In the **Select File** dialog, go to the location where the `SDCARD.dd` SD card image file is present, select it, and click on **Finish**:

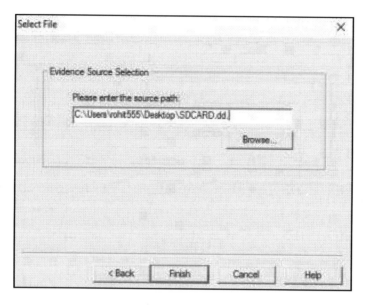

Selecting the image file for analysis in FTK Imager

4. The contents of the SD card image are then shown in the **View** pane. You can browse through the folders by clicking on the + sign. When a folder is highlighted, the contents are shown on the right pane. When a file is selected, its contents can be seen in the bottom pane. As shown in the following screenshot, the deleted files are also shown with a red X over the icon:

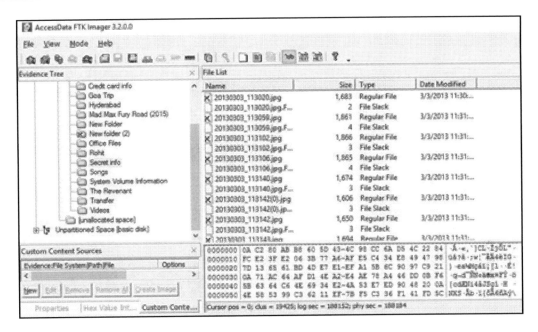

Deleted files shown with a red cross over the icons in FTK Imager

5. To copy the deleted files to the workstation, right-click on the marked file and select **Export Files...**, as shown in the following screenshot:

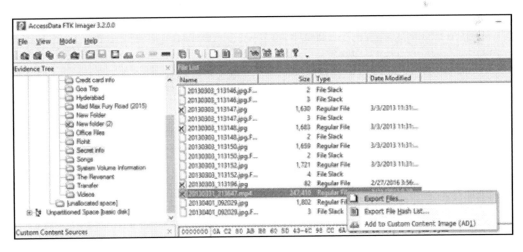

Recovering deleted images in FTK Imager

It is also recommended to check whether the device has any backup applications or files installed. The initial release of Android did not include a mechanism for users to back up their personal data. Hence, several backup applications were used extensively by users. Using these apps, users have the ability to back up their data either to the SD card or to the cloud. For example, the **Super Backup** app contains the options to back up call logs, contacts, SMS, and more, as shown in the following screenshot:

The Super Backup Android app

Upon detection of a backup application, the forensic examiners must attempt to determine where the data is stored. Usually, the backup folder path is the internal SD card. The folder path is also present in the backup app's settings. The data saved in a backup may contain important information, and thus, looking for any third-party backup app on the device would be very helpful.

Recovering data deleted from internal memory

Recovering files that are deleted from Android's internal memory (such as SMS, contacts, app data, and more) is not supported by all analytical tools and may require manual carving. Unlike some media containing common file systems, such as SD cards, the file system may not be recognized and mounted by forensic tools. Also, the examiner cannot get access to the raw partitions of the internal memory of an Android phone unless the phone is rooted. The following are some of the other issues that the examiner may face when attempting to recover data from the internal memory on Android devices:

- To get access to the internal memory, you can try to root the phone. However, the rooting process might involve writing some data to the /data partition, and this process could overwrite the data of value on the device.
- Unlike SD cards, the internal file system here is not FAT32 (which is widely supported by forensic tools). The internal file system could be YAFFS2 (in older devices), EXT3, EXT4, RFS, or something proprietary built to run on Android. Therefore, many of the recovery tools designed for use with Windows file systems won't work.
- Application data on Android devices is commonly stored in the SQLite format. While most forensic tools provide access to the database files, they may have to be exported and viewed in a native browser. The examiner must examine the raw data to ensure that the deleted data is not overlooked by the forensic tool.

The discussed reasons make it difficult, but not impossible, to recover the deleted data from the internal memory. The internal memory of Android devices holds a bulk of the user data and the possible keys to your investigation. As previously mentioned, the device must be rooted in order to access the raw partitions. Most of the Android recovery tools on the market do not highlight the fact that they only work on rooted phones. Let's now take a look at how we can recover deleted data from an Android phone.

Recovering deleted files by parsing SQLite files

Android uses SQLite files to store most data. Data related to text messages, emails, and certain app data is stored in SQLite files. SQLite databases can store deleted data within the database itself. Files marked for deletion by the user no longer appear in the active SQLite database files. Therefore, it is possible to recover the deleted data, such as text messages, contacts, and more. There are two areas within a SQLite page that can contain deleted data-- unallocated blocks and free blocks.

Most of the commercial tools that recover deleted data scan the unallocated blocks and free blocks of the SQLite pages. Parsing the deleted data can be done using the available forensic tools, such as **Oxygen Forensics SQLite Viewer**. The trial version of the SQLite Viewer can be used for this purpose; however, there are certain limitations on the amount of data that you can recover. You can write your own script to parse the files for deleted content, and for this, you need to have a good understanding of the SQLite file format. The link `http://www.sqlite.org/fileformat.html` is a good place to start. If you do not want to reinvent and want to reuse the existing scripts, you can try the available open source Python scripts (`http://az4n6.blogspot.in/2013/11/python-parser-to-recover-deleted-sqlite.html`) to parse the SQLite files for deleted records.

For our example, we will recover deleted SMSs from an Android device. Recovering deleted SMSs from an Android phone is quite often requested as part of forensic analysis on a device, mainly because text messages contain data, which can reveal a lot of information. There are different ways to recover deleted text messages on an Android device. First, we need to understand where the messages are being stored on the device. In Chapter 9, *Android Data Extraction Techniques*, we explained the important locations on the Android device where user data is stored. Here is a quick recap of this:

- Every application stores its data under the /data/data folder (again, this requires root access to acquire data)
- The files under the location, /data/data/com.android.providers.telephony/databases, contain details about the SMS/MMS

Under the mentioned locations, text messages are stored in an SQLite database file, which is named mmssms.db. Deleted text messages can be recovered by examining this file. Here are the steps to recover deleted SMSs using the mmssms.db file:

1. On the Android device, enable the USB debugging mode and connect the device to the forensic workstation. Using the adb command-line tool, extract the databases folder present at /data/data/ by issuing the adb pull command:

```
C:\android-sdk\platform-tools>adb.exe pull /data/data/com.android.providers.telephony/databases C:\temp
pull: building file list...
pull: /data/data/com.android.providers.telephony/databases/telephony.db-journal -> C:\temp/telephony.db-journal
pull: /data/data/com.android.providers.telephony/databases/telephony.db -> C:\temp/telephony.db
pull: /data/data/com.android.providers.telephony/databases/nwk_info.db-journal -> C:\temp/nwk_info.db-journal
pull: /data/data/com.android.providers.telephony/databases/nwk_info.db -> C:\temp/nwk_info.db
pull: /data/data/com.android.providers.telephony/databases/mmssms.db-shm -> C:\temp/mmssms.db-shm
pull: /data/data/com.android.providers.telephony/databases/mmssms.db-wal -> C:\temp/mmssms.db-wal
pull: /data/data/com.android.providers.telephony/databases/mmssms.db -> C:\temp/mmssms.db
7 files pulled. 0 files skipped.
3242 KB/s (6177288 bytes in 1.860s)
```

Once the files are extracted to the local machine, use the Oxygen Forensics SQLite Viewer tool to open the `mmssms.db` file.

2. Click on the table named `sms` and observe the current message under the **Tables** data tab in the tool.

3. One way to view the deleted data is by clicking on the **Blocks containing deleted data** tab, as shown in the following screenshot:

Recovering deleted SMS messages

Similarly, other data residing on Android devices that store data in SQLite files can be recovered by parsing for deleted content. When the preceding method doesn't provide access to the deleted data, the examiner should look at the file in raw hex file for data marked as deleted, which can be manually carved and reported.

Recovering files using file-carving techniques

File carving is an extremely useful method in forensics because it allows data that has been deleted or hidden to be recovered for analysis. In simple terms, file carving is the process of reassembling computer files from fragments in the absence of file system metadata. In file carving, specified file types are searched for and extracted across the binary data to create a forensic image of a partition or an entire disk. File carving recovers files from the unallocated space in a drive based merely on file structure and content without any matching file system metadata. Unallocated space refers to the part of the drive that no longer holds any file information indicated by the file system structures, such as the file table.

Files can be recovered or reconstructed by scanning the raw bytes of the disk and reassembling them. This can be done by examining the header (the first few bytes) and footer (the last few bytes) of a file.

File carving methods are categorized based on the underlying technique in use. The header-footer carving method relies on recovering the files based on their header and footer information. For instance, for JPEG files that start with 0xffd8 and end with 0xffd9. The locations of the header and footer are identified and everything between those two endpoints is carved. Similarly, the carving method based on the file structure uses the internal layout of a file to reconstruct the file. However, the traditional file-carving techniques, such as the ones that we've already explained, may not work if the data is fragmented. To overcome this, new techniques, such as smart carving, use the fragmentation characteristics of several popular file systems to recover the data.

Once the phone is imaged, it can be analyzed using tools, such as **Scalpel**. Scalpel is a powerful open source utility to carve files. This tool analyzes the block database storage, identifies the deleted files, and recovers them. Scalpel is file-system independent and is known to work on various file systems, including FAT, NTFS, EXT2, EXT3, HFS, and more. More details about Scalpel can be found at: `https://github.com/sleuthkit/scalpel`. The following steps explain how to use Scalpel on an Ubuntu workstation:

1. Install Scalpel on the Ubuntu workstation using the `sudo apt-get install scalpel` command.

2. The `scalpel.conf` file present under the `/etc/scalpel` directory contains information about the supported file types, as shown in the following screenshot:

```
scalpel.conf ✕
# GRAPHICS FILES
#--------------------------------------------------------------------------
#
#
# AOL ART files
#       art       y       150000    \x4a\x47\x04\x0e            \xcf\xc7\xcb
#       art       y       150000    \x4a\x47\x03\x0e            \xd0\xcb\x00\x00
#
# GIF and JPG files (very common)
#       gif       y       5000000   \x47\x49\x46\x38\x37\x61         \x00\x3b
#       gif       y       5000000   \x47\x49\x46\x38\x39\x61         \x00\x3b
# █     jpg       y       200000000 \xff\xd8\xff\xe0\x00\x10         \xff\xd9
#
#
# PNG
#       png       y       20000000  \x50\x4e\x47?   \xff\xfc\xfd\xfe
#
#
# BMP    (used by MSWindows, use only if you have reason to think there are
#        BMP files worth digging for. This often kicks back a lot of false
#        positives
```

The scalpel configuration file

This file needs to be modified in order to mention the files that are related to Android. A sample `scalpel.conf` file can be downloaded from: `https://www.nowsecure.com/tools-and-trainings/#viaforensics`. You can also uncomment the files and save the `conf` file to select file types of your choice. Once this is done, replace the original `conf` file with the one that is downloaded.

3. Scalpel needs to be run along with the preceding configuration file on the dd image being examined. You can run the tool using the command shown in the following screenshot by inputting the configuration file and the dd file. Once this command is run, the tool starts to carve the files and build them accordingly:

```
unigeek@ubuntu:~$ scalpel -c /home/unigeek/Desktop/scalpel-android.conf /home/un
igeek/Desktop/userdata.dd -o /home/unigeek/Desktop/rohit
Scalpel version 1.60
Written by Golden G. Richard III, based on Foremost 0.69.

Opening target "/home/unigeek/Desktop/userdata.dd"

Image file pass 1/2.
/home/unigeek/Desktop/userdata.dd: 100.0% |**************|    3.9 MB    00:00 ETA
Allocating work queues...
Work queues allocation complete. Building carve lists...
Carve lists built.  Workload:
gif with header "\x47\x49\x46\x38\x37\x61" and footer "\x00\x3b" --> 0 files
gif with header "\x47\x49\x46\x38\x39\x61" and footer "\x00\x3b" --> 2 files
jpg with header "\xff\xd8\xff\xe0\x00\x10" and footer "\xff\xd9" --> 71 files
jpg with header "\xff\xd8\xff\xe1" and footer "\x7f\xff\xd9" --> 1 files
png with header "\x50\x4e\x47\x3f" and footer "\xff\xfc\xfd\xfe" --> 0 files
png with header "\x89\x50\x4e\x47" and footer "" --> 71 files
sqlitedb with header "\x53\x51\x4c\x69\x74\x65\x20\x66\x6f\x72\x6d\x61\x74" and
footer "" --> 0 files
email with header "\x46\x72\x6f\x6d\x3a" and footer "" --> 0 files
doc with header "\xd0\xcf\x11\xe0\xa1\xb1\x1a\xe1\x60\x00" and footer "\xd0\xcf\
x11\xe0\xa1\xb1\x1a\xe1\x00\x00" --> 0 files
doc with header "\xd0\xcf\x11\xe0\xa1\xb1" and footer "" --> 0 files
htm with header "\x3c\x68\x74\x6d\x6c" and footer "\x3c\x2f\x68\x74\x6d\x6c\x3e"
 --> 1 files
pdf with header "\x25\x50\x44\x46" and footer "\x25\x45\x4f\x46\x0d" --> 0 files
pdf with header "\x25\x50\x44\x46" and footer "\x25\x45\x4f\x46\x0a" --> 0 files
wav with header "\x52\x49\x46\x46\x3f\x3f\x3f\x3f\x57\x41\x56\x45" and footer ""
 --> 0 files
amr with header "\x23\x21\x41\x4d\x52" and footer "" --> 0 files
```

Running the Scalpel tool on a dd file

4. The `output` folder that was specified in the preceding command now contains lists of folders that are based on the file types, as shown in the following screenshot. Each of these folders contains data that is based on the folder name. For instance, `jpg 2-0` contains files related to the .jpg extension that has been recovered:

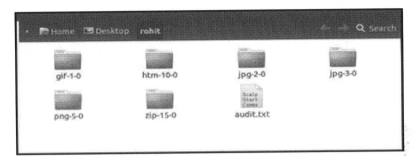

Output folder after running the Scalpel tool

5. As shown in the preceding screenshot, each folder contains recovered data from the Android device, such as images, PDF files, ZIP files, and more. While some pictures are recovered completely, some are not recovered fully, as shown in the following screenshot:

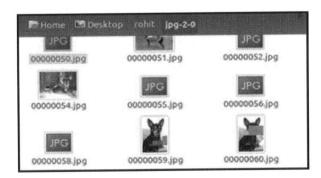

Recovered data using the Scalpel tool

Applications such as **DiskDigger** can be installed on Android devices to recover different types of files from both the internal memory and SD cards. DiskDigger includes support for JPG files, MP3 and WAV audio, MP4 and 3GP video, raw camera formats, Microsoft Office files (DOC, XLS, and PPT), and more. However, as mentioned earlier, the application requires root privileges on the Android device in order to recover the content from the internal memory. Thus, file-carving techniques play a very important role in recovering important deleted files from the device's internal memory.

Recovering contacts using your Google account

You can also restore the contacts on the device using the Restore Contacts option through the Google account that is configured on the device. This would work if the user of the device has previously synced their contacts using the **Sync Settings** option available in Android. This option synchronizes the contacts and other details and would store them in the cloud. A forensic examiner with legal authority or proper consent can restore the deleted contacts if they can get access to the Google account configured on the device. Once the account is accessed, perform the following steps to restore the data:

1. Log in to your Gmail account.
2. Click on **Gmail** in the top-left corner and select **Contacts**, as shown in the following screenshot:

The Contacts menu in Gmail

3. Click on **More**, which is present above the contacts list.

4. Click on **Restore Contacts**, and the following screen will appear:

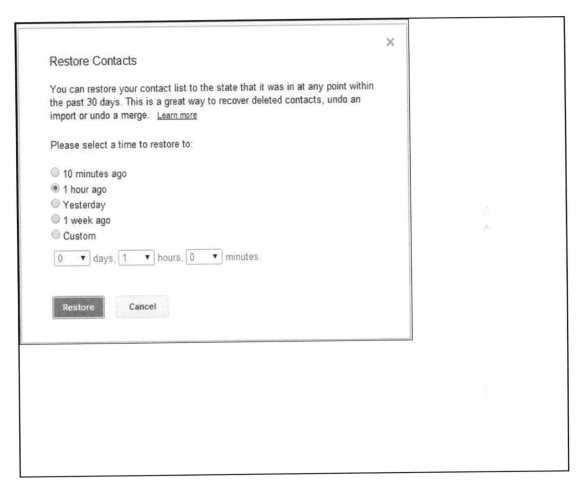

The Restore Contacts dialog box

5. You can restore the contact list to the state that it was in at any point within the past 30 days using this technique.

Summary

Recovery of the deleted data on Android devices depends on various factors, which heavily rely on access to the data residing in the internal memory and SD card. While the recovery of deleted items from external storage, such as an SD card, is easy, the recovery of deleted items from the internal memory takes considerable effort. SQLite file-parsing and file-carving techniques are two methods that are used to recover deleted data extracted from an Android device.

The next chapter discusses forensic analysis of Android apps, malware, and the reverse engineering of Android apps.

11
Android App Analysis, Malware, and Reverse Engineering

Third-party applications are commonly used by smartphone users. Android users download and install several apps from app stores such as Google Play. During forensic investigations, it is often helpful to perform an analysis of these apps to retrieve valuable data and to detect any malware. For instance, a photo vault app might lock sensitive images present on a device. Hence, it would be of great significance to have the knowledge to identify the passcode for the photo vault app. Also, apps such as Facebook, WhatsApp, Skype, and so on, are widely used these days, and they are often the source of valuable data that aids in cracking a case. Hence, it is important to know what kind of data these apps store and the location of this data. While the data extraction and data recovery techniques discussed in earlier chapters provide access to valuable data, app analysis would help us gain information about the specifics of an application, such as preferences and permissions. In this chapter, we will cover the following topics:

- Analyzing some of the most widely used Android apps to retrieve valuable data
- Techniques to reverse engineer an Android application
- Android malware

Analyzing Android apps

On Android, everything the user interacts with is an application. While some apps are preinstalled by the device manufacturer, others are downloaded and installed by the user. For example, even routine functions, such as contacts, calls, SMS, and so on, are performed through their respective apps. Thus, Android app analysis is crucial during the course of an investigation. Several third-party apps, such as WhatsApp, Facebook, Skype, Chrome browser, and so on, are used widely, and they handle a lot of valuable information. Depending on the type of application, most of these apps store sensitive information on the device's internal memory or SD card. Analyzing them may provide information about the location details of the user, their communication with others, and more. Using the forensic techniques described earlier, it is possible to get access to the data stored by these applications. However, a forensic examiner needs to develop the necessary skills to convert the available data into useful data. This is achieved when you have a comprehensive understanding of how the application handles data.

As discussed in previous chapters, all applications store their data in the /data/data folder by default. Apps also store certain other data on the SD card, if they want to, by asking permission at the time of installation. Information about applications present on the device can be gathered by inspecting the contents of the /data/data folder, but this is not straightforward. As an alternative, you can inspect the packages.list file present under /data/system. This file contains information about all the apps along with their package names and data path, as shown in the following screenshot:

```
C:\android-sdk\platform-tools>adb.exe shell
root@android:/ # cd /data/system
root@android:/data/system # cat packages.list
com.google.android.location 10021 0 /data/data/com.google.android.location
com.android.defcontainer 10026 0 /data/data/com.android.defcontainer
com.sec.android.gallery3d 10092 0 /data/data/com.sec.android.gallery3d
com.sec.android.fotaclient 10041 0 /data/data/com.sec.android.fotaclient
com.monotype.android.font.helvneuelt 10052 0 /data/data/com.monotype.android.font.
com.sec.android.motions.settings.panningtutorial 10067 0 /data/data/com.sec.androi
com.fmm.dm 10128 0 /data/data/com.fmm.dm
android.googleSearch.googleSearchWidget 10049 0 /data/data/android.googleSearch.g
com.android.providers.calendar 10087 0 /data/data/com.android.providers.calendar
com.android.bluetooth 10083 0 /data/data/com.android.bluetooth
```

Content of the packages.list file

We will now cover various third-party apps that are widely used and handle valuable data. The following apps are covered only to make the reader familiar with the kind of data that can be extracted and the possible locations where the data can be obtained.

Facebook Android app analysis

The Facebook Android app is one of the most widely used social networking applications. It stores the information under the `/data/data` folder, with the `com.facebook.katana` package name. The following details provide an overview of the kind of information that can be gathered across various files:

- **Facebook contacts**: Information about the user's Facebook contacts can be retrieved by analyzing the `contacts_db2` database, which is present under the following path:
  - **Path**:
    `/data/data/com.facebook.katana/databases/contacts_db2`
  - The `contacts_db2` database (SQLite file) contains a table named contacts, which has most of the information, such as their first names, last names, display names, and URL for display picture.
- **Facebook notifications**: Information about a user's notifications can be gathered by analyzing the `notification_db` database, which is present under the following path:
  - **Path**:
    `/data/data/com.facebook.katana/databases/notifications_db`
  - The `gql_notifications` table present under the preceding path holds the information. The `seen_state` column confirms whether a notification has been seen or not. The `updated` column points to the time when the notification was updated. The `gql_payload` column contains the notification and the sender information.
- **Facebook messages**: A Facebook message conversation may be of crucial importance in several cases and can be viewed by analyzing the `threads_db2` database:
  - **Path**:
    `/data/data/com.facebook.katana/databases/threads_db2`

- **Videos from newsfeed**: The `/video-cache` folder contains videos downloaded from the user's newsfeed. Note that these are not the videos posted by the user, but rather they are the videos that appeared on their newsfeed:
    - **Path**: `/data/data/com.facebook.katana/files/video-cache`

- **Images from newsfeed**: The `/images` folder contains various images that appear on the user's profile, such as the ones from their newsfeed and contact profile pictures. Several directories are present within this folder and images may be stored in formats other than `.jpg`, such as `.cnt`:
    - **Path**: `/data/data/com.facebook.katana/cache/images`

- **Newsfeed data**: The `newfeed_db` database contains data shown to the user on their newsfeed. As shown in the following screenshot, analyzing this database would provide valuable information, such as when a particular story was loaded by the device (the `fetched_at` column), if a particular story was seen by the user (the `seen_state` column), and where the corresponding files of a story are stored on the device (the `cache_file_path` column):
    - **Path**: `/data/data/com.facebook.katana/databases/newsfeed_db`

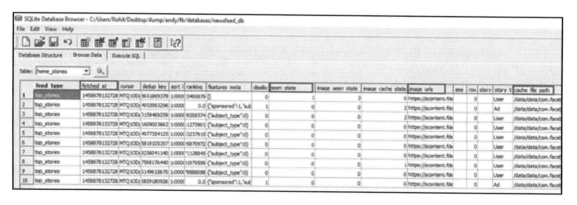

The Facebook newsfeed.db file analyzed in SQLite browser

In the preceding screenshot, `fetched_at` specifies the date and time when this information is fetched. Notice that the app uses Linux epoch time, also known as Unix time or Posix time, to store this information. This format is used very often by multiple apps and, hence, is worth taking a look at. Linux epoch time is stored as the number of seconds (or milliseconds) since midnight on January 1, 1970. There are several online sites, such as `https://www.epochconverter.com/`, that can readily convert the Linux epoch time into normal format.

WhatsApp Android app analysis

WhatsApp is the most popular chat (audio and video) messaging service, and is used by more than a billion people across the globe. It stores the information under the /data/data folder, with the package name com.whatsapp. The following is an overview of the important files that are of interest from a forensic perspective:

- **User's profile pic**: The user's profile picture is saved with the filename me.jpg and is present under the following path:
    - **Path**: /data/data/com.whatsapp/me.jpg
- **User's phone number (associated with WhatsApp)**: The me file present under the main folder contains the phone number that is associated with the user's WhatsApp account. Note that this may or may not be the phone number that is associated with the SIM:
    - **Path**: /data/data/com.whatsapp/me
- **Contacts profile pic**: The /avatars directory has thumbnails of profile pictures of the user's contacts (who use WhatsApp):
    - **Path**: /data/data/com.whatsapp/files/Avatars
- **Chat messages**: All the message-related information, including chats and sender details, is present in the msgstore.db file, which is present at the following location:
    - **Path**: /data/data/com.whatsapp/databases/msgstore.db
- **WhatsApp files**: Most of the files shared with WhatsApp, such as images, videos, and audio messages, are stored on the SD card in the following location:
    - **Path**: /sdcard/WhatsApp/Media

Both sent and received files are stored separately here with their respective folder names.

Skype Android app analysis

Skype is an app that offers video chat and voice call services. The application's data is stored under the /data/data folder, with the package name com.skype.raider. The following are important artifacts that can be extracted by analyzing the Skype app:

- **Username and IP address**: The shared.xml file present under the following path contains information about the username and the last IP address that connected to Skype:
    - **Path**: /data/data/com.skype.raider/files/shared.xml

- **Profile picture**: The user's profile picture is present in the `/thumbnails` directory, whose path is as follows:
    - **Path**:
      `/data/data/com.skype.raider/files/<username>/thumbnails/`
- **Call logs**: Information about call logs made from Skype is available in the `main.db` file. Analyzing this file gives us a lot of information:
    - **Path**:
      `/data/data/com.skype.raider/files/<username>/main.db/`
        - For example, the `duration` table provides information about call duration, the `start_timestamp` field gives the start time of a call, and the `creation_timestamp` field indicates when the call is initiated (this includes unanswered calls). The `type` column indicates whether the call was incoming (value= 1) or outgoing (value= 2).
- **Chat messages**: The `messages` table present in the `main.db` file contains all the chat messages. The `author` and `from_dispname` columns provide information about who wrote the message. The `timestamp` column shows the date/time of the message. The `body_xml` column contains the content of the message:
    - **Path**:
      `/data/data/com.skype.raider/files/<username>/main.db/`
- **Files transferred**: The `Transfers` table contains information about transferred files, such as the filename, the size of the file, and their location on the device:
    - **Path**:
      `/data/data/com.skype.raider/files/<username>/main.db/`
        - The actual images or files received will be stored in an SD card. If a file is downloaded, it would be in the `Downloads` folder in the root of the SD.
- **Group chats**: The `ChatMembers` table shows a list of users who are present in a particular chat. The `adder` column shows the user who initiated the conversation:
    - **Path**:
      `/data/data/com.skype.raider/files/<username>/main.db/`

Gmail Android app analysis

Gmail is a widely used email service offered by Google. The application data is saved under the `/data/data` folder, with the package name `com.google.android.gm`. The following are important artifacts that can be extracted by analyzing the Gmail app:

- **Account details**: The XML files present under `/shared_prefs` confirm the email account details. Details of other accounts, which are linked to the current email, can be identified from the `Gmail.xml` file:
    - **Path**:
      `/data/data/com.google.android.gm/cache/<username>@gmail.com`

- **Attachments**: Attachments that are recently used in both sending and receiving emails are saved to the `/cache` directory. This is valuable because it gives access to items deleted from the email too. Each row also contains a `messages_conversation` value. This value can be compared with the `conversations` table to an attachment with the email it was included within. The `filename` column identifies the path on the device where the file is located. The following is the exact path for this folder:
    - **Path**:
      `/data/data/com.google.android.gm/cache/<username>@gmail.com`

```
127|root@android:/data/data/com.google.android.gm/cache/t████████@gmail.com # ls
04 Vulnerabilities-1.pptx
04 Vulnerabilities-2.pptx
05 XSS-1.pptx
05 XSS.pptx
06 SQLi.pptx
07 CSRF & Others.pptx
831105_08_Final_AJ-1.docx
831105_08_Final_AJ.docx
805387_04_16-1.png
805387_04_16-2.png
805387_04_16-3.png
805387_04_16-4.png
```

List of attachments present under Gmail's cache directory

- **Email subject**: The subject of this email can be recovered by analyzing the `conversations` table present in the `mailstore.<username>@gmail.com.db` file:
  - **Path**:
    `/data/data/com.google.android.gm/databases/mailstore.<username>@gmail.com.db`
- **Search history**: Any text searches that were made within the app are stored in the `suggestions.db` file present at the following location:
  - **Path**:
    `/data/data/com.google.android.gm/databases/suggestions.db`

Google Chrome Android app analysis

Google Chrome is the default web browser in Nexus and many other devices, and it is used widely to browse the internet. The application data is present under the `/data/data` folder, with the package name `com.android.chrome`. The following are important artifacts that can be extracted by analyzing the Gmail app:

- **Profile picture**: The profile picture of the user is stored with the filename `Google Profile Picture.png` in the following location:
  - **Path**:
    `/data/data/com.android.chrome/app_chrome/Default/Google Profile Picture.png`
- **Bookmarks**: The `Bookmarks` file contains information about all the bookmarks synced with the account. Details, such as the site name, URL, and the time when it was bookmarked, can be gathered by analyzing this file:
  - **Path**:
    `/data/data/com.android.chrome/app_chrome/Default/Bookmarks`
- **Browsing history**: The `History.db` file contains the user's web history stored in the various tables. For example, as shown in the following screenshot, the `keyword_search_terms` table contains information about the searches that were made using the Chrome browser:

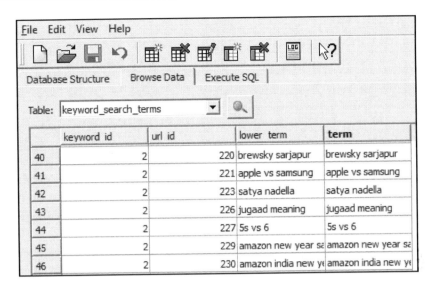

Google Chrome browsing history

- The `segments` table contains a list of sites visited by the user (but not all of the sites). It's interesting to note that Chrome stores the data belonging to not just the device, but the account in general. In other words, information about sites visited from other devices using the same account is also stored on the device. For example, the `URLs` table contains the browsing history for a Google account across several devices.
- **Path**:
  `/data/data/com.android.chrome/app_chrome/Default/History`

- **Login Data**: The `Login Data` database contains login information of different sites saved in the browser. The site URL, along with the username and password, is stored in the respective tables:
  - **Path**:
    `/data/data/com.android.chrome/app_chrome/Default/Login Data`

- **Frequently visited sites**: The `Top Sites` database contains a list of frequently visited sites:
  - **Path**:
    `/data/data/com.android.chrome/app_chrome/Default/Top Sites`

- **Other data**: Other information, such as the phone numbers or email addresses entered by the user during form fills across different sites, is stored in the `Web Data` database. Tables present within this database contain autofill data:
    - **Path**:
    `/data/data/com.android.chrome/app_chrome/Default/Web Data`

Reverse engineering Android apps

The examiner may need to deal with applications that stand as a barrier to accessing the required information. For instance, take the case of the gallery on a phone that is locked by an *AppLock* application. In this case, in order to access the pictures and videos stored in the gallery, you first need to enter the passcode to the *AppLock*. Hence, it would be interesting to know how the *AppLock* app stores the password on the device. You might look into the SQLite database files. However, if they are encrypted, then it's hard to even tell that it's a password. Reverse engineering applications would be helpful in such cases where you want to better understand the application and how the application stores the data.

To state it in simple terms, reverse engineering is the process of retrieving source code from an executable. Reverse engineering an Android app is done in order to understand the functioning of the app, data storage, the security mechanisms in place, and more. Before we proceed to learn how to reverse engineer an Android app, here is a quick recap of the Android apps:

- All the applications that are installed on the Android device are written in the Java programming language.
- When a Java program is compiled, we get bytecode. This is sent to a dex compiler, which converts it into a Dalvik bytecode.
- Thus, the class files are converted to dex files using a dx tool. Android uses something called **Dalvik virtual machine (DVM)** to run its applications.
- JVM's bytecode consists of one or more class files depending on the number of Java files that are present in an application. Regardless, a Dalvik bytecode is composed of only one dex file.

Thus, the dex files, XML files, and other resources that are required to run an application are packaged into an Android package file (an APK file). These APK files are simply collections of items within ZIP files. Therefore, if you rename an APK extension file to `.zip`, then you will be able to see the contents of the file. However, before you can do this, you need to get access to the APK file of the application that is installed on the phone. Here is how the APK file corresponding to an application can be accessed.

Extracting an APK file from an Android device

Apps that come preinstalled with the phone are stored in the `/system/app` directory. Third-party applications that are downloaded by the user are stored in the `/data/app` folder. The following method helps you gain access to the APK files on the device; it works on both rooted and nonrooted devices:

1. Identify the package name of the app by issuing the following command:

```
C:\android-sdk\platform-tools>adb.exe shell pm list packages
package:android
package:android.googleSearch.googleSearchWidget
package:com.android.MtpApplication
package:com.android.Preconfig
package:com.android.apps.tag
package:com.android.backupconfirm
package:com.android.bluetooth
package:com.android.browser
package:com.android.calendar
package:com.android.certinstaller
package:com.android.chrome
package:com.android.clipboardsaveservice
package:com.android.contacts
package:com.android.defcontainer
package:com.android.email
package:com.android.exchange
package:com.android.facelock
```

List of package names present on the device

As shown in the preceding command-line output, the list of package names is displayed. Try to find a match between the app in question and the package name. Usually, the package names are very much related to the app names. Alternatively, you can use the Android Market or Google Play to identify the package name easily. The URL for an app in Google Play contains the package name, as shown in the following screenshot:

Facebook App in Google Play Store

2. Identify the full pathname of the APK file for the desired package by issuing the following command:

```
C:\android-sdk\platform-tools>adb.exe shell pm path com.android.chrome
package:/data/app/com.android.chrome-1.apk
```

3. Pull the APK file from the Android device to the forensic workstation using the `adb pull` command:

```
C:\android-sdk\platform-tools>adb.exe pull /data/app/com.android.chrome-1.apk C:\temp
3706 KB/s (42168820 bytes in 11.110s)
```

You can also use applications such as **ES Explorer** to get the APK file of an Android application. Now, let's analyze the contents of an APK file. An Android package is a container for an Android app's resources and executables. It's a zipped file that contains the following files:

- `AndroidManifest.xml`: This contains information about the permissions and more
- `classes.dex`: This is the class file converted to a dex file by the dex compiler
- `Res`: The application's resources, such as the image files, sound files, and more, are present in this directory
- `Lib`: This contains native libraries that the application may use
- `META-INF`: This contains information about the application's signature and signed checksums for all the other files in the package

Once the APK file is obtained, you can proceed to reverse engineer the Android application.

Steps to reverse engineer Android apps

APK files can be reverse engineered in different ways to get the original code. The following is one method that uses the `dex2jar` and JD-GUI tools to gain access to the application code. For our example, we will examine the `com.twitter.android-1.apk` file. The following are the steps to successfully reverse engineer the APK file:

1. Rename the APK extension to ZIP to see the contents of the file. Rename the `com.twitter.android-1.apk` file to `twitter.android-1.zip`, and extract the contents of this file using any file archiver application. The following screenshot shows the files extracted from the original file `twitter.android-1.zip`:

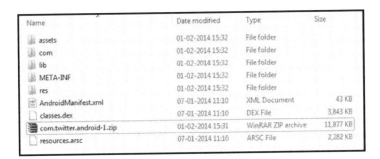

Extracted files of an APK file

2. The `classes.dex` file discussed in the earlier sections can be accessed after extracting the contents of the APK file. This dex file needs to be converted to a class file in Java. This can be done using the `dex2jar` tool.

3. Download the `dex2jar` tool from https://github.com/pxb1988/dex2jar, drop the `classes.dex` file into the `dex2jar` tools directory, and issue the following command:

```
C:\Users\Rohit\Desktop\Training\Android\dex2jar-0.0.9.15>d2j-
dex2jar.bat classes.dex dex2jar classes.dex -> classes-dex2jar.jar
```

4. When the preceding command is successfully run, it creates a new `classes - dex2jar.jar` file in the same directory, as shown in the following screenshot:

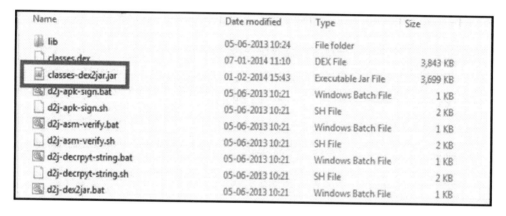

Name	Date modified	Type	Size
lib	05-06-2013 10:24	File folder	
classes.dex	07-01-2014 11:10	DEX File	3,843 KB
classes-dex2jar.jar	01-02-2014 15:43	Executable Jar File	3,699 KB
d2j-apk-sign.bat	05-06-2013 10:21	Windows Batch File	1 KB
d2j-apk-sign.sh	05-06-2013 10:21	SH File	2 KB
d2j-asm-verify.bat	05-06-2013 10:21	Windows Batch File	1 KB
d2j-asm-verify.sh	05-06-2013 10:21	SH File	2 KB
d2j-decrpyt-string.bat	05-06-2013 10:21	Windows Batch File	1 KB
d2j-decrpyt-string.sh	05-06-2013 10:21	SH File	2 KB
d2j-dex2jar.bat	05-06-2013 10:21	Windows Batch File	1 KB

The classes-dex2jar.jar file created by the dex2jar tool

5. To view the contents of this JAR file, you can use a tool such as **JD-GUI**. As shown in the following screenshot, the files present in an Android application and the corresponding code can be seen:

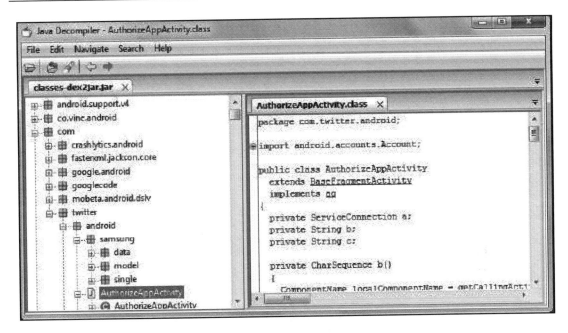

The JD-GUI tool

Once we get access to the code, it is easy to analyze how the application stores the values, permissions, and more information that may be helpful to bypass certain restrictions. When malware is found on a device, this method to decompile and analyze the application may prove useful, as it will show what is being accessed by the malware and provide clues to where the data is being sent. The following sections focus on Android malware in detail.

Android malware

As Android's market share continues to increase, so do attacks or malware targeted at Android users. Mobile malware is a broad term that refers to a piece of software that performs unintended actions and includes Trojans, spyware, adware, ransomware, and others. According to Pulse Secure, 97 percent of mobile malware is focused at the Android operating system (`https://www.scmagazineuk.com/updated-97-of-malicious-mobile-malware-targets-android/article/535410/`). As per statistics released by G DATA software, almost 4,900 new Android samples are being discovered every day. The following URL will take you to a sample screenshot that shows the rise of Android malware over the past few years, referenced from `https://www.gdatasoftware.com/blog/2017/04/29712-8-400-new-android-malware-samples-every-day`.

One of the primary reasons for this situation is that, unlike Apple's App Store, which is tightly controlled by the company, Google's Play Store is an open ecosystem without any detailed upfront security reviews. Malware developers can easily move their apps to Play Store and thereby distribute their apps. Google now has a malware-detecting software named Google Bouncer, which will automatically scan an uploaded app for malware, but attackers have figured out several ways to remain undetected. Moreover, Android officially allows the loading of apps downloaded over the internet (side-loading), unlike iOS, which does not allow unsigned apps. For example, as shown in the following screenshot, when the **Unknown sources** option is selected on an Android device, it allows the user to install apps that are downloaded from any site over internet:

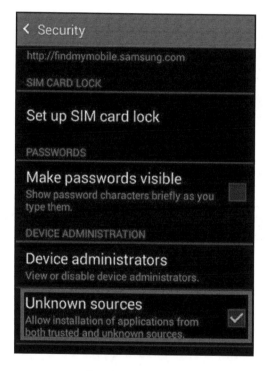

Side-loading option in Android

The third-party app stores that host Android apps are known to be hubs of malware. This prompted Google to roll out the *Verify Apps* feature starting from Android 4.2, which scans apps locally on Android devices to look for malicious activities, such as SMS abuse. As shown in the following screenshot, the Verify apps feature may warn the user, or in some cases may even block the installation. However, this is an opt-in service, so users can disable this feature if they choose to:

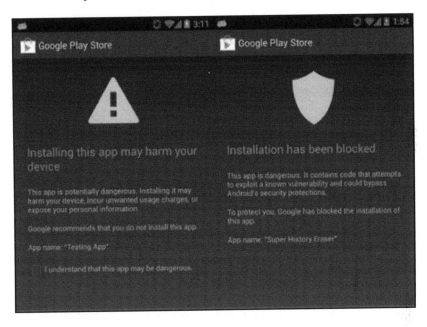

Verify apps feature in Android

Once malware gets into a device, it can perform dangerous actions, some of which are listed, as follows:

- Send and read your text messages
- Steal sensitive data, such as pictures, videos, and credit card numbers
- Manipulate files or data present on the device
- Send SMS to a premium-rated number
- Infect your browser and steal any data typed into its **Change device** settings
- Wipe all data present on the device
- Lock the device until a ransom is paid
- Display advertisements continuously

Advanced malware is also capable of rooting the device and installing new apps. For example, the Android Mazar malware, discovered in Feb 2016, spreads via text messages and is capable of gaining administrator rights on phones, allowing it to wipe handsets, make calls, or read texts.

 A full list of Android malware families and their capabilities is available at https://forensics.spreitzenbarth.de/android-malware/.

How does malware spread?

An Android device can be infected with malware in several different ways. The following are some of the possible ways:

- **Repackaging legitimate application**: This is the most common method used by attackers. The attacker first downloads a legitimate application, disassembles it, then adds their malicious code, and reassembles the application. The new malicious application now functions exactly as the legitimate application does, but it also performs malicious activity in the background. This kind of application is commonly found in the third-party Android app stores and is downloaded by many people.

- **Exploiting Android vulnerabilities**: In this scenario, an attacker exploits the bugs or the vulnerabilities that are discovered in the Android platform to install their malicious application or to perform any unwanted actions. For example, installer hijacking, identified in 2015, has been exploited by attackers to replace an Android application with malware during installation.

- **Bluetooth and MMS propagation**: Malware is also spread via Bluetooth and MMS. The victim receives the malware when the device is in discoverable mode, for example, when it can be seen by other Bluetooth-enabled devices. In the case of MMS, the malware is attached to the message just as computer viruses are sent through email attachments. However, in both these methods, the user has to agree, at least once, to run the file.

- **App downloading malicious update**: In this case, the app originally installed does not contain any malicious code, but a function present within the code will download malicious commands at runtime. This can be done via a stealthy update or user update. For example, the Plankton malware uses stealthy updates that directly download a JAR file from a remote server and do not need any user permission. In the case of user updates, the user has to allow the app to download the new version of the app.

- **Remote install**: The attacker may compromise the credentials of the user's account on the device and thereby remotely install apps on the device. This generally happens in targeted scenarios and is less frequent compared to the previous two methods just described.

Identifying Android malware

From a forensic perspective, it's important to identify the presence of any malware on the device prior to performing any analysis. This is because malware can alter the state of the device or contents on the device, thereby making the analysis or the results inconsistent. Information about various types of Android malware apps and their descriptions is provided at `https://forensics.spreitzenbarth.de/android-malware/`. There are tools available on the market that can analyze the physical extraction to identify malware. For example, Cellebrite UFED Physical Analyzer has BitDefender's anti-malware technology, which scans for malware. As shown in the following screenshot, once the physical image is loaded into the tool, the file can be scanned for malware.

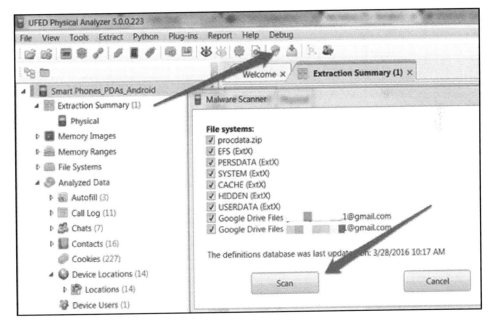

Scanning for malware in UFED Physical Analyzer

Once the scan starts, the BitDefender software tries to unpack the .apk files and looks for infected or malicious files. The process is automatic and the tool points to the malicious apps, as shown in the following screenshot:

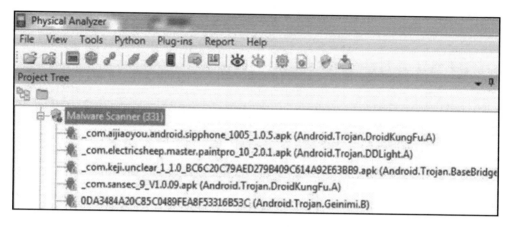

Malware scanner results in UFED Physical Analyzer

The tool simply points out that something malicious is present on the device. The forensic investigator has to then manually confirm whether this is a valid issue by analyzing the respective application. This is where the reverse engineering skills that were discussed in previous sections need to be leveraged. Once the application is reverse engineered and code is obtained, it is recommended that you take a look at the AndroidManifest.xml file to find out the app permissions. This will be helpful for understanding where the app stores the data, what resources it is trying to access, and more. For example, a Flashlight application does not need read/write access to your SD card data, or to make a call.

```
<uses-permission android:name="android.permission.ACCESS_COARSE_LOCATION">
</uses-permission>
<uses-permission android:name="android.permission.ACCESS_FINE_LOCATION">
</uses-permission>
<uses-permission android:name="android.permission.ACCESS_NETWORK_STATE">
</uses-permission>
<uses-permission android:name="android.permission.ACCESS_WIFI_STATE">
</uses-permission>
<uses-permission android:name="android.permission.CALL_PHONE">
</uses-permission>
<uses-permission android:name="android.permission.CAMERA">
</uses-permission>
<uses-permission android:name="android.permission.GET_ACCOUNTS">
</uses-permission>
<uses-permission android:name="android.permission.INTERNET">
</uses-permission>
<uses-permission android:name="android.permission.MANAGE_ACCOUNTS">
</uses-permission>
<uses-permission android:name="android.permission.READ_CONTACTS">
</uses-permission>
<uses-permission android:name="android.permission.READ_PHONE_STATE">
</uses-permission>
<uses-permission android:name="android.permission.USE_CREDENTIALS">
</uses-permission>
<uses-permission android:name="android.permission.VIBRATE">
</uses-permission>
<uses-permission android:name="android.permission.WRITE_SETTINGS">
</uses-permission>
<uses-permission android:name="android.permission.WRITE_EXTERNAL_STORAGE">
</uses-permission>
```

Permissions in the AndroidManifest.xml file

It's also important to note that the tool may not identify a valid case if the details are obfuscated in the `.apk` file. Hence, as a forensic investigator, it's important to develop the necessary skills to reverse engineer any suspicious apps and analyze the code to identify malicious behavior. In some investigations, the nature of the malware that is present on a device may also result in arriving at certain crucial conclusions, which may affect the outcome of the case. For example, consider an internal investigation in a corporation that involves sending abusive messages to other employees. Identifying malware on the device that sends the messages would help to solve the case.

Summary

Android app analysis helps a forensic investigator to look for valuable data in relevant locations on a device. Reverse engineering Android apps is the process of retrieving source code from an APK file. Using certain tools, such as `dex2jar`, Android apps can be reverse engineered in order to understand their functionality and data storage, identify malware, and more. Identifying malware present on a device is crucial, as it may affect the outcome of an investigation. Tools such as UFED Physical Analyzer come with BitDefender software, which can automatically scan for malware. The next chapter covers performing forensics on Windows Phone devices.

12
Windows Phone Forensics

Windows Phones are becoming more widely used, and they may be encountered during forensic investigations. These devices are the most affordable on the market, so understanding how to acquire, analyze, and decode data from Windows Phones is important. Locating and interpreting digital evidence present on these devices requires a specialized knowledge of the Windows Phone operating system, and may not always be possible. Commercial forensic and open source tools provide limited support for acquiring user data from Windows devices. As Windows Phones do not occupy much of the mobile market space, most forensic practitioners are unfamiliar with the data formats, embedded databases used, and other artifacts that exist on the device. This chapter provides an overview of Windows Phone forensics, describing various methods of acquiring and examining data on Windows mobile devices.

In this chapter, we will cover the following topics:

- Windows Phone OS
- Windows Phone security
- Jailbreaking
- Windows Phone forensic acquisition and analysis

Windows Phone OS

Windows Phone is a proprietary mobile operating system developed by Microsoft. It was launched as a successor to Windows Mobile, but it does not provide backward compatibility with the previous platform. Windows Phone was launched in October 2010 with Windows Phone 7. The version history of the Windows Phone operating system then continued with the release of Windows Phone 7.5, Windows Phone 7.8, Windows Phone 8.1, and Windows Phone 10.

Despite the fact that Microsoft claim they have stopped developing this mobile operating system, excluding security patches, you are likely to face it as a mobile forensic examiner.

The following sections will provide more details about Windows Phone, its features, and its underlying security model.

Unlike Android and iOS devices, Windows Phone comes with a new interface, which uses so-called **tiles** for apps instead of icons, as shown in the following figure. These tiles can be designed and updated by the user:

The Windows Phone home screen

Similar to other mobile platforms, Windows Phone allows for the installation of third-party apps. These apps can be downloaded from the Windows Phone Marketplace, which is managed by Microsoft. When comparing the number of apps available for iOS and Android devices, Windows Phone pales in comparison. However, applications are available and the examiner should expect to see them on Windows Phone devices.

Windows Phone introduced new features, making it more similar to other smartphones as compared to Windows Mobile:

- **Cortana**: This is the personal assistant for the device. It was introduced in Windows 8.1 and is still present on Windows 10 devices. Cortana aids the user by fielding questions using Bing, setting reminders, sending texts, and essentially using all the functionality to provide the user with a better and easier experience. Everything that Cortana does leaves a trace on the device.
- **Wallet**: This stores credit card accounts, boarding passes, tickets, coupons, and more.
- **Geofence and advanced location settings**: These provide the user with additional protection as the phone can detect when it is out of a trusted zone and may lock itself.
- **Additional features**: These are features such as live tiles, enhanced colors, and quiet hours.

Other common applications associated with Windows Phone include OneDrive (formerly SkyDrive), OneNote, and Office 365 synchronization. OneDrive provides the user with access to all of their documents and files from any device. OneNote is essentially the same, but it acts as a notebook or diary. Office 365 provides the user with constant access to their email, calendar, contacts, and more across multiple devices.

The introduction of data synchronization across multiple devices makes our job as forensic examiners difficult. It is our job to determine how the evidence was placed on the device. Is it possible to definitively state how an artifact was placed on a device? To be honest, this depends. Nobody wants to hear this response, but a lot of factors must be considered. What is the app? What OS is running on the device? What is the artifact? For example, let's consider SkyDrive. If the device contains documents from SkyDrive, the original author should be contained within the metadata. This, together with examining whether or not the content was shared to the device, may provide a glimpse into how the artifact was created. However, when examining a calendar entry when Office 365 is in place, it may be impossible to state whether the user created the entry on their phone, PC, or laptop. The synchronization is instantaneous, and status flags stating where the artifact was created do not always exist. If this artifact is indeed the *smoking gun* of the investigation, you need to apply your skills to uncover other artifacts that support your findings. Digging deeper into the data is required.

Security model

The security model of Windows Phone is designed to make sure that the user data present on the device is safe and secure. The following sections provide a brief explanation of the concepts on which Windows Phone security is built.

Chambers

Windows Phone is heavily built on the principles of least privilege and isolation. This has been consistent since the inception of Windows Phone 7. To achieve this, Windows Phone introduced the concept of **chambers**. Each chamber has an isolation boundary where processes can run. Depending on the security policy of a specific chamber, a process running in this chamber has the privilege of accessing the OS's resources and capabilities (`https://www.msec.be/mobcom/ws2013/presentations/david_hernie.pdf`). There are four types of security chambers. The following is a brief description of each one of them:

- **Trusted Computing Base (TCB)**: The processes here have unrestricted access to most Windows Phone resources. This chamber has privileges to modify policies and enforce the security model. The kernel runs in this chamber.

- **Elevated Rights Chamber (ERC)**: This chamber is less privileged than the TCB chamber. It has privileges to access all resources except the security policy. This chamber is mainly used for services and user-mode drivers, which provide functionality intended for use by other applications on the phone.
- **Standard Rights Chamber (SRC)**: This is the default chamber for preinstalled applications, such as Microsoft Outlook Mobile 2010.
- **Least Privileged Chamber (LPC)**: This is the default chamber for all the applications that are downloaded and installed through the Marketplace Hub (which is also known as the Windows Phone Marketplace).

Encryption

Windows Phone 8 introduced BitLocker technology to encrypt all user data that is stored on the device via AES 128-bit encryption. The user can simply flip the switch to enable this feature, and all of their data residing on the internal storage of the device is encrypted. In addition, the user can encrypt their SD card, assuming the device has one, and set a password or PIN on their device. Should all of these locks and the encryption be enabled, accessing the data on this device may be impossible, unless the password is recovered.

Capability-based model

Capabilities are defined as the resources on the phone (camera, location information, microphone, and more) associated with security, privacy, and cost. The LPC has a minimal set of access rights by default. However, this can be expanded by requesting more capabilities during the installation. Capabilities are granted during the app installation and cannot be modified or elevated during runtime. For this reason, it is difficult to side-load applications or force custom bootcode to the device to gain forensic access, as it is normally rejected prior to bootup.

To install an app on a Windows Phone, you need to sign in to Marketplace with a Windows Live ID. During installation, apps are required to ask the user for permission before using certain capabilities, an example of which is shown in the following screenshot:

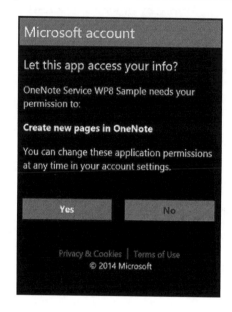

Windows app requesting user permissions (https://i-msdn.sec.s-msft.com/dynimg/IC752370.png)

This is similar to the permission model in Android. This gives the user the freedom to learn about all the capabilities that an application has before installing the application. The list of all capabilities is included in the `WMAppManifest.xml` application manifest file, which can be accessed through Visual Studio or other methods that are defined at `https://docs.microsoft.com/en-us/previous-versions/windows/apps/ff769509(v=vs.105)`.

App sandboxing

Apps in Windows Phone run in a sandboxed environment. This means every application on Windows Phone runs in its own chamber. Applications are isolated from each other and cannot access the data of other applications. If any app needs to save information to the device, it can do so using the isolated storage, which is restricted from access by other applications. Also, the third-party applications installed on Windows Phone cannot run in the background; that is, when the user switches to a different application, the previously used application is shut down (although the application state is preserved). This ensures that the application cannot perform activities such as communicating over the internet when the user is not using the application. These restrictions also make Windows Phone less susceptible to malware, but never assume that any device is safe. It is just more challenging for malware to function on these devices.

Windows Phone filesystem

The Windows Phone filesystem is more or less similar to the filesystems used in Windows 7, Windows 8, and Windows 10. From the root directory, one can reach different files and folders that are available on this device. From a forensic perspective, the following are some of the folders that can yield valuable data. All the listed directories are located in the root directory:

- **Application data**: This directory contains data of preinstalled apps on the phone, such as Outlook, Maps, and Internet Explorer.
- **Applications**: This directory contains the apps installed by the user. The isolated storage, which is allocated or used by each app, is also located in this folder.
- **My Documents**: This directory holds different Office documents, such as Word, Excel, or PowerPoint files . The directory also includes configuration files and multimedia files, such as music or videos.
- **Windows**: This directory contains files that are related to the Windows Phone operating system.

The acquisition method used here will determine the amount of filesystem access that the examiner has to the device. For example, a physical image may provide access to several partitions that can be recovered from the data dump. We are looking at a Windows Phone 10 device that contains 27 partitions in the following screenshot. Partitions **26** (**MainOS**) and **27** (**Data**) contain the relevant data:

```
⊞ ▦ DPP (1) [8MB]
⊞ ▦ MODEM_FSG (2) [1MB]
⊞ ▦ MODEM_FS1 (3) [1MB]
⊞ ▦ MODEM_FS2 (4) [1MB]
⊞ ▦ MODEM_FSC (5) [0MB]
⊞ ▦ DDR (6) [0MB]
⊞ ▦ SSD (7) [0MB]
⊞ ▦ UEFI_BS_NV (8) [0MB]
⊞ ▦ UEFI_RT_NV (9) [0MB]
⊞ ▦ SBL1 (10) [0MB]
⊞ ▦ DBI (11) [0MB]
⊞ ▦ UEFI (12) [2MB]
⊞ ▦ RPM (13) [0MB]
⊞ ▦ TZ (14) [0MB]
⊞ ▦ WINSECAPP (15) [0MB]
⊞ ▦ TZAPPS (16) [16MB]
⊞ ▦ BACKUP_SBL1 (17) [0MB]
⊞ ▦ BACKUP_DBI (18) [0MB]
⊞ ▦ BACKUP_UEFI (19) [2MB]
⊞ ▦ BACKUP_RPM (20) [0MB]
⊞ ▦ BACKUP_TZ (21) [0MB]
⊞ ▦ BACKUP_WINSECAPP (22) [0MB]
⊞ ▦ BACKUP_TZAPPS (23) [16MB]
⊞ ▦ PLAT (24) [8MB]
⊞ ▦ EFIESP (25) [32MB]
⊞ ▦ MainOS (26) [1476MB]
⊞ ▦ Data (27) [5847MB]
```

Windows Phone 10 partitions

While most artifacts will exist in the **Data** partition, it is always best practice to capture and analyze both when possible.

The **MainOS** partition in the preceding screenshot, partition **26**, contains the system data from the Windows Phone. As in all Windows investigations, the system data contains artifacts relevant to investigations.

In this example, partition 27 contains the **User** or **Data** partition. Depending on the device, the partition numbers may vary. In our example, the **Data** partition is shown in the following figure as partition **27**. Here, the SMS, email, application data, contacts, call logs, and internet history were recovered using mobile forensic tools. These methods will be discussed later in this chapter:

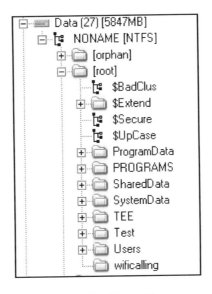

Windows Phone 10 Data partition

Windows Phone also maintains the **Windows registry**, a database that stores environment variables on the operating system. The Windows registry is basically a directory that stores settings and options for the Microsoft operating system. Windows Phone is no different. When examining a Windows Phone, an examiner will expect to see the NTUSER.dat, SAM, SYSTEM, SOFTWARE, SECURITY, and DEFAULT hives. While these hives may be unique to the phone, they can be examined just like traditional Windows registry hives.

A detailed case investigation is included in a paper by Cynthia Murphy. This involves a criminal case of a home invasion and sexual assault, and details the efforts of great minds in the forensic community to uncover artifacts that assisted in closing the investigation. Sometimes, the mobile device is the most important artifact pertaining to the case. For more information, refer to https://www.sans.org/reading-room/whitepapers/forensics/ windows-phone-8-forensic-artifacts-35787.

Data acquisition

Acquiring data from a Windows Phone is challenging for forensic examiners, as the physical, file system, and logical methods that were defined in previous chapters are not greatly supported. In addition to this, the phone may need to be at a specific battery charge state (%) in order for the commercial tool to recognize and acquire the device. This is often one of the most difficult steps in acquiring Windows Phones.

One of the most common techniques implemented by commercial tools attempting data acquisition is to install an application or agent on the device, which enables two-way communication for commands to be sent to the device in order to extract data. This could result in certain changes on the device; nevertheless, this is still forensically sound if the examiner follows standard protocols and has tested the validity of the tool being used. These protocols include proper testing to ensure no user data is changed (and if changed, documenting what occurred), validation of the method on a test device, and documenting all steps taken during the acquisition process. For this acquisition method to work, the app needs to be installed with the privileges of the SRC. This may require the examiner to copy the manufacturer's DLLs, which have higher privileges, into the user app. This allows the app to access methods and resources that are usually limited to native apps. In addition to this, the device must be unlocked, or these methods may not work.

Most examiners rely on forensic tools and methods to acquire mobile devices. Again, these practices are not as supported for Windows Phones. Keep in mind that to deploy and run an app on Windows Phone, both the device and the developer must be registered and unlocked by Microsoft. This restriction can be bypassed by unlocking the device using a public jailbreak for Windows Phone 8 to 10 devices.

For quite a long time, JTAG and chip-off acquisitions were the only options to acquire most Windows Phones. Everything changed in January 2015: Cellebrite implemented an acquisition module which allowed mobile forensic examiners to extract data on the physical level from most Lumia devices.

Later, the Windows Phone Internals project presented a way to unlock the bootloader of some Lumia devices, including 520, 521, 525, 620, 625, 720, 820, 920, 925, 928, 1020, and 1320. This made physical acquisition of these devices possible. You can learn more about the project here: https://www.wpinternals.net/.

Commercial forensic tool acquisition methods

There are a few commercial tools available that offer support for the acquisition of Windows Phone devices. Cellebrite UFED offers support to acquire Windows Phone devices using the physical, file system, and logical methods. To determine whether the device you are examining is supported by the tool, you can download and use the UFED Phone Detective mobile app, which is available for free both in App Store and Google Play:

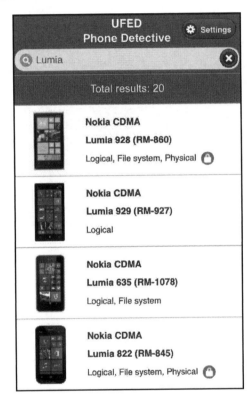

Searching for supported Lumia devices

Some of these acquisition methods are more robust, obtain a full physical dump of the data, and can bypass some lock codes on specific devices. However, some device support includes simply extracting contacts and pictures from the device. It is important for the examiner to realize that specific steps must be taken as directed by the tool. Acquiring these devices is not easy, and often the examiner will find that the tool will not be successful.

When the tool seems to fail, attempt to acquire the device using the Smartphone/PDA option offered in UFED. To do this, follow these steps:

1. Launch UFED4PC and select **Mobile Device**.
2. Select **Browse Manually**.
3. Select **Smartphones**.
4. Select the Windows device that you are attempting to acquire.
5. Try all the methods that are offered, starting with physical, file system, and logical (in that order, where possible):

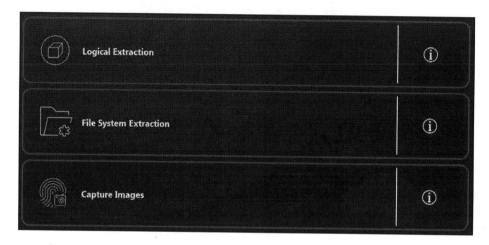

Extraction methods

6. Follow all the remaining steps and try all offered acquisition methods until successful.

Cellebrite may alert you that the acquisition is not successful for several reasons. When this occurs, try every option to ensure you have exhausted the commercial options available. An example of an acquisition attempt in UFED4PC is shown as follows:

1. Launch UFED4PC.
2. Select your **Make** and **Model** for the device.
3. Select the **Physical**, **File System**, or **Logical** acquisition method (offerings will vary depending on the device model).

In this example, only the **Logical** acquisition was supported. Two methods are available. The first option uses a cable, and the second uses Bluetooth. In this example, a special UFED cable is required. I selected the UFED cable first, as Bluetooth requires that additional changes be made to the phone during pairing:

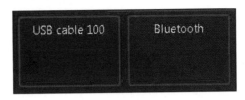

UFED4PC Logical extraction options

When attempting to acquire the device with USB cable 100, only multimedia files were accessible.

Then, attempt the same acquisition, but select **Bluetooth**. Follow the instructions to pair the device to the forensic workstation:

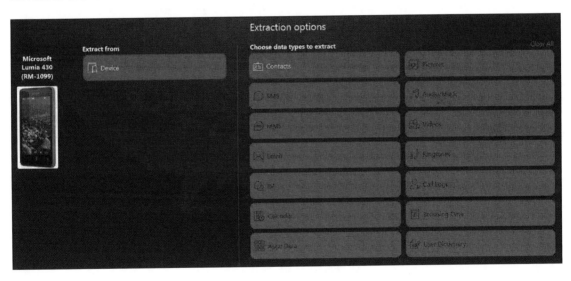

UFED4PC extraction options (Bluetooth)

With this acquisition method, we were able to obtain contacts. Note that there was not a method offered to obtain **SMS**, **MMS**, **Email**, **IM**, **Calendar**, **Call Logs**, **Apps Data**, and others. It is suggested you repeat the generic methods listed in the previous screenshot using the **Smartphone** option in UFED4PC.

Extracting data without the use of commercial tools

On an unlocked device, it may be possible to run an app that can extract the user data present in the phone. This device may have to be jailbroken for this to work. Several apps that do this are available, and they depend on the version of Windows running on the phone and the version on your forensic PC. Two apps will be covered in this section. The first is **TouchXperience** and the second is **Windows Phone app for Desktop**.

The TouchXperience app, which comes with the **Windows Mobile Device Manager** (**WMDM**), can be used for this purpose. WPDM is the management software for Windows Phone 7. The TouchXperience client app extracts data, such as the filesystem, from the mobile device, and WPDM retrieves this data and converts it into a human-readable graphical format. The following are the steps that will help a forensic examiner extract user data present on an unlocked Windows Phone device:

1. Download Windows Phone SDK 7.1 and the Zune software on the forensic workstation, and install it (`https://www.microsoft.com/en-us/download/details.aspx?id=27570`).

2. Download the Windows Phone Device Manager on the workstation, and launch `WPDeviceManager.exe` (`http://www.touchxperience.com/windows-phone-device-manager/`).

3. Connect the device to the workstation, and it should be detected automatically. If it is not detected, make sure that a passcode is not set on the device. If it is, this process may fail if the passcode is unknown.

4. Windows Phone Device Manager will automatically install the TouchXperience app when the phone is connected for the first time. Make sure that you set what the software is allowed to do on the device (that is, make sure not to change the user data, update date/time settings, or do anything else that will modify the user data). Make sure to document that TouchXperience was installed in order to extract data from the Windows Phone, as standard forensic methods provide little support for these devices.

Thereafter, the following screen is presented, providing access to a vast number of files that are present on the device:

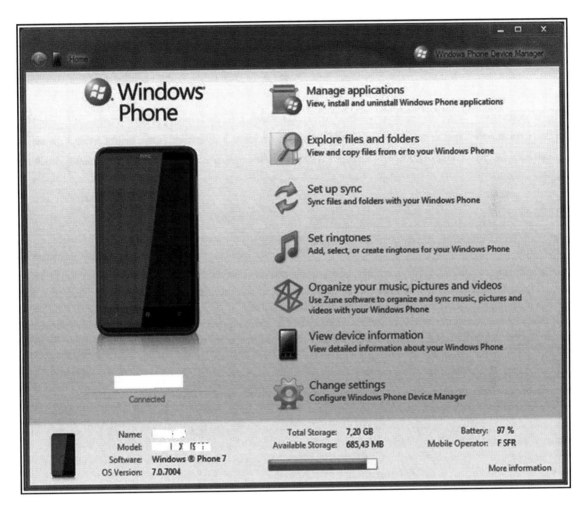

Windows Phone Device Manager

The home screen displays information about the model of the phone, OS version, and more. Click on **Manage applications** to see the information about installed apps on the device, as shown in the next screenshot. WPDM also provides other functionality, such as media management and synchronization of files and folders. From a forensic point of view, the file explorer is the most interesting part of this software. It provides read, write, and executable access to most of the files that are present on the Windows Phone 7 device:

Name	Publisher	Installed On	Size	Version
Installed Applications				
TouchXplorer	Julien Schapman	28/02/2011	664,91 KB	1.0.0.0
TouchXperience	Julien Schapman	28/02/2011	2,42 MB	1.0.2.0
Bluetooth	Julien Schapman	28/02/2011	587,02 KB	1.0.0.0
Config. avancée	Julien Schapman	28/02/2011	1,31 MB	1.1.0.1
Éditeur de registre	Julien Schapman	28/02/2011	1,29 MB	1.1.0.0
Purchased Applications				
Config Connexion	HTC Corporation		913,10 KB	1.0.0.0
Convertisseur	HTC Corporation		1,82 MB	1.0.0.0
HTC Hub	HTC Corporation		18,04 MB	1.0.0.0

Windows Phone Device Manager – the Manage applications screen

Using this acquisition technique, you can access two types of data: system data and application data. System data is mainly the data that is required to run the device, and application data is the data created and used by different applications that are installed on the device. While system data may not contain data relevant to your investigation, application data is very valuable. Regardless, all data should be acquired from any smartphone, as the examination must be complete and capture all the data contained on the device when possible. The following sections discuss the steps to be followed to extract application data from a Windows Phone device. The application data will contain the bulk of the user-created data, and it will provide the most value to your investigation.

Windows Phone app for Desktop works like the app that we just defined, but it supports the Windows Phone 8 device. Note that both the phone and the SD card can be accessed. The user relies on this app to transfer and sync files, similarly to how iPhone users rely on iTunes. Examiners rely on this app as a method to extract user artifacts when all other options are exhausted. When attempting to acquire data from the SD card, please refer to the methods discussed later in this chapter:

Windows Phone app for Desktop

Other options for Windows 8.1 include the **Windows Phone App** and **Phone Companion App** for Windows 10 devices. These apps provide the user with additional functionality and allow for the copying of files from the PC to the device and/or SD card.

SD card data extraction methods

Windows Phones may contain removable SD cards. These cards may be secured with a key that prevents the SD card from being removed and used, or accessed via other devices (phones, cameras, computers, and more). This is different from the key that is created if the user encrypts the SD card. Brute force and dictionary attacks can be run on user-encrypted SD cards to attempt to access the data. When examining a Windows Phone, it is best to research the device to see whether SD card security will be a factor when acquiring data from the device. If so, simply follow the preceding steps and acquire the SD card data through the phone during forensic extraction; or refer to the following chart.

For devices where the SD card can be removed, you have two scenarios to consider. If the device is on, should you acquire the phone and the SD card as is? If the device is off, should you remove the SD card and acquire the device using FTK Imager? The answer is: it depends. In forensics, we use this statement frequently, but it remains true. If you leave the device on, it must be isolated from the network to ensure that it is not remotely accessed and immediately acquired, or the battery will drain and, ultimately, the device may power down. If the device is off and you remove the SD card, you must ensure that the card remains tied to the device itself and is acquired both externally and internally to ensure all data is captured. In a normal situation, the following chart suggests the recommended steps to handle SD cards that are found in Windows Phones:

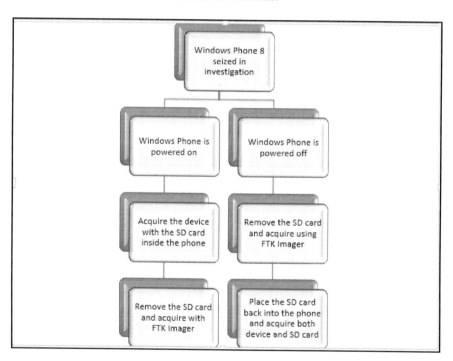

Most commercial forensic tools will offer to extract data from SD cards. Often, the phone extraction will only be data residing on the SD card. This is often the case when there is no support for a specific Windows Phone. If the SD card is not recognized by the tool and the data is not extracted, it is likely that the SD card has been encrypted by the user, and the password for the device is different from the password for the SD card. When this occurs, try to crack the passcode and reacquire the device. Note that cracking a passcode on an SD card may not always be possible, but it's worth a shot using brute force and dictionary attacks as you would on a standard hard drive or external device.

When acquiring an SD that has been removed from a Windows Phone, FTK Imager is a free and reliable option to create a forensically sound image that can be examined in a variety of tools. To create an SD card image, follow these steps:

1. Remove the SD card from the device and make sure to document all identifiers on the card and the phone to ensure that they are not permanently separated.
2. Insert the SD card into a **write blocker** and insert this into your forensic workstation.
3. Launch FTK Imager.
4. Select **File** and then select **Create Disk Image**.
5. Select **Physical Drive**:

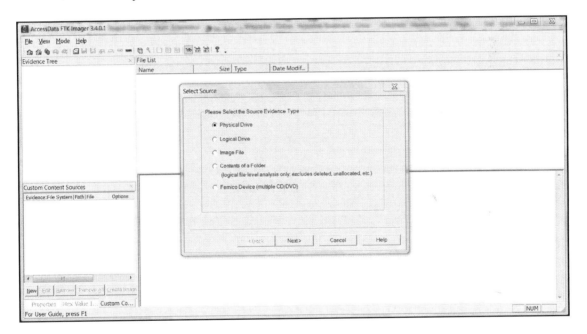

FTK Imager – creating a disk image

6. Use the drop-down list to select the correct device.

Look at the make and size to ensure that you are acquiring the correct device.

7. Select **Finish**.

8. Click on **Add** and select the image type. For this example, **Raw (dd)** is going to be used, as it is supported by most commercial and open source methods for analysis:

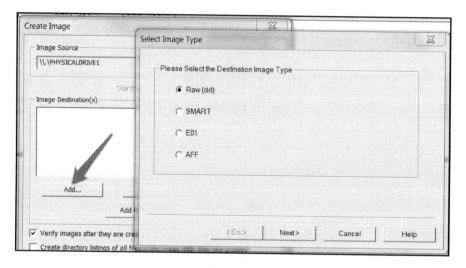

FTK Imager – selecting the image type

9. Enter the relevant case information and select **Next**. This can be skipped.
10. Select the image destination:

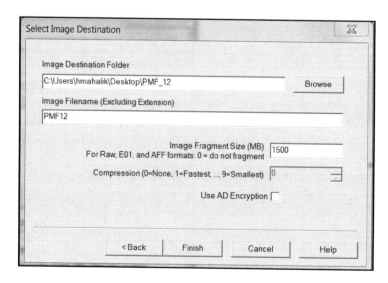

FTK Imager – saving your image file

11. Select **Finish** and then select **Start**. It is recommended that you verify images after they are created.

Once complete, your results will be displayed. We will cover analyzing the SD card data in the following sections.

Key artifacts for examination

In this section, we are going to introduce you to the location of some of the most common Windows Phone forensic artifacts, including contacts, SMS, and call and internet history.

Extracting contacts and SMS

All the contacts and incoming and outgoing short messages (SMS) in Windows Phone 7–10 are stored in the file named `store.vol`, which is present under the `\Application Data\Microsoft\Outlook\Stores\DeviceStore` (Windows 7) and `Users\WPCOMMSERVICES\APPDATA\Local\Unistore` (Windows 8-10) directories. An example of a Windows 10 `store.vol` file is shown in the following screenshot:

[current folder]	2015-04-06 20:07:11 EDT	2015-04-06 20:07:11 EDT	2015-04-06 20:07:11 EDT	2017-05-20 12:13:54 EDT
[parent folder]	2017-05-23 10:16:20 EDT	2017-05-23 10:16:20 EDT	2017-05-23 10:16:20 EDT	2017-05-20 12:13:37 EDT
store.vol	2015-04-06 20:07:30 EDT	2015-04-06 20:07:30 EDT	2017-05-20 12:13:54 EDT	2017-05-20 12:13:54 EDT
USS.chk	2015-04-06 20:07:30 EDT	2015-04-06 20:07:30 EDT	2017-05-20 12:13:54 EDT	2017-05-20 12:13:54 EDT
USS.log	2015-04-06 20:07:30 EDT	2015-04-06 20:07:30 EDT	2017-06-05 13:37:25 EDT	2017-06-05 13:37:25 EDT
USS00005.log	2017-07-26 18:53:09 EDT	2017-07-26 18:53:09 EDT	2017-05-20 12:13:54 EDT	2017-05-20 12:13:54 EDT
USSres00001.jrs	2017-05-20 12:13:54 EDT	2017-05-20 12:13:54 EDT	2017-05-20 12:13:54 EDT	2017-05-20 12:13:54 EDT
USSres00002.jrs	2017-05-20 12:13:54 EDT	2017-05-20 12:13:54 EDT	2017-05-20 12:13:54 EDT	2017-05-20 12:13:54 EDT
USStmp.log	2017-07-07 16:25:07 EDT	2017-07-26 18:53:09 EDT	2017-05-20 12:13:54 EDT	2017-05-20 12:13:54 EDT

The store.vol file in a Windows Phone

Extracting call history

Call history data can currently be extracted from the `Phone` file. It's important to note that the file doesn't have an extension and is located at `\Users\WPCOMMSERVICES\APPDATA\Local\UserData\`. Here is an example of a Windows 10 `Phone` file:

[current folder]	2015-04-06 20:07:11 EDT	2015-04-06 20:07:11 EDT	2015-04-06 20:07:11 EDT	2017-05-20 12:13:54 EDT
[parent folder]	2017-05-23 10:16:20 EDT	2017-05-23 10:16:20 EDT	2017-05-23 10:16:20 EDT	2017-05-20 12:13:37 EDT
FavoriteData.xml	2017-07-21 20:18:19 EDT	2017-07-21 20:18:19 EDT	2017-06-12 17:31:43 EDT	2017-06-12 17:31:43 EDT
FavoriteData.xml.tmp	2017-07-21 20:18:19 EDT	2017-07-21 20:18:19 EDT	2017-06-12 17:31:43 EDT	2017-06-12 17:31:43 EDT
Phone	2015-04-06 20:07:30 EDT	2015-04-06 20:07:30 EDT	2017-05-20 12:13:54 EDT	2017-05-20 12:13:54 EDT
UDM.chk	2015-04-06 20:07:30 EDT	2015-04-06 20:07:30 EDT	2017-05-20 12:13:54 EDT	2017-05-20 12:13:54 EDT
UDM.log	2015-04-06 20:07:30 EDT	2015-04-06 20:07:30 EDT	2017-05-20 12:13:54 EDT	2017-05-20 12:13:54 EDT
UDM00001.log	2017-07-19 08:17:25 EDT	2017-07-19 11:03:33 EDT	2017-05-20 12:13:54 EDT	2017-05-20 12:13:54 EDT
UDMres00001.jrs	2017-05-20 12:13:54 EDT	2017-05-20 12:13:54 EDT	2017-05-20 12:13:54 EDT	2017-05-20 12:13:54 EDT
UDMres00002.jrs	2017-05-20 12:13:54 EDT	2017-05-20 12:13:54 EDT	2017-05-20 12:13:54 EDT	2017-05-20 12:13:54 EDT
UDMtmp.log	2017-07-19 11:03:33 EDT	2017-07-19 11:03:33 EDT	2017-07-19 11:03:33 EDT	2017-07-19 11:03:33 EDT

The Phone file in a Windows Phone

Extracting internet history

Internet history can be extracted from the `WebCacheV01.dat` located at `\Users\DefApps\APPDATA\Local\Microsoft\Windows\WebCache\`. Here is an example of a Windows 10 `WebCacheV01.dat` file:

[current folder]	2017-07-25 20:40:46 EDT	2017-07-25 20:40:46 EDT	2017-07-25 20:40:46 EDT	2017-05-20 12:13:55 EDT
[parent folder]	2017-05-20 12:36:23 EDT	2017-05-20 12:36:23 EDT	2017-05-20 12:36:23 EDT	2017-05-20 12:13:30 EDT
V01.chk	2015-04-06 21:41:57 EDT	2015-04-06 21:41:57 EDT	2017-05-20 12:13:55 EDT	2017-05-20 12:13:55 EDT
V01.log	2015-04-06 21:41:57 EDT	2015-04-06 21:41:57 EDT	2017-07-19 12:24:21 EDT	2017-07-19 12:24:21 EDT
V0100016.log	2017-07-25 20:40:46 EDT	2017-07-25 20:40:46 EDT	2017-07-20 20:10:03 EDT	2017-07-20 20:10:03 EDT
V01res00001.jrs	2017-05-20 12:13:55 EDT	2017-05-20 12:13:55 EDT	2017-05-20 12:13:55 EDT	2017-05-20 12:13:55 EDT
V01res00002.jrs	2017-05-20 12:13:55 EDT	2017-05-20 12:13:55 EDT	2017-05-20 12:13:55 EDT	2017-05-20 12:13:55 EDT
V01tmp.log	2017-07-24 17:23:26 EDT	2017-07-25 20:40:46 EDT	2017-06-21 12:17:53 EDT	2017-06-21 12:17:53 EDT
WebCacheV01.dat	2015-04-06 21:41:57 EDT	2015-04-06 21:41:57 EDT	2017-05-20 12:13:55 EDT	2017-05-20 12:13:55 EDT

The WebCacheV01.dat file in a Windows Phone

These files can be examined manually, for example, with a hex viewer, or can be parsed automatically with mobile forensic tools. Here is the `WebCacheV01.dat` file parsed with Magnet AXIOM:

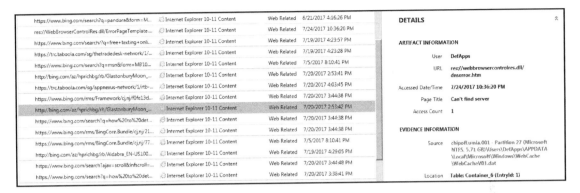

WebCacheV01.dat file parsed with Magnet AXIOM

Summary

Acquiring data from Windows Phone devices is challenging, as they are secure, and commercial forensic tools and open source methods do not provide easy solutions for forensic examiners. Multiple tools, chip-off, JTAG, and the methods defined in this book are some of the methods that provide access to user data on Windows Phone devices. Often, you will find that Windows Phone devices require multiple extraction methods to acquire accessible data. The biggest challenge is getting access to the device to acquire the data. Once the data is available, all the extracted information can be analyzed by the examiner.

Again, the device must not contain a passcode. It must be unlocked (jailbroken or rooted) to use non-commercial methods, and it may be modified by the examiner in order to extract the data using the methods defined in this chapter. While some may challenge us and say that these methods are not common in forensic practices, they must realize that these methods may be the only way to obtain user data from Windows Phone devices.

13
Parsing Third-Party Application Files

Third-party applications have taken the smartphone community by storm. Most smartphone owners have more than one app on their device that they rely on to chat, game, get directions, or share pictures. According to `https://www.statista.com/statistics/276623/number-of-apps-available-in-leading-app-stores/`, there are almost 4 million apps existing worldwide for the various smartphones. Apple's App Store offers approximately 2.2 million apps, Google Play offers 2.8 million, Amazon offers 600,000, and Windows offers 670,000. This number is expected to grow exponentially through 2018.

The goal of this chapter is to introduce you to the various applications seen on Android, iOS devices, and Windows Phones. Each application will vary due to versions and devices, but their underlying structures are similar. We will look at how the data is stored and why preference files are important to your investigation.

We will cover the following topics in detail in this chapter:

- Different third-party applications
- How applications are stored on iOS devices
- How applications are stored on Android devices
- Windows Phone 8 application storage
- How to use both commercial and open source solutions to parse application data

Third-party application overview

Third-party applications are an integral part of mobile device investigations; often, the key artifacts seem to exist within an application. This requires the examiner to understand where application data is stored on the device, how application data is saved for that platform, and which tool best helps uncover the evidence. Manual parsing is often a key factor when examining third-party applications on any smartphone. While some commercial tools, such as Magnet IEF, are known for application parsing support, no tool is perfect and it's virtually impossible for tools to keep up with the frequent updates that are released for each application. Most often, you'll find that the commercial tools available parse the most popular applications on the market. For example, when Facebook purchased WhatsApp, Cellebrite, IEF, and Oxygen Forensics started supporting this application. Facebook is extremely popular, but data isn't always extracted or parsed, due to security features that are built into the app—this is where all apps differ. Our best advice is to test, test, and test! You can download an app, populate data, and examine the results to see how your view of the evidence compares to your actual evidence. This practice will enable you to understand how updates change the artifacts, how evidence locations change, and how to manually extract artifacts that your tools are missing. Additionally, reverse-engineering an app and analyzing its code will help you to identify where the data is stored and how it is stored.

Most applications do not require a data plan for use; they can fully function via a Wi-Fi network, which means that apps can still function if a person travels to a region in which their device would not usually work. For example, when I travel, I rely on Skype, Viber, and WhatsApp to call and text family and friends. To use these apps, all that is required is that my smartphone is connected to Wi-Fi.

We have already addressed some third-party application extraction and analysis tips in this book. In addition to this, we discussed the files that need to be examined to understand and analyze application data in Chapter 5, *iOS Data Analysis and Recovery*, Chapter 10, *Android Data Analysis and Recovery*, Chapter 11, *Android App Analysis, Malware, and Reverse Engineering*, and Chapter 12, *Windows Phone Forensics*. This chapter will dive deeper into the applications and relevant files, and will prepare the examiner for the analysis of these artifacts. Each application has a purpose. Most tools provide support for the most popular application in each category. The rest is up to you. A quick look at the applications presented by Oxygen Detective is shown in the following screenshot. As expected, these are not all of the applications that are present on the device; rather, these are just the ones that the tool knows how to parse:

Example of applications parsed by Oxygen

Chat applications

Chat applications are among the most common applications on the market. These applications provide users with the ability to chat outside the standard SMS services offered by the network service provider and device, and are sometimes more secure. By secure, we mean that the apps may offer encryption, private profiles, private group chats, and more. Additionally, these apps enable the user to message others without the need for a data plan, as Wi-Fi provides all the access that they need. Tango, Facebook Messenger, WhatsApp, Skype, and Snapchat are some of the more popular applications.

Parsing artifacts from chat applications is not always simple. Often, multiple tools and methods will be required to extract all of the data within them. Commercial tools may only parse a portion of the data, forcing the examiner to learn how to examine and recover all data or miss evidence. Oxygen Detective is being used to parse chat messages from Tango on an Android device in the following screenshot. Note that the message does not show the image in the table. However, this image can be *pieced* back into the message, as shown in the following screenshot, to provide the total picture of what was being shared in a conversation. In this example, the graphic was located and is shown with an arrow pointing to the message to which it belongs. This was a manual process and was not performed by the tool:

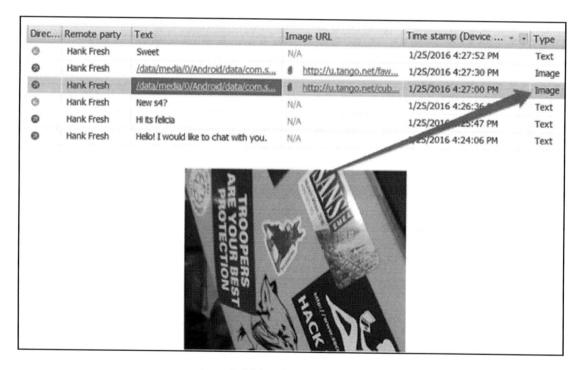

An example of piecing application chat logs back together

GPS applications

Most users branch out from their standard phone apps for GPS support. This includes getting directions to locations and obtaining maps for areas of interest. Common GPS applications include Waze and Google Maps. Waze goes beyond just providing directions, as it also alerts the user to road hazards, traffic, and police officers that are along the path they are driving:

The Waze application

Other applications that store location information include Twitter, Instagram, Facebook, and Foursquare. These applications enable a user to alert friends and followers to their location when they create a post or share an image or video. All of these transactions are tracked within the app. Understanding this is key to uncovering additional artifacts that are not reported by your forensic tool.

When examining location information from GPS applications, it is best to assume that you need to manually examine the databases and preference files that are associated with that application. We recommend using your forensic tool to triage the data on the device and then dive deeply into the artifacts, which will be discussed later in this chapter. An example of Waze being parsed by UFED Physical Analyzer is in the following screenshot. Here, we can see that the user had 5 favorite locations, 74 mapped locations, and 70 recent directions. All of this information must be manually verified if it pertains to the investigation. This is because the tool cannot determine whether the user typed the address, whether it was suggested, or whether the user even traveled to that location. Proper skills are required by the examiner to tie a user to a specific location, and this takes more than a forensic tool.

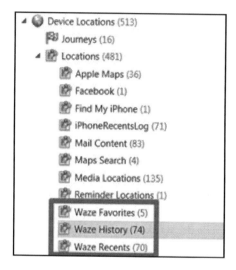

The Waze application in UFED physical analyzer

Secure applications

If data is secure and self-destructing, did it ever even exist? Ignore the claims of data retention and hunt for that data, as these apps often make claims that are simply untrue. Although applications are designed with security in mind, updates are released quickly and quality assurance checks may not be strong enough to catch everything. On occasion, you will find an app with an encrypted or nonexistent database, but the file includes a **journal**, **write-ahead logs**, or **shared memory files** that contain portions of chats that were supposed to be encrypted. In addition to this, the user can save media files that are shared, take screenshots of conversations, and do much more. Often, you may uncover the images, audio, and video files that were shared and supposed to be encrypted.

Some popular secure messaging applications include Telegram, Wickr, and Signal. Some of these are encrypted, where nothing is recoverable. However, this all depends on the device, the OS running on the smartphone, and the version of the app. The security level of these apps is publicly advertised, but again, take this with a grain of salt. You should always assume that there could be a vulnerability in the app that may provide you with access forensically. Dig for this evidence!

Information on how secure some of these apps are can be found at: `https://www.eff.org/secure-messaging-scorecard`.

Financial applications

Applications that utilize financial information, such as credit card information and personal banking, are required to be encrypted and secure. iOS devices will not acquire these apps without an Apple ID and password. Even if you have the user's Apple ID and password, the data extracted should still be encrypted. Some examples of financial applications include Google Wallet, Windows Phone Wallet, PayPal, Apple Pay, and In-App Purchases. When you examine a device, you may see that the app was installed with the associated application metadata, but account information and transactions will not be accessible.

Social networking applications

Commercial support for social networking applications is strong as they are the most popular apps downloaded from app stores. These applications allow users to make posts, share locations, chat publicly and privately, and essentially catalogue their lives. Common social networking applications include Facebook, Twitter, and Instagram. Often, users will enable one app, such as Instagram, to have access to Facebook and Twitter so that posting is seamless. Thus, when examining devices, the user may find multiple copies of the same file or conversation due to the sharing that takes place between apps.

When examining these apps with commercial tools, it is common for chats and contacts to be parsed, meaning that other data may be overlooked. Again, this means the examiner must look at the data dump to ensure that nothing is missed. As an example, we are going to take a look at Twitter. This application stores a lot of information that may require more than one tool to parse. Additionally, the user may have to manually examine the database files to ensure that all artifacts have been recovered.

Let's take a look at what the tool was able to extract. As stated several times in this book, start with what the tool is telling you is installed, and then formulate keywords and methods to dig deep into the file system. We can see the user account information for Twitter, as well as the file path where this data is being extracted, in the following screenshot:

Twitter as parsed by Oxygen Detective

The next logical step is to view what the tool can tell you about the application and how it was used. Oxygen Detective provided the following information for Twitter account usage. Note that both public tweets and private messages (DMs) are recovered:

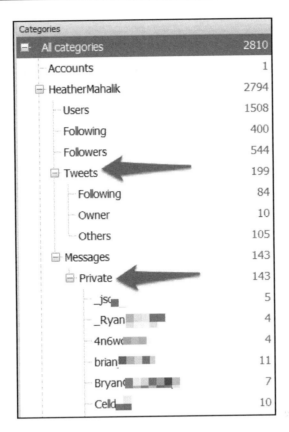

Twitter usage by Oxygen Detective

After examining what was parsed by the tool, the database files should be examined to ensure nothing was missed. This is not always simple, as each account and function may have a unique database. By function, we mean that contacts may be stored in one database while chats and account information are stored in another. Once you become more familiar with common applications, you will know where to look first. At the time of writing this book, the following databases were the most relevant:

- `Global.db`: This database contains account information, such as the username
- `<User-id>.db`: This database contains notifications, messages, contacts, and statuses

In the following screenshot, we can see all of the databases that are associated with Twitter. Again, start with what you know and dig deeper:

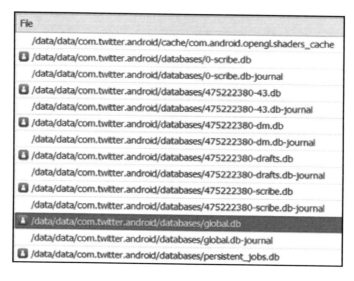

Twitter databases containing user activity

Each database may contain unique data that can be parsed for additional artifacts. These applications also contain unique `user_id` values, which can be used as keywords to search for other devices with traces of communication within an investigation. In the following example, we can see `user_id` values, the creation date (UNIX timestamp), and the data, which is the result of private messaging on Twitter:

user_id	created	data
475222380	1404903823000	I—O?u? jcI wonder if the person that asked us for ...
29574511	1404905109000	I—Tl?` j~No, I'm with myself at E ▇ ▇ ▇ly ca...
475222380	1404913177000	I—s3B jaWe need test data. Not really doing resea...
29574511	1404913470000	I—tQ??oDo you want just the chats? I can toss togeth...
475222380	1404916910000	I—□q? j?It's not even for me. A student asked me if I h...
29574511	1454683850000	I §W@??┤•jHShoot me your address and I'll try to get th...

Twitter private messaging artifacts

Custom queries can be written to parse Twitter databases of interest. A good example of how to do this is shown as follows. This query is specific to parsing Twitter contacts:

```
SELECT
_id AS "Index", user_id, username,
name,
datetime (profile_created/1000,'UNIXEPOCH','localtime') AS "Profile
Created",
description AS "Twitter Description", web_url,
location, followers,
friends AS "Following",
users.statuses AS "Number of Tweets",
datetime (profile_created/1000,'UNIXEPOCH','localtime'), image_url,
datetime (updated/1000,'UNIXEPOCH','localtime') AS "Profile Updated",
datetime (friendship_time/1000,'UNIXEPOCH','localtime') AS "Became Friends"
FROM users
```

Encoding versus encryption

The terms encoding and encryption are used so frequently when discussing applications and smartphone data that they are often confused. Encoding is essentially the process of obfuscating a message or piece of information to appear as raw code. In some cases, the goal of encoding is to make the data unrecognizable to the computer or the user. In reality, the primary goal of encoding is to transform the input into a different format using a publicly available scheme. In other words, anyone can easily decode an encoded value. Encryption, however, transforms the data using a key in order to keep its content confidential. So, encrypted text can only be reversed if you have the key. Most applications claim that they encrypt data or that the data is never saved to disk. While this is true for some, most are simply encoded. Encoding options can vary, but the most common option for smartphone data is **Base64**. Messaging apps often rely on Base64 encoding to make the data appear to be hidden or *safe*. A common artifact of Base64 is the padding of the data with an = when the encoded bytes are not divisible by three.

Until a little over a year ago, Oxygen Forensics and Autopsy were two of the few tools that support the decoding of Base64 payloads from applications derived from smartphones. For these tools to parse the data, they must support the application containing the encoding. Currently, MSAB, UFED Physical Analyzer, and Magnet IEF also provide Base64 decoding support.

An example of Base64-encoded messages is shown in the following screenshot. This data is from the Tango chat application:

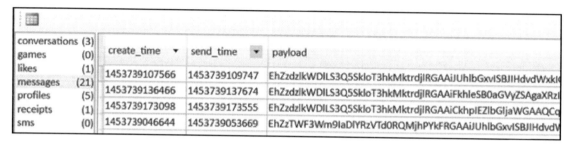

Base64-encoded Tango messages

Encryption is a bit more difficult as the app itself may not even provide access to the encrypted data. For example, you may find that the database directory or the cells containing the encrypted data are simply empty. Occasionally, you will have access to the encrypted blobs within the databases, but this data cannot always be decrypted. Again, when you face encrypted data, look elsewhere. Have you examined the journal and write-ahead logs? Have you examined the cache and media directories? Have you examined the SD card? These are common questions you will often have to ask yourself to ensure you are not relying on your forensic tools too much and that you are covering your bases to ensure nothing is overlooked. As we've explained, start with what you know. We know that the cache and database directories store user data, so this is a great place to start your manual examination, as you can see in the following screenshot:

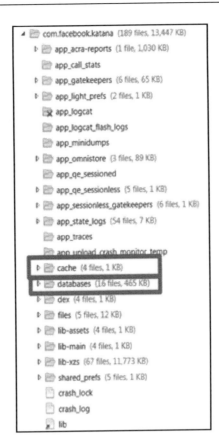

Data storage locations for applications

Application data storage

Almost all applications rely on SQLite for data storage. These databases can be stored internally on the device or on the SD card for relevant phones. When SQLite is used, temporary memory files are commonly associated to each database to make SQLite more efficient. These files, which were previously mentioned, are **write-ahead logs** (**WAL**) and **shared memory files** (**SHM**). These files may contain data that is not present in the SQLite database. Few tools will parse this information, but the ones that are offered by Sanderson Forensics will get you started. Go to
`http://sandersonforensics.com/forum/content.php?261-Timelining-events-in-a-WAL-based-SQLite-DB` for more information. We can see several WAL and SHM files associated with various WhatsApp database files in the following screenshot:

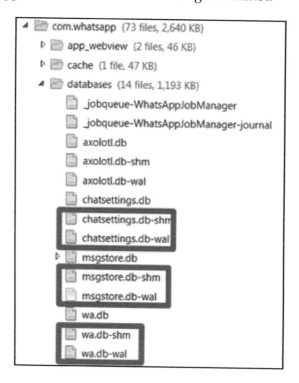

An SHM file and WAL example

In addition to SQLite databases, other devices rely on Plist, XML, JSON, and DAT files for application data storage, account data storage, purchase information, and user preferences. These files will be discussed in the Android, iOS, and Windows Phone sections of this chapter.

iOS applications

Apple relies on SQLite and Plist as common locations for application data storage. On occasion, JSON files will be used for application data. Examining applications recovered from an iOS device can be overwhelming. We suggest you start with what you know and what your tool is telling you. Examine the Installed Applications listed by your tool of choice. From here, go directly to the applications directory and ensure that nothing is being overlooked. When a user deletes an app, the databases often remain and the link to the installed application is simply broken. Examining all areas of the iOS device will prevent the examiner from missing data:

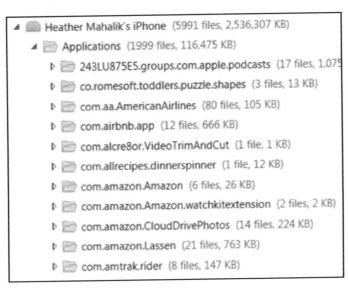

Installed applications on an iPhone

After examining the installed applications, search the `Library` and `Documents` directories for any relevant Plist files that may contain application artifacts. Finally, examine the `Media` directory on the iPhone as well as the one associated with the app to recover additional artifacts, such as shared photos, videos, audio files, and profile pictures. In the following screenshot, we are examining the `Media` directory associated to the WhatsApp application:

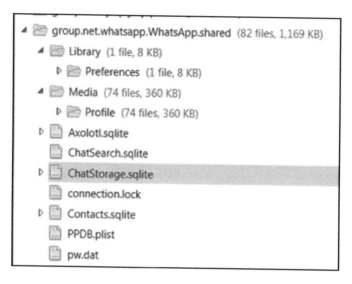

Application data on an iPhone

Android applications

Android devices rely heavily on SQLite for application storage. The preference files for each application are often in the DAT or XML file formats. More so than an iOS device, examining applications on an Android may be one of the most tedious tasks. This is due to the various locations that data may be stored in. The best place to start is with a tool that will provide a listing of what is installed on the device. Next, go to the subdirectories off the `/Root` directory. Remember, these applications may possess unique names and may be difficult to locate.

You may have to research the application to gain a better understanding of the filenames that are associated with each of them. The following screenshot is an example of application directories on an Android device:

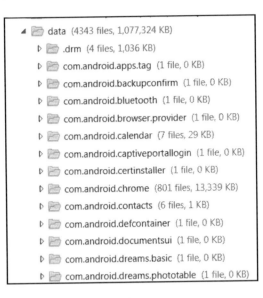

Application data on an Android device

Each of these application directories will contain a lot of data to examine. We recommend starting with the `Databases` and `Cache` directories and then expanding your analysis to other locations on the device. The next locations to examine include the `Media` and `Cache` partitions. If the data appears to be missing or is claimed to have been deleted, do not forget to examine the `Downloads` directory on the device and SD card.

Application data can exist in several locations in the `Media` directories. Using a tool, such as UFED Physical Analyzer, which provides keyword-searching capabilities spanning beyond parsed items, will really help in locating artifacts pertaining to specific applications. We are looking at the large amount of data stored in the `Media` directory on an Android device in the following screenshot. This data is unique from what is stored in the application directories which were discussed previously. Each location needs to be thoroughly examined to ensure nothing is missed. It is important that you take what you learned in previous chapters to analyze Android application data:

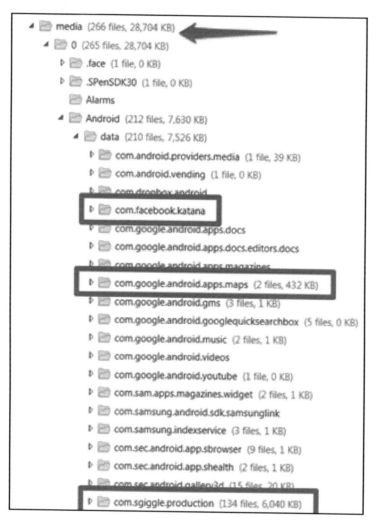

Unique application data in the Media directory

Windows Phone applications

Applications found on Windows Phones are no different to those found on iOS and Android devices. SQLite is the most common format used for data storage. However, not all devices allow for SQLite files to be stored internally on the phone. For these devices, all application data will be found on the SD card. Some may view this as lucky because it saves us from having to examine several locations on the device, but the SD card and the applications themselves may be encrypted.

Where possible, it is best to remove the SD card and acquire it using a forensic tool. When this is not possible, the next best method would be to try to acquire the SD card through the phone using a forensic tool. Again, this will often result in missed data. As a final effort, live analysis can be completed by mounting the device and using Windows Explorer to view the applications stored on the device and SD card, as discussed in `Chapter 12`, *Windows Phone Forensics*.

Forensic methods used to extract third-party application data

Almost all commercial tools will attempt to support the extraction of third-party applications. We recommend that you test your tools thoroughly and often, if you rely on tool output for your investigative results. This is because the apps are updated so frequently that it is nearly impossible for the tools not to miss something. You must learn about the applications, how they work, and how the devices store data for each app. We strongly recommend that you use your tool to triage the case and then dive into the data to manually extract anything that the tools miss. Make sure that you only include factual data in your forensic report and not everything that the tools parse, as the tools cannot decipher the difference between device and human creation. Only a trained examiner can do this with confidence.

Commercial tools

As you have seen in this book, there are many tools that can handle the job of smartphone forensics. However, there are a few that really shine when it comes to parsing application data. Magnet IEF, Oxygen Detective, Forensics Suite, and UFED Physical Analyzer are a few that do a good job of recovering data from the application categories discussed in this chapter. We will take a quick look at how to leverage each of these tools to parse application data. Keep in mind that these tools will not find every application and will not parse all data for applications.

Oxygen Detective

Oxygen Detective can be used to examine application data. For this example, we are assuming the acquisition is complete and we are simply attempting to analyze the data. Note that Oxygen is capable of acquiring and analyzing smartphones. In this example, we acquired the device with Cellebrite UFED and analyzed it with Oxygen. To load a data dump of a device and examine its application artifacts, follow these steps:

1. Launch Oxygen Detective.
2. Select the **Import File** option and choose your image. Multiple image formats are supported for ingestion into Oxygen.
3. After parsing is complete, start examining the parsed applications:

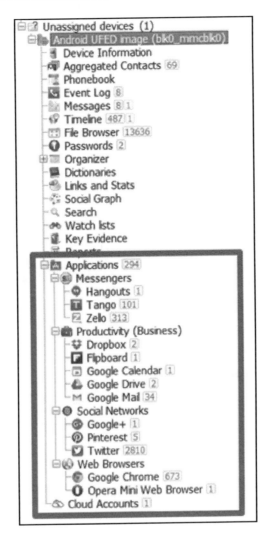

The Oxygen Detective application view

4. Next, start examining applications of interest by clicking on the application and examining all of the associated files.

5. Once you select the application, you will be presented with the data that was parsed and the full file path from where the data was extracted. Use this path to manually verify the findings. We are looking at the Pinterest application in the following screenshot. Note how the container, file, and table of interest are provided and hyperlinked for the user. The tool is even encouraging you to dig deeper and verify the findings:

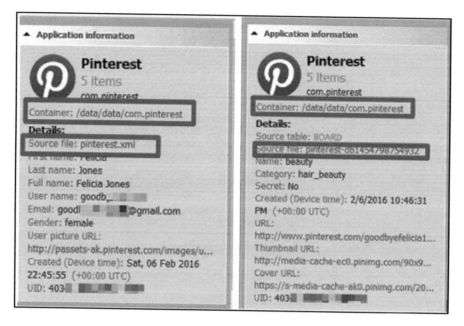

Oxygen Detective Pinterest example

Oxygen Detective has built-in features for keyword searching, bookmarking, and reporting. In addition, the SQLite Database and Plist Viewer will provide you with a method for examining relevant application data

6. Report all account information, chats, messages, locations, and any other data of interest, as this provides relevance to your investigation.

Magnet IEF

Magnet IEF has been known as one of the leaders in internet and application parsing for digital media. They are just as strong with mobile devices. Again, one tool cannot do the job, but IEF proves to be the strongest and parses the most applications from Android, iOS, and Windows Phones. The downside to this tool is that we are forced to rely on the reported artifacts, as the file system is not normalized and provided for manual examination. To use IEF to examine application artifacts, follow these steps:

1. Launch IEF and then select **MOBILE** (note that if **MOBILE** is grayed out, you need to obtain a license that provides mobile support from Magnet Forensics):

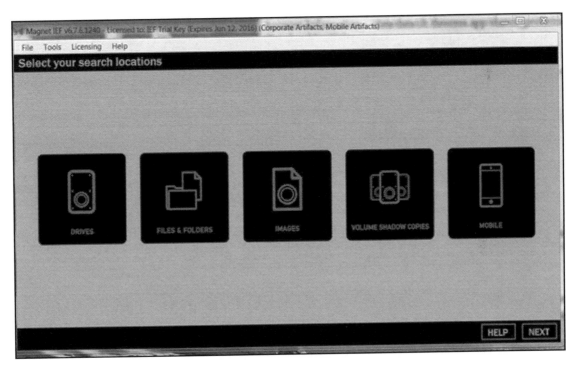

Magnet IEF

2. Select **IMAGES** and navigate to your image file. More than one image can be loaded and parsed at the same time.

3. Select **NEXT** and determine what you want to parse. We recommend selecting **CHECK ALL**:

Magnet IEF supported artifacts

4. Browse to the location where you wish to save the case file and select **Find Evidence**.

5. Once complete, the IEF Report Viewer will be displayed, as follows:

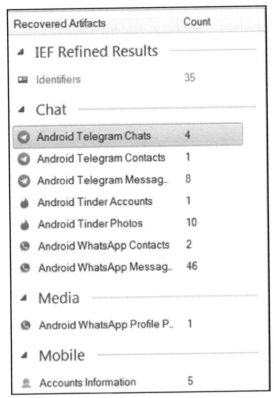

Recovered Artifacts	Count
⊿ IEF Refined Results	
▣ Identifiers	35
⊿ Chat	
⊘ Android Telegram Chats	4
⊘ Android Telegram Contacts	1
⊘ Android Telegram Messag…	8
⬧ Android Tinder Accounts	1
⬧ Android Tinder Photos	10
⬤ Android WhatsApp Contacts	2
⬤ Android WhatsApp Messag…	46
⊿ Media	
⬤ Android WhatsApp Profile P…	1
⊿ Mobile	
⬤ Accounts Information	5

Application Artifacts in Magnet IEF

The first step in examination is to review what has been parsed by IEF. In the preceding screenshot, we can see that Telegram was parsed. Start your examination in the most relevant location. For example, if you are looking for **Telegram Chats**, go right to that location and start examining the artifacts. Note that **Messages** and **Chats** are pulled into two different categories. This is common when private messaging is used. All relevant application containers should be examined. Additionally, IEF provides the full file path from which the data was recovered. Use another tool to navigate to this file for verification and manual examination.

IEF also provides logical keyword search (it will search what it can parse and nothing else), bookmarking, and reporting. Make sure that you only report factual application artifacts and incorporate this into your final forensic report.

UFED Physical Analyzer

Physical Analyzer is one of the most well-known mobile forensic tools on the market. This tool is one of the best platforms to manually conduct an examination in addition to leveraging the data parsed by the tool. For application analysis, Physical Analyzer is good at parsing chats and contacts for each supported application. For data that is not parsed, Physical Analyzer provides an analytical platform that enables the user to browse the file system to uncover additional artifacts. Keyword searching is robust in this tool and is capable of searching raw Hex as well as parsed data. In addition, a SQLite viewer is included.

To conduct a forensic examination of application data in Physical Analyzer, follow these steps to get started:

1. Launch Physical Analyzer by double-clicking on the UFED shortcut image file or by double-clicking the tool icon.
2. Load the image file and wait until parsing completes.
3. Examine the parsed artifacts, as shown in the following screenshot. For this example, we are examining **Tango**. Physical Analyzer recovered **Tango** data in **Chats**, **Contacts**, **Installed Applications**, **Passwords**, and **User Accounts**:

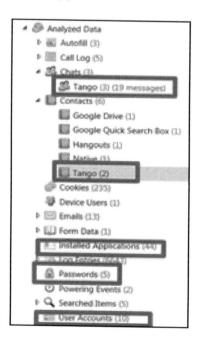

Tango as parsed by Physical Analyzer

We recommend examining what is parsed and referring to the hyperlink of where the data is being extracted. Navigate to this path and then examine the entire application directory.

To find the application directory, leverage built-in keyword searching capabilities to aid in the investigation. Remember, you may have to conduct research to determine the file names associated to the app if this is not apparent. Tango, for example, does not use the term Tango in the file paths or filenames. The directory is `.sgiggle` and the primary database is `tc.db`. This makes our job harder because we can't simply search for Tango and get accurate results.

Open source tools

For those on a budget, it is possible to examine application data from smartphones using open source solutions and cheap tools. These solutions are more difficult to use, and they are often not the answer for those new to forensics who need the assistance of a tool in data extraction and analysis. Examining application data is tedious, and if you do not know where to look, it's likely you will need to spend some money to get a head start. Tools, such as **Andriller**, can be purchased for around $500. While this is not free, it's also not $10,000, which is what some of the other commercial tools cost. In the following section, we will cover a few of our favorite tools that are useful in parsing application data from smartphones.

Autopsy

Autopsy is one of the best tools for examining Android and Windows Phones. Unfortunately, iOS parsing is not provided in Autopsy. Autopsy can be downloaded from `http://sleuthkit.org/autopsy/`. When using Autopsy, the Android Analyzer module will parse some application data from the device. This module is unique in that it is currently the only tool that parses **WordsWithFriends**, a gaming application, and was the first tool, other than Oxygen Forensics, to provide Base64 decoding support for Tango chat messages. Some say that Autopsy is the free solution for those who cannot afford Physical Analyzer.

To use Autopsy, download the software and install it on a Windows machine and follow these instructions. Make sure that you are always using the latest version:

1. Launch Autopsy.
2. Create a new case:

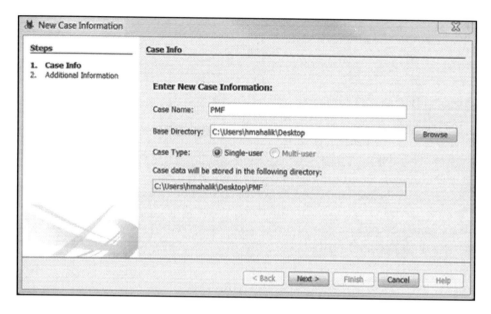

Autopsy case creation

3. Select **Next** and then click on **Finish**.
4. Navigate to your image file and select **Next**.
5. Select the modules that you wish to run. **Keyword Search** and **Android Analyzer** will be the most fruitful for an Android device. These modules can also be run after the image is ingested. The **Keyword Search** will prove to be just as robust as Physical Analyzer:

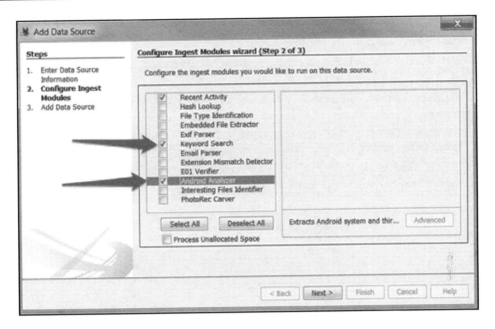

Autopsy module selection

Ingest Modules are tools built into Autopsy that can be run when the case has started or at any point afterwards. The default modules in this version of Autopsy are as follows:

- **Recent Activity**: This extracts recent user activity such as web browsing, recently used documents, and installed programs.
- **Hash Lookup**: This identifies known and notable files using supplied hash databases, such as a standard NSRL database. It also allows importing custom hash databases.
- **File Type Identification**: This matches file types based on binary signatures.
- **Archive Extractor**: This extracts archive files (`.zip`, `.rar`, `.arj`, `.7z`, `.gzip`, `.bzip2`, `.tar`). It automatically extracts these file types and puts their contents into the directory tree.
- **EXIF Parser**: This ingests JPEG files and retrieves their EXIF metadata.
- **Keyword Search**: This performs file indexing and periodic search using keywords and regular expressions in lists. It allows the loading of custom keywords/lists.
- **Email Parser**: This module detects and parses `mbox` and `pst/ost` files and populates e-mail artifacts in the blackboard.

- **Extension Mismatch Detector**: These are flag files that have a non-standard extension based on their file types.
- **E01 Verifier**: This validates the integrity of E01 files.
- **Android Analyzer**: This extracts Android system and third-party app data.
- **Interesting Files Identifier**: This identifies interesting items, as defined.

Autopsy provides access to file system data faster than any commercial or open source tool available. Knowing where to go from there is the hard part. So, again, start with anything that is in the extracted content and then dive into the file system to examine the files discussed in this book and any relevant application data, as shown in the following screenshot:

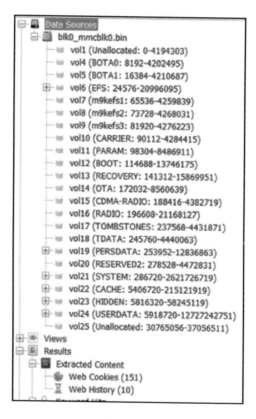

Autopsy results

Once you have identified applications of interest, start with what is parsed and then examine the relevant database, cache, and preference files. At the time of writing, Autopsy does not have an SQLite viewer available. All databases must be exported and examined in a SQLite viewer. We like SQLite Forensic Browser, which has been discussed in this book.

Autopsy was able to parse Tango chat messages and contacts in a similar way to Physical Analyzer, IEF, and Oxygen. The following screenshot shows the results of the decoded messages:

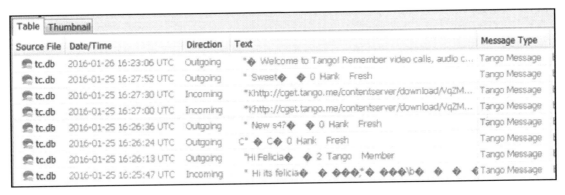

Tango decoded by Autopsy

Other methods of extracting application data

One of the easiest ways to parse application data is to create custom SQLite queries and Python scripts to parse data of interest. We have discussed several suggestions and examples of queries and scripts throughout this book. Python is one of the best solutions because it is free and we have full access to its libraries. One thing to keep in mind is that our scripts have to be updated frequently to keep up with application updates. Also, make sure your encoding schemas are correct to prevent application artifacts from being missed or not interpreted correctly.

In addition to Python scripts, free parsers that support application extraction already exist. WhatsApp Extract is a free tool for both Android and iOS that will extract WhatsApp application data from devices. Often, this free tool will extract more data than the commercial solutions, depending on the permissions the user allocated during installation. Others, such as *Mari DeGrazia* (http://az4n6.blogspot.in/p/downloads.html) and *Adrian Leong* (https://github.com/cheeky4n6monkey/4n6-scripts), have developed scripts to parse applications, recover deleted data from SQLite free pages, decode Base64, and more. We recommend using what is already available before developing your own.

Summary

Many apps are not what they claim to be. Never trust what you read about apps, as quality assurance testing across apps is not consistent, and we have determined several vulnerabilities and security flaws over the years that provide us with methods of piecing application data back together. In addition, application updates will change the way we need to look at the data found. Understanding each smartphone and how it stores application data is the first step towards successfully examining applications on smartphones. Knowing that updates may change data locations, encoding, and encryption, as well as how your tool functions, is one of the hardest concepts for examiners to grasp. It is your job to learn the capabilities of the application to uncover the most data from the mobile device.

Understanding how an application works is hard enough without having to consider how to extract artifacts. As you have read in this book, there are many ways to parse data from smartphones. One tool is never enough, and the reality is that mobile forensics can be expensive. We hope that we have provided you with a practical guide that teaches you how to acquire and analyze artifacts that are recovered from smartphones. Take what you've learned and apply it immediately to your methods to conduct mobile forensics or use it to make you more prepared in your next job. Remember that practice, testing, and training will make you better at your job and will help you perfect the art of mobile forensics.

Other Books You May Enjoy

If you enjoyed this book, you may be interested in these other books by Packt:

Mastering Mobile Forensics
Soufiane Tahiri

ISBN: 978-1-78528-781-7

- Understand the mobile forensics process model and get guidelines on mobile device forensics
- Acquire in-depth knowledge about smartphone acquisition and acquisition methods
- Gain a solid understanding of the architecture of operating systems, file formats, and mobile phone internal memory
- Explore the topics of of mobile security, data leak, and evidence recovery
- Dive into advanced topics such as GPS analysis, file carving, encryption, encoding, unpacking, and decompiling mobile application processes

Mobile Forensics Cookbook
Igor Mikhaylov

ISBN: 978-1-78528-205-8

- Retrieve mobile data using modern forensic tools
- Work with Oxygen Forensics for Android devices acquisition
- Perform a deep dive analysis of iOS, Android, Windows, and BlackBerry Phone file systems
- Understand the importance of cloud in mobile forensics and extract data from the cloud using different tools
- Learn the application of SQLite and Plists Forensics and parse data with digital forensics tools
- Perform forensic investigation on iOS, Android, Windows, and BlackBerry mobile devices
- Extract data both from working and damaged mobile devices using JTAG and Chip-off Techniques

Leave a review - let other readers know what you think

Please share your thoughts on this book with others by leaving a review on the site that you bought it from. If you purchased the book from Amazon, please leave us an honest review on this book's Amazon page. This is vital so that other potential readers can see and use your unbiased opinion to make purchasing decisions, we can understand what our customers think about our products, and our authors can see your feedback on the title that they have worked with Packt to create. It will only take a few minutes of your time, but is valuable to other potential customers, our authors, and Packt. Thank you!

Index

H

hardware model
  identifying 34, 35, 36, 37
HFS Plus filesystem
  reference 49
HFS Plus volume
  about 50
  structure 51
Hierarchical File System (HFS) 49

I

iBackup Viewer
  download link 102
iBSS
  reference 69
iCloud backups
  extracting 112
  working with 110
iExplorer
  about 37
  reference 104
image
  adding, to Autopsy 274, 276, 277
  analyzing, Autopsy used 278, 279
imaging the device 264
initialization vector (IV) 108
Integrated Circuit Card Identifier (ICCID) 98
inter-process communication (IPC) 195
internal memory
  deleted data, recovering from 287
internal storage 248
International Mobile Equipment Identity (IMEI) 98
internet history
  extracting 340
iOS applications 357
iOS architecture
  about 55
  Cocoa Touch layer 55
  Core OS layer 55
  Core Services layer 55
  Media layer 55
iOS database files
  address book contacts 126
  address book images 128

calendar events 132
call history 130
consolidated GPS cache 136
notes 133
photo metadata 135
Safari bookmarks and cache 134
Short Message Service (SMS) 131
Voicemail 137
iOS devices
  operating modes 64
iOS security
  about 56
  Activation Lock 59
  Address Space Layout Randomization (ASLR) 58
  Code Signing 57
  data execution prevention (DEP) 59
  data protection 58
  data wipe 59
  encryption 58
  face ID 57
  passcodes 57
  privilege separation 58
  sandboxing 57
  stack-smashing protection 58
  touch ID 57
IP-BOX 3 72
iPad hardware 45
iPad models
  about 43, 44
  reference 43
iPad Pro
  reference 45
iPhone hardware 42, 43
iPhone models
  about 34
  features 38
  reference 34
iPhone operating system 54
iPhone releases
  features 39, 40
iThmb Converter
  reference 144
iTunes backup
  about 92

70376878R00224

Made in the USA
San Bernardino, CA
28 February 2018